RELIGION AND THE SOCIAL ORDER

South Florida-Rochester-Saint Louis
Studies on Religion and the Social Order
EDITED BY
Jacob Neusner   William Scott Green   William M. Shea

RELIGION AND THE SOCIAL ORDER
What Kinds of Lessons Does History Teach?
edited by
Jacob Neusner

RELIGION AND THE SOCIAL ORDER

WHAT KINDS OF LESSONS DOES HISTORY TEACH?

edited by
Jacob Neusner

WITHDRAWN

Scholars Press
Atlanta, Georgia

RELIGION AND THE SOCIAL ORDER
What Kinds of Lessons Does History Teach?

edited by
Jacob Neusner

Published by Scholars Press
for the University of South Florida, University of Rochester,
and Saint Louis University

Funds for the publication of this volume were provided by

The Tyson and Naomi Midkiff Fund for Exellence
of the Department of Religious Studies at the University of South Florida

The Max Richter Foundation of Rhode Island

and

The Tisch Family Foundation of New York City

Library of Congress Cataloging in Publication Data

Neusner, Jacob, 1932–
    Religion and the social order : what kinds of lessons does history
teach? / Jacob Neusner.
        p.   cm. — (South Florida-Rochester-Saint Louis studies on
religion and the social order ; 11)
    Includes index.
    ISBN 0-7885-0054-6 (alk. paper)
    1. Religion and sociology. 2. Religion—Study and teaching.
I. Title. II. Series: South Florida-Rochester-Saint Louis studies
on religion and the social order ; v. 11.
BL60.N425   1994
291.1'7—dc20   94-33696
                                                CIP

Printed in the United States of America
on acid-free paper

CONTENTS

VII.
Unconventional Evidence Pertaining to Times Past
and Its Lessons for Contemporary Sensibility

VIII.
A Theological Perspective
on the Social Study of Religion in History

Introduction

Using historical, humanistic disciplines, rather than contemporary, social scientific ones, addressing the records of the past in all of their diverse media of preservation, we take up an acutely contemporary problem of learning. We want to know about the relationship between religions and the societies that organize themselves around said religions. How do religions give definition to the social entities that practice them? How do societies impose their traits upon their religions? This is a question of reciprocal relationship, and, in this context of humanistic learning, it falls into two parts.

First, what can we know? That is, of course, a question of historical knowledge. And what we know out of the past hardly compares with what we can find out in the acutely present tense of contemporary society. The limits of our knowledge about the past – adventitious and unpredictable and sometimes scarcely palpable – impose themselves upon the questions that we frame to begin with. Here, then, we want to articulate the limits of knowledge: what can we know from one kind of evidence, what from another, meaning, what are the sorts of questions we may bring to data of a given order. If the data take the form of dance, for instance, then we shall have to learn how to formulate questions that the dance illuminates; and if the data take the form of buildings, then we want to know how buildings formulate the religious system and bring it to concrete expression; and if the data take the form of graphic arts, then we shall ask what we may learn from graphic arts. So our goal is to attain self-awareness: how do our data impose their pattern upon our imagination, so that we ask questions our data dictate and scarcely imagine questions that they do not provoke.

Second, what is at stake in what we can know? Here we have in mind to ask, given the diverse programs of learning shaped in response to the character of the data of (to use our examples) dance, on the one side, buildings on the second, and graphic arts, on the third, how may we compare what these kinds of data tell us with the results of the more conventional data yielded by ordinary written sources or archaeological sources; and the contrast, of course, between history of religion resting on written sources and characterization of the material culture, inclusive of religion, resting on archaeological evidence, has also to be drawn. The issues of method, broadly construed, then work themselves out in studies of particular problems: religions and the data that convey those religions. While we pursue understanding of religion, what we study is religions, one by one; but ours is a generalizing science, so in meetings such as that recorded here, we attempt to transcend the limits of religions and speak about religion. Now to the particulars of this conference book.

These papers[1] seek understanding of the importance of religion in the definition of the social order. The topic, the way in which religion defines, and is defined by, society, takes as its premise that religion is public, something that a "we" does together. That is why we may analyze religion, not only record and report on its assertions as to fact or faith. The particular problem brought to bear upon that topic is, how do the data of the world before this morning govern our research into, and perspective on, the social side of faith. Ordinarily, to pursue such an inquiry people examine with the tools of contemporary social science – sociology and demography, anthropology and economics, politics and psychology. Today's world testifies day by day to the formative power of religion in the politics of nations and the social life of peoples; many of us identify religion as the single most powerful force in the definition of events in many parts of the world, and most people acknowledge its critical importance in world history, past and present. To explain humanity's character and the consequences thereof, we have therefore to form a theory for ourselves of what religion is and how it works.

But what about times past? The historians of religion whose papers are presented here work in a wide range of religions, Judaism, Christianity, Islam. But they share the burden of using evidence out of the past to try to understand how religion shaped and was shaped by the society that preserved that evidence. We who work in history of religions undertake a task of interpretation of considerable difficulty, because we bring our questions to writings produced to take up issues remote from our day and perspective. In another age, the task of intellect found definition in the phrase, "faith seeking understanding." Our task enlists understanding – the disciplines of academic learning – seeking to make some sense of the this-worldly realities of faith that have endured out of another world altogether. In focusing upon the social dimension of matters, the facts of the here and now, we take up the this-worldly

---

[1]Read at the University of South Florida conference, Religion and the Social Order: The Lessons of History, February 19-22, 1994.

chapter of matters, embodying for these few days the quest for understanding seeking to make sense of faith in concrete terms: Precisely how does religion work? The particular chapter of that larger quest calls upon scholars to explain their work on the study of religion and the social order by asking them to transcend the givens and speculate on the unknown possibilities of imagination.

"What kinds of lessons does history teach?" is a simple way of asking, what do diverse classes of evidence on the social role of religion in worlds before our own, or in contemporary worlds other than our own, tell us, and how may we compare the sorts of inquiries one class of evidence permits with those of others? We seek perspective on how the character of the evidence on which we work dictates the kinds of questions we ask. This we do by speculating on the sorts of questions we should formulate in response to evidence of a different character altogether. The challenge is to form a dialectic between what we think we know and what we imagine we might further know.

The papers address a particular problem: how can we in the history of religion gain perspective upon our work, our methods. Solving that problem requires an act of imagination: Are there other questions, other premises and methodological perspectives, besides the ones I presently use, for the study of the data on which I work? Have the data before me defined my methods and limited my questions, so imposing constraints upon my imagination that have to be identified and overcome? Contemporary social science, ever alert to issues of method, gives ample evidence of the value of methodological self-consciousness. Historians of religion, by contrast, prove less reflective concerning the methods used in the study of the relationship of religion and society. While drawing upon history and sociology, archaeology and literature, anthropology and the arts in music and dance, the conference focuses upon the academic discipline of the study of religion, to which these areas of humanistic and social scientific learning contribute in important ways. The papers analyze the kinds of questions people presently address to various types of evidence – written and archaeological, for example. They identify types of evidence just now gaining attention – other than written or archaeological – in the study of how religion makes its impact upon society. All the papers are meant to treat the special subject as exemplary and each of the scholars is asked to speculate beyond the area of his or her expert knowledge.

So each of the substantive papers is meant to be exemplary, with a particular body of data, whether contemporary Islam or the ancient Near East, serving to illustrate a type of inquiry that today is undertaken. The papers further draw into the framework of humanistic study the kinds of questions pursued by contemporary social science. The goal of the conference is to offer perspective on the study of religion and the social order, so that specialists in the use of one kind of evidence may broaden their perspective upon the work they now are doing and formulate research problems in response to the inquiries of others, working on altogether different types of evidence. "What kinds of lessons does history teach?" is a simple way of asking, what do diverse classes of evidence on the social role of religion in worlds before our own, or other than our own, tell us, and how may we compare the sorts of inquiries one class of evidence permits with those of some others? And in what ways do we gain perspective, from the achievements of contemporary social science, on pre-contemporary data and the studies they make possible? A few concrete definitions now are called for.

WHAT DO WE MEAN BY "RELIGION AND THE SOCIAL ORDER?" In times past, as in our own day, whole nations, ethnic groups in various places, communities and societies of various kinds, have formulated through religious systems their theories of the social order they embody. These religious systems, comprising a statement of a worldview (ethics), a way of life (ethos), and a definition of the social group that sees the world in accord with the one and realizes in every day life the other (ethnos), then set forth the social order of those nations, ethnic groups, communities, or societies. Now, when we view religion as a fact of social life, what we want to know is, how do religious systems of the social order impart to a social group that sense of structure and meaning that holds people together and explains to them who they are and what they do together?

We look for the answer to that question in a very specific set of data: the data that tell us the ecology of a religion: what facts of the social environment dictate the problems a group has to work out, what issues have to be faced by a nation or ethnic group, community or society or church, for its members to live their lives, for its social order to hold together. The ecology of a religious group helps us to interpret the religious theory of the social order that that group finds illuminating, the group's explanation of itself, its way of life, its worldview. It follows that the relationships between the ideas that people hold about themselves and the world that they make for themselves and the world in which they live – these relationships form an important problem in the academic study of religion. The phrase, "religion and the social order," then refers to the investigation of how religions define and explain the lives of social groups, from nations to small church-communities. A principal task of the academic study of religion requires us to ask about the relationship between the ideas that people hold and the social world that they create, and that is the focus of this conference concerning diverse scholars' ways of dealing with that crucial question.

THE GOALS SET FOR THE PRINCIPALS OF THE PROGRAM: Our goals therefore are these:

1. we are trying, as specialists in a given topic and method, to generalize beyond the limits of our data and experience;

2. we are attempting, as experts on some one body of evidence, to think in broad terms about the problems of method we are solving in our particular cases, and how we may learn from how others define and solve problems using other data of the same class as our data, for example, literary data;

3. we want to gain perspective on our work by comparing what we do with materials of a historical character with what a contemporary social scientist does with materials of an acutely contemporary type;

4. we seek to explore the possibilities of making not only descriptive but normative statements, moving from understanding to matters of judgment.

This conference serves the further, and critical, purpose of introducing our students to the character of scholarship by showing what working scholars do in the conduct of their enterprise. And that means, how working scholars set themselves challenges, pursue their education, above all, seek always to surpass themselves.

THE UNITS OF THE PROGRAM: The papers hold together – surprisingly well, given their diverse topics – because each asks about the social dimension of the topic. For the great social scientist, Andrew Greeley, that question comes naturally. But how the social reading of the gospels illuminates the religious world of earliest Christianity, which Bruce D. Chilton explains, hardly proves so self-evident to the generality of readers. The quest for the hard facts of history, if any, that has dominated the study of the Hebrew Scriptures or Old Testament hardly can have led us to anticipate a paper that transcends historical fact in a search for social construction, such as H. Kent Richards has contributed. The way in which contemporary politics defines the description of the history of a religion once more shows the powerful force of today's societies upon our appreciation of yesterday's, as John Esposito demonstrates. Whether or not our data tell us anything at all about religion, or whether a given society possessed anything comparable to what we call religion in our own – that hitherto unasked question distinguishes Erica Reiner's remarkable and reflective paper. The definition of the past by appeal to matters that agitate the present comes to the fore in the fresh insights of Robert Ellwood. William Green's paper rightly comes at the outset, therefore, with its systematic exposition of the way in which our own country's political culture shapes our vision of all things, including, not incidentally, religion. In these ways the colleagues from other universities take up the concerns that animate our own shared intellectual program at the University of South Florida.

While the papers join together in a fundamental and broadly characteristic program, each pursues its own topic with all the precision and specificity that authentic scholarship always requires. The book falls into eight parts. We begin with a statement that defines the terms at hand. We then ask about the use of literary evidence for the study of religion and the social order. This is in two parts: the study of the Bible, then the study of principal documents of post-biblical Judaism. We privilege the Holy Scriptures, because of their paramount position in contemporary religious life. The two papers examine the role of social entities in the formation of Scripture. The third part asks about how from what the sources tell us we may proceed to what they take for granted, and how we may identify the deepest layers of consciousness and thought by examining the connections people make and the conclusions they draw from the self-evidence of those connections. From there, in the fourth part, we turn from literary evidence – sacred Scriptures – to the study of public behavior in matters of power and politics, past and present, in the analysis of religion and the social order. We proceed to unconventional evidence for the same task.

Having treated the study of religion attested by one kind of evidence – literary or political behavior – we move on to the mixture of two distinct types of evidence adduced in the same inquiry, the literary and the archaeological. Here we come back once more to Scripture, but we turn also to that complex body of evidence, literary and archaeological, that ancient Mesoptamia has bequeathed to us in the study of a social world quite discontinuous from our own. Here we ask whether, out of the past, we are able to study religion at all. From times past we return to our own day, with three quite distinct perspectives, the social scientific, the analytical, and the normative. The first of the three contemporary papers on religion and the social order asks how the acutely contemporary work of sociology and demography may be contemplated for the world before our own day. The second examines principal figures in the study of how religion and society relate through myth and symbol – a study of how the past has been represented and what we learn about the present from the re-presentation of the past. The third introduces the necessary conclusion. Religion is not only a generalizing science, but because of the nature of what is studied, it also is, and should be, a conclusion-drawing one. One kind of conclusion is placed on display here.

WHAT DO WE WANT TO KNOW IN ASKING ABOUT THE KINDS OF LESSONS HISTORY TEACHES? By "history" we mean simply, all time, from prehistorical ages to the day before yesterday. The study of materials that tell us about religious life before our own times, whether written or not, whether artistic or archaeological or musical or theatrical, contrast with the kinds of data that inform us about religion today. And, many will agree, the study of religion and the social order, often called simply "religion and society," achieves its solid results in contemporary sociology of religion. Using the hard data of demography and other statistical materials, sociologists of religion have produced important accounts of the role of religion in contemporary America – Professor Andrew Greeley is the outstanding figure in this area, but only one among a number of important scholars. As a result, when we examine how religion shapes a society and forms its principal institutions, life patterns, and operative values, we have considerable insight formed into the immediate present. The sorts of data that yield that insight – how important religion is in peoples' lives and decisions, what aspects of their affairs prove to respond to religious beliefs or ways of seeing things and which ones do not, how the cultural life of various groups brings to expression even in secular ways religious perspectives on relationships and the like – these data are of one kind: the hard facts of public opinion polling, surveys of action and attitude, and the like.

EPISTEMOLOGICAL ISSUES: But what about the data that derive from times past, meaning, from any time prior to yesterday? These data, broadly construed, we may call "historical," with the proviso that by "historical data" we mean something considerably more diverse than simply archival sources, the written records of the past, on the one side, and the evidence of material culture, the archaeological detritus of the past, on the other. These two principal sources for the study of religion in society before our own time and place have of course to be examined when we want to know what kinds of lessons about religion and the social order history teaches. But religion comes to realization in a great many other kinds of sources as well, and these other permanent records of the religious world tell us about the past in a different way from the conventional literary and archaeological data. Such sources, also historical, include architecture and the graphic arts, symbolic arts, music, dance, the design of cities and of clothing, the presentation of theater and of mime, the telling of stories and the expression of the faith through ritual. There is scarcely a medium to be excluded from the ways by which a religious system of the social order may make its statement. So when we ask, "what kinds of lessons does history teach," we want to know, precisely what do we know about religion in past time from the entire range of data, conventional and unconventional, and various mixes of such data, that attest to the day before yesterday.

WHAT WE HOPE TO ACHIEVE: GAINING NEW PERSPECTIVE ON THE STUDY OF RELIGION AND SOCIETY: The conference thus aims at addressing the future of research, with special interest in the identification of appropriate problems and methods in the study of diverse kinds of data, conventional, unconventional, and mixed, in character. What can we who work mainly with historical materials do, and what can we not do, in the study of religion and the social order? We know not only what contemporary social science, sociology and anthropology, but also economics, psychology, and so on, are able to accomplish: the questions they ask, the kinds of data they use, the answers they present. Are there questions we can ask that they cannot ask? Are there questions they can ask that we cannot ask? Where do we who work with pre-contemporary data find the limits, but also the openings, of our work, with special reference to the social and public side of religion?

Our conference focuses in particular upon one dimension of religion, which is religion and the social order. We want to form an agenda of questions that guide us to new kinds of data and show us how diverse kinds of data – the conventional and the unconventional – together contribute to a coherent account of how religion shapes and integrates societies. At the same time, we want to draw into the study of religion beyond the acutely contemporary moment – that is, the history of religion, broadly construed – perspective deriving from contemporary social science. Social science in sociology and demography, political science, economics, psychology, and other areas gathers data out of today's facts and interprets those data; a program of questions has been shaped that responds to the character of those data. Now that we are re-forming the academic study of religion in times past to take account of data of an other-than-immediately-contemporary character (hence, in a broad sense, "historical") and also data that are not in writing or in material culture along with data that are, data that are not in the cultures of the West along with those that are, we have a new problem. It is to bring to our study that perspective on the study of religion and society that social science uniquely provides. Readers of this volume will decide how far along the path toward our never-to-be-attained goal we have come in these papers.

AN ACADEMIC RESPONSE TO THE CHALLENGE OF MULTI-CULTURALISM: A major challenge – not a problem, but a welcome challenge – facing American universities in the next generation will be a constructive response to the entirely legitimate demand that every constituency in our social order find a comfortable home in the academic curriculum of the universities. "Multi-culturalism" stands for many things, constructive and deplorable. Properly understood, the humanities, which concern themselves with the imagination and intellect of diverse civilizations over time, by definition realize the ideals of inclusive and comprehensive attention to all that counts – and nothing that does not – for which the word "multi-culturalism" stands in many settings. The humanities have been multicultural in sympathy and practice before the generality of opinion recognized that diversity and broad sympathy mark the condition of humanity. So in the nature of things it is in the humanities that we address the traditions of learning that are particular to different countries and ethnic groups, regions and races; the challenge of multi-culturalism faces humanities scholars.

Some humanistic disciplines serve better than others to accomplish the task of inclusion. When universities organize as free-standing units black studies or Jewish studies or Chicano studies or women's studies and the rest, they reinforce the exclusive character of the curriculum throughout; they make no effort to draw from diverse learning and experience lessons for a common inquiry. If mostly blacks study Afro-American subjects, with others coerced by degree requirements to do so, or if Jewish studies form an intellectual ghetto for ethnic celebration, then the university finds itself deprived of what it requires from the legacy of learning and experience that these formerly excluded groups, among many, owe to the common concern. So the public interest requires that multi-culturalism find its task in inclusion, not exclusion, in the tearing down of walls constructed by special pleading and the self-evidence of racism (ethnic traits, for instance).

Where to accomplish this task in a manner more in keeping with the character of the data that are studied than in the study of religion? The natural meeting place is, of course, the study of religion, which exists to present the particularities of distinct cultures and regions and races and ethnic groups and nations, but also to find the general rules that pertain to them all. The study of religion was multi-cultural before multi-culturalism defined a principal mission of university learning – scholarship and teaching – as it now does. The fact that, in these pages, so vast a range of human experience, over time and space and circumstance, may be examined, so wide a perspective and so broad a vision may come to bear, shows what religion can do to include everybody and exclude nobody.[2] Here again, readers of these papers

---

[2]The textbook for world religions and American religions courses that I edited, *World Religions in America. An Introduction* (Louisville, 1994: Westminster/John Knox Press), translates into a concrete course of study these same claims about the character of the study of religion to accomplish the goals of multi-culturalism.

will decide for themselves whether we have taken a step toward the goal
of showing how many religions may contribute to the study of religion,
so, in one area of learning and sensibility, how many diverse kinds of
social experience may help everyone to understand the social world
viewed whole and in an integrated aspect.

Within the disciplines that form the study of religion under academic
auspices – both humanistic and social scientific – those that take up data
of an other-than-social-scientific character, such as history of religion,
philology, literature of religion, philosophy of religion, archaeology, the
study of religion documented not by material culture but by music,
dance, theater, poetry, story (myth), graphic arts and plastic arts, and the
like are the disciplines that know how to address specificities of gender,
race, ethnic group, class, and the like. These disciplines are now defining
themselves in the context of the challenge of the hour and some time to
come: how to encompass a much wider sample of groups (defined
variously), how to deal with a much broader range of types of data, than
we presently address.

A HUMANISTIC RESPONSE TO THE CHALLENGE OF
CONTEMPORARY SOCIAL SCIENCE RESEARCH ON RELIGION: Social
scientists have defined exceedingly successful methods to deal with
religion in the world today. Data other than that of an acutely
contemporary venue, by contrast, are addressed in some few ways, and
not all of these are fully articulated as to method and conception,
research program and problematic. The humanities in the study of
religion need to formulate a self-conscious program of methods that can
yield generalizations and insights on religion and the social order in
times past, comparable in breadth of vision to, though different in shape
and structure from, the great achievements of social science in our
century. To do this, we need to ask successful scholars of the study of
religion in times past to think about the kinds of questions they maintain
their data permit them to address, and to compare the research programs
resting on those kinds of data with the ones undertaken by contemporary
social science, on the one side, and by disciplines working on different
sorts of data from those on which they labor, on the other. In other
words, it is time to do some work of methodological comparison and
contrast: what kinds of questions can I ask of the data on which I work,
how do my questions compare to those of others working on
contemporary or other than contemporary data, with methods particular
to data or methods aimed at generalization across cultural lines: what

---

That textbook is one that I could have conceived and organized only in the
setting of the University of South Florida or an equivalent place: a full-service
university on the urban frontier.

methods will govern the study of religion as a public fact of the social order in the day that has come, when the diverse kinds of social orders have found a legitimate and welcome place within the academy.

Since this book presents the public record of a conference, there is no pretense at a systematic and internally coherent argument for a single proposition. But the connections between the papers are not to be missed. Each participant takes seriously the challenge of rethinking not just research but the formulation of the agendum of research. All address a single subject and take seriously its definition; everyone sets forth an answer to the problem in connection with that subject that framed our interest. So while the book does not unfold in a single connected statement, from beginning to end, the papers are intended to, and I believe do, join together in treating one subject and pursuing one problematic. A mark of success will be future conferences that ask specialists to address a common problem in a manner intelligible to specialists in other areas, on the one side, and students of the subject, on the other.

Acknowledgments

I organized this conference because I have found at the University of South Florida a coherent intellectual program that would sustain such a project: a critical mass of scholars, all working on a single coherent problem, each in his or her own area of specialization to be sure. That distinguished colleagues contributed their learning and energy to the project, furthermore, underscores the broad interest that that problem has attracted. While some study religion to investigate its intellectual propositions, and others its psychological foundations, and still others its capacity to form and inform the life of social groups, we take as our problem religion in times past and in its most public aspect: that which a group of people do together, the statement that they make through their religion, the facticity of religion as a principal and often paramount component of the social life of humanity.

My first thanks go to the scholars, both American and from overseas, who took up the burden and challenge of thinking about our question in the setting of their areas of special knowledge. In addition to those represented in this book, others, from Europe and the State of Israel, joined us and shared in our discussions. The contributions of each are appreciated, and I take pride in having created an occasion for discussions of worth and illumination.

Since ours is one of America's largest universities, facing the challenge of the urban frontier in ways in which, in times past, the state universities took up the challenge of the agricultural frontier, it is particularly important that the academic study of religion establish its place in what I believe is a trend-setting center of learning. The engagement in this project of the new President, Provost, and Dean, as well as of the University's distinguished Honors Program, augurs well for a subject that, elsewhere, struggles to cope with powerful negative pressures. It is the intellectual vitality of the study of religion, the critical importance of the questions that that study takes up, that in the end will – and should – dictate the fate of the field. The conference recorded here means to make a statement in response to the challenge every field must address, and the University's senior administration manifestly has given our field a cordial hearing. For this uncommon grace we express special gratitude. It is not to be taken for granted.

The students who formed an integral part of the work and for whom I organized the conference to begin with derive from three distinct streams of our University's vast constituency. First are the honors students. A University of South Florida Honors Program seminar focused on studying in advance most of the papers of the conference. The undergraduates, both in the Honors Program and Religious Studies majors, worked diligently and intelligently in preparing themselves for this project. Second are the graduate students for the Master of Arts in the Department of Religious Studies. Some of the graduate students who participated in the seminar contributed responses to the papers. The students, undergraduate and graduate, served as hosts for the conference and chaired many of the sessions. I take great pride in their commitment to learning and the hard work they invested in preparing themselves to participate. Once more I appreciate the opportunities for scholarship, expressed in both publication and teaching, occasioned by the educational task at hand. As to all of the undergraduates in the seminar and the graduate students, a simple word of praise suffices from a veteran professor. I have not taught better students in thirty-five years of college teaching, nor can I recall more sheer pleasure in teaching than these wonderful young people gave me. Third are the senior citizens, retired professors and physicians, who participated in the seminar and contributed their learning and wisdom. They represent the special wealth of Florida, its natural resource.

Funds to support the conference and its activities, both social and collegial, came from a number of sources. It remains to express thanks to those foundations and individuals that made possible both the conference and also the preparation and the publication of this book. These are as follows: The Earhart Foundation, Ann Arbor, Michigan; The Max Richter Foundation of Rhode Island; G.G. Meisels, Provost of the University of South Florida; Rollin Richmond, Dean of the College of Arts and Sciences of the University of South Florida; Stuart Silverman, Director of the Honors Program of the University of South Florida; and further staff support and assistance from William Heller, Dean of the University of South Florida at St. Petersburg, and his staff, particularly Mrs. Julie Gillespie; the Library of the University of South Florida at St. Petersburg, and particularly Mr. Jerry Notaro, who took responsibility for video-taping the proceedings for the University Archives at University of South Florida at St. Petersburg and for televising them on the City of St. Petersburg Municipal Cable Channel.

The secretarial staff of the Department of Religious Studies at the University of South Florida in Tampa, and their counterparts at the University of South Florida in St. Petersburg, undertook many tasks, small and large, and carried them out promptly, efficiently, and with much good will. No one can take for granted the kind of ongoing support that a project such as this requires, and I am especially thankful to people whose professionalism shades over into commitment.

All concerned also thank the newly elected President of the University of South Florida, Mrs. Betty Castor, for serving as chairman of the inaugural event, and for the other senior leadership of the University, the Provost, the Dean of the College of Arts and Science, and the Dean of University of South Florida at St. Petersburg, who on successive days of work welcomed our conference colleagues. That eagerness to salute and encourage our work signals that the administration of this University takes seriously humanistic learning in general, and the academic study of religion in particular, and promises a bright future for this subject in this place.

The Finnish Academy made possible the participation of Professor Karl-Johan Illman and Dr. Siv Illman, both of the Theology Faculty at Åbo Akademi, Åbo/Turku, Finland, Finland's Swedish-language university. During my protracted stay as Gästforskarprofessor, Visiting Research Professor, at Åbo Akademi's Research Institute, I was able to review the program of this conference with the Illmans, who made many useful suggestions, and I especially appreciate their making the long journey to join in our proceedings. Other overseas guests of the conference, from Europe and the State of Israel, as well as Canadian and American colleagues who participated, enjoyed their universities' support in attending the meeting, for which we are grateful.

No work of mine can omit reference to the exceptionally favorable circumstances in which I conduct my research as Distinguished Research Professor in the Florida State University System at the University of South Florida. I organized this conference and therefore edited this book as part of my labor of research scholarship, expressed through both publication and teaching at the University of South Florida, which has afforded me an ideal situation in which to conduct a scholarly life. I express my thanks for not only the advantage of a Distinguished Research Professorship, which for a scholar must be the best job in the world, but also of a substantial research expense fund, ample research time, and some stimulating and cordial colleagues. In the prior chapters of my career, I never knew a university that prized professors' scholarship and publication and treated with respect those professors who actively and methodically pursue research.

The University of South Florida, among all ten universities that comprise the Florida State University System as a whole, exemplify the high standards of professionalism that prevail in publicly-sponsored higher education in the United States and provide the model that privately-sponsored universities would do well to emulate. Here there are rules, achievement counts, and presidents, provosts, and deans honor and respect the University's principal mission: scholarship, scholarship alone – both in the classroom and in publication. Here at last I find integrity governing in the lives of people true to their vocation and their mission.

Jacob Neusner
DISTINGUISHED RESEARCH PROFESSOR OF RELIGIOUS STUDIES
UNIVERSITY OF SOUTH FLORIDA
TAMPA

I.

RELIGION AND AMERICA'S SOCIAL ORDER

1

Religion and the Social Order: The Tasks of the Study of Religion

William Scott Green
University of Rochester

To be able to see and describe the world as it is, you have to be ready to be always dealing with things that are complicated, confused, impure, uncertain — all of which runs counter to the usual idea of intellectual rigor.

Pierre Bordieu

Our host for this conference has given us an exceptional and creative intellectual assignment. He asks us to slip the bonds of our scholarly preparation — which trained us never to stray very far from our primary data — and to speculate, to imagine freely. Our assignment is nothing less than to transcend the limits of our evidence, to make historical remains — whether textual or artifactual — testify against themselves, to reveal what they ignore and to display what they cover up about the interplay between religion and the social order.

My task in particular is to sketch the coutours of our assigned inquiry. This is a daunting and unnerving assignment. Reflection on religion and the social order has a massive and rich intellectual history and scholarly literature, and the problem is an absolutely key component in the classics of social and psychoanalytic theories. Moreover, the basic categories of our topic, "religion" and "social order," are themselves abstractions grounded in these diverse theories. Thus, what "religion" and "social order" mean depends very much on what we mean when we use the categories. Different understandings of each category shape how the category is conceived to interract with the other. For example, definitions that cast religion in terms of ultimacy, transcendence, or all-pervasive meaning may actually ground the social order in religion, while definitions that distinguish religion in terms of lesser variables — such as interraction with superhuman beings — may do just the reverse. Likewise, the concept of "social order" can admit of a wide range of denotations — from class structure to symbolic interraction.

The difficulties of sketching the boundaries of our topic do not stop there. Even if we could achieve analytical and definitional uniformity with regard to "religion" and "social order," we would still encounter difficulties with the third component of our quest: history. Because they are survivals from the past, the data of any historical period are necessarily partial, both overdetermined and random. For any given period of the past, we hear too much from and about some people, and too little from and about others. It follows that our picture of any historical reality is always imbalanced, schematic, and incomplete. We build our historical constructions on the foundations we find, and our structures are always either too straight or lopsided.

Since the problem of the past's limited testimony about itself confronts all understandings of religion and the social order equally, perhaps we should begin reflecting on our problem here. Our aim is to achieve both sight of and insight into a reality our data do not display. To do so, we have to get beyond the apparently unavoidable objectification and schematization of historical reconstruction and description. The question is how to do that. Perhaps no contemporary thinker has worried and written more effectively about this problem than the French sociologist and social theorist Pierre Bordieu. According to Richard Jenkins, Bordieu's work begins with the understanding that all descriptions of social life, whether historical or contemporary, operate between two extremes. The first is objectivity, the world of authoritative rules of practice, articulated conventions of behavior, and endorsed cultural principles, the world of public pattern and regularity — the world lived , we might say, from the outside in. The second is subjectivity, the personal world of the individual social being, the world of unselfconscious habit and spontaneity, of strategy and innovation, of practical knowledge and action — the world lived, as it were, from the inside out. Bordieu decries the fact that social science must operate with these two alternatives because he judges them both to be artificial. Objectivity as a goal or mode of analysis produces static, artificial descriptions that mistake the normative for the actual. For example, in his study of marriage practices in Berber village society, Bordieu discovered that only three to four per cent of the polulation followed the practice of parrallel cousin marriage, although such practice was the cultural norm. Alternatively, subjectivity presupposes a false intimacy. He writes, "One cannot live the belief associated with profoundly different conditions of existence, that is, with other games and other stakes, still less give others the means of reliving it by the sheer power of discourse. Those who want to believe with the beliefs of others grasp neither the objective truth nor the subjective experience of belief" (Jenkins: 50-51). Bordieu appears to be claiming that it is impossible to grasp another social world through the intellectual operations of objectivity or subjectivity. Rather, to make sense of social behavior, he claims, we need to recognize the mix of "subjective dispositions" within objective constraints, to understand the ways in which real social life is a mix of expectation and circumstance, rules and spontaneity. Bordieu seems to say that we cannot experience the social practice of others. Our possibility of understanding another social world, then, comes in the recognition that we are like the people we study because we know how to operate our culture as they know how to operate theirs. Hence, Bordieu calls for what he labels the "objectification of objectfication," an intellectual move in which we treat ourselves as if we were "other," and put our own cultural practices to the tests to which we subject others. This helps us to see how constructed, and culturally specific, our accounts of social reality are. For Bordieu, the description of society contains a couble vision, a dual complexity. The world we are in, which we know imperfectly in one way, and the world we want to describe, which we know imperfectly in another way, need to be worked together.

The remainder of this essay is an attempt to demonstrate, with a fairly elaborated pedagogical example of a familiar historical case, the dense complexity, the double embeddedness of present and past, that I understand Bordieu to describe. I focus on a pedagogical example in order to begin close-up, with the culture I understand best. First, I will focus on some aspects of the interaction of religion and the social order within our own contemporary sphere of action. Second, I will ask how the study of religion contributes to, subverts, reproduces, or is irrelevant to that interraction. Third, I will move from the present to a consideration of religion and the social order in a well-known but pivotal historical context. In the end, I hope the example will show us what is at stake for the study of religion in the question this conference has invited us to consider. [1]

II

Perhaps no issue so preoccupies the contemporary college campus as does the question of difference. Like the proverbial glossary of the Eskimos' words for snow, the academic lexicon for difference is extensive

---

[1]The remainder of this article is reprinted with permission from *The Journal of the American Academy of Religion,* Winter, 1994, 1191-1207.

and nuanced. Whether we use the language of political correctness, multiplicity, diversity, multiculturalism, otherness, identity politics, or the politics of recognition, learning how to make sense of, and to live with, people who — in fundamental ways — are not like us (whoever *we* are!) has become a central concern of the curriculum, the co-curriculum, and residential life.

The increasing diversity of students and faculty is both a primary cause and result of a major shift in academic self-consciousness, particularly in the humanities and social sciences. The proliferation of new, ideology- and confession-driven fields of study has altered our sense of where and how we teach and learn, and even of the nature of knowledge itself. Perhaps the academy once conceived and presented itself as a center of neutral inquiry and dispassionate cerebral discourse. If so, no longer. American colleges and universities now offer an educational context of concentrated pluralism, in which students, faculty, and administrators encounter and assess divergent and often conflicting theories, methods, experiences, points of view, and intellectual loyalties. The contemporary educated American is marked no less by possession of an erudite and analytical intellect than by the capacities to engage in and negotiate with argued conviction. To be educated is to know how to understand, experience, and respect difference.

Religion has been a bit player in the intellectual drama of the past decade. Rather, the curricular struggles over cultural diversity and inclusiveness have been fought out primarily in the arenas of gender, ethnicity, sexual orientation, and national origin, and principally in the fields of history, sociology, and literature. In some instances religion has been deliberately excluded from the enterprise. For example, biblical texts[2] have been derided as part of the established canon that needs to be overturned. Some campuses have tagged Judaism — whose classic writings remain substantially unrepresented and underrepresented in college curricula, particularly in the American south and midwest — as part of the majority's culture and banished it from the multicultural agenda. Christianity, of course, has taken its own set of multicultural hits, both without and within the study of religion. Moreover, when curriculum committees, governmental agencies, and foundations do include religion in discussions about diversity, they tend to lump religion with other forms of difference — race, gender, ethnicity, etc. — as if all were species of the same genus. But surely being a Buddhist, being gay, and being African-American constitute fundamentally dissimilar ways in

---

[2]Despite occasional protestations to the contrary from the AAR's leadership, biblical studies is a highly visible and numerically very significant component of the study of religion.

which human beings identify and understand themselves in, and are identified and understood by, American society. As K. Anthony Appiah observes, these "collective social identities matter to their bearers and to others in different ways. Religion, for example, unlike all the others, entails attachments to creeds or commitment to practices" (150). Far from enhancing religion, these catalogues of difference can obscure, and even deny, religion's distinctive traits.

The relative absence of religion and the study of religion from America's recent debates about difference is ironic but hardly unprecedented. For reasons too familiar to need rehearsal here, religion remains a highly charged and awkward subject in American public discourse and in American education. Though there are signs of change, religion's quest for legitimacy and recognition in American higher education has always seemed something of a struggle, and many scholars and fields treat religion as the humanities' country cousin. The judgment of the historian R. Laurence Moore that "no centrally important component of American life is more regularly neglected in synthetic accounts of American history than religion" (9) could be applied, *mutatis mutandis,* to other fields as well. But why curse the darkness yet again? Rather, let us ask, What would religion and its study contribute to America's multicultural debate, the so-called "culture wars?" Three points of particular relevance immediately suggest themselves. First, religion shapes American pluralism in distinctive ways. Second, the study of religion illustrates the kind of education we think we need now. Third, religion, particularly western religion, has been our primary school for difference. Let us take these up in turn.

Religion and American Pluralism

The American doctrine of freedom of religion grounds and in many ways justifies American pluralism — the very national trait that generates the demographic, intellectual, and curricular developments described above. The First Amendment to the Constitution guarantees three basic American freedoms: religion, speech, and the press. Americans often overlook the conjunction of the three in same amendment. Just as free speech and a free press distinctively shape and define American politics, society, and culture, so too does freedom of religion. By naming religion and marking it off for special consideration, the Constitution embeds the notion of religion in American culture. Because of the First Amendment, religion is a native category for Americans , a basic, culturally significant classification that we routinely and intuitively use to make sense of the world and explain what is happening to us. That there is religion and that religion matters are axioms of American life.

The presence of religion on the First Amendment's list extends freedom to communities as well as to individuals. Because the category of religion includes both individual conscience — the freedom to believe — and collective behavior — the freedom (within some limits) to live those beliefs — religious liberty implies the freedom , and perhaps the right, of communities to work to survive. Whatever its initial intent (which may have been limited to Protestant denominations) the First Amendment's restriction of government control over religion places difference — both individual and collective — at the heart of the nation's character. In a fundamental respect, America's initial conversation about difference should be — must be — a discourse about religion.

The First Amendment guarantees that America will have more than one religion and affirms that religion is a legitimate, legally protected form of difference in American society. Americans are supposed to differ from one another religiously. Indeed, it is no exaggeration to suggest that our national ability not merely to abide but to sanction difference — to affirm difference as a social benefit — derives from our constitutional commitment to religious freedom. To be sure, America's diversity of population — its status as an immigrant nation — precedes the Constitution. But the First Amendment shapes a distinctive American attitude towards diversity by depicting difference as a cultural good, as something to be appreciated, defended, and preserved. In the form of religious difference, pluralism — particularly on questions of value — characterizes our national life. In America, whatever else religion is about, it is about the freedom to be different.

Religion and Education

These factors help to explain why the study of religion is particularly well-suited to the kind of education we think we need now. Education is society's primary mode of socialization and acculturation. It is where Americans acquire not only necessary information and skills, but also a basic sense of American culture and its endemic pluralistic structure and values. Higher education has a share in this responsibility and a stake in this mission. College learning, therefore, cannot be incongruous to the culture to which it prepares students to contribute; it must aim to equip them for the real circumstances they will encounter. To provide the foundation for work and life in an increasingly diverse and divided society, college study must educate about difference and for tolerance. Because of the First Amendment's doctrine of religious freedom, America has engaged in a two hundred year experiment in tolerating difference, an exercise in pluralism that has succeeded more often than it has failed. To appreciate how American pluralism works in particular requires understanding the place of religion in American culture and society. But understanding religion's privilege in America depends on knowing what is at stake in religion itself.

Scholars of religion often explain the educational pertinence of our field by claiming that the study of religion is inherently cross-cultural and comparative. The claim is accurate in principle since the goal of the field is to explain the general category "religion" (as linguistics tries to explain "language"), and the general category cannot be understood through one religion alone. But cross-cultural comparison is practiced in only some sectors of the study of religion, and then in very specific ways. Most of us spend most of our careers achieving expertise in one religion, and even people who study two do not consistently or necessarily do so comparatively. Moreover, cross-cultural comparison is carried out in other disciplines as well, particularly anthropology, history, and comparative literature. Rather than cross-cultural comparison, what gives the study of religion particular educational relevance just now is the way religion anchors difference in conviction.

Increasingly in the humanities and social sciences, accepted modes of analysis and interpretation are being joined and often challenged by what we might call experiential foundationalism. Fields of study have emerged that are grounded in the experience of a group or community in the world. Typically, the group's experience is one of disregard by the larger culture. That experience is refined, abstracted, and developed into a set of questions, perspectives, and lenses that are applied to any and all other topics and phenomena and expose them in fresh and interesting ways. The sociologist Todd Gitlin explains:

> Each [group] felt it had a distinct world to win — first by establishing that its group had been suppressed and silenced; then by exhuming buried work and exploring forms of resistance; and, finally, by trying to rethink society, literature, and history from the respective vantages of the silenced, asking what the group and, indeed, the entire world would look like if those hitherto excluded were now included. (315)

This can be called experiential foundationalism because the core experience on which the field builds is epistemologically unassailable. We can interrogate, for example, claims made by women or African-Americans, or Jews for and about their experience in the world, but we cannot deny the experience. These new fields of learning begin in conviction and develop into argument. Experiential foundationalism may have found fresh expression in the rest of the humanities and social sciences during the past decade, but it is nothing new in the study of religion. Indeed, the appeal and persistence of religions lie partially, if not principally, in their conviction of the fundamental correctness of their vision of reality, which both shapes and is generated by their adherents' experience in the world. Religions are compelling because of their affirmations of certitude and truth, because of their refusal to compromise on basic convictions, and because of the extent of their claims on the human person. Unlike other aspects of culture — politics or philosophy, for example — religion tends to extend its reach, to be comprehensive in scope. In nearly all societies, the cultural construction we call religion exhibits enormous range of expression. For instance, religion attacks all the senses — not only in speech and writing, but also in art, music, and dance, in smell and taste, in ethics, sexuality, and intellect. Most religions have cosmologies and eschatologies, theories of nature, birth, gender, marriage, suffering, and death. Few political systems, social ideologies, or philosophies have such a reach or exhibit religion's capacity to make definitive demands on the total human being. As Moore puts it, "Religion, even conceived as a very earth-bound cultural construction, yields a different sort of allegiance than most other things, whatever the close analogues" (9).

Because the study of religion deals with whole worlds, intersecting worlds, and worlds within worlds, the field offers no Archimedean cognitive point and advocates no single analytical perspective. Rather, the study of religion, as the encounter between and among religions, is de-centered. There are always at least two standpoints — frequently divergent, often conflicting, occasionally contradictory. In the study of religion, analysis and interpretation are processes of intellectual negotiation, movements from somewhere to somewhere, rather than judgments made from a stable analytical center. The most demanding work of the field is to make sense of consequential ways of living and influential modes of experience that are alien and even threatening to us — particularly in religions we think we know well . The absence of a fixed analysis or normative interpretive focus strengthens the study of religion by forcing our work of understanding to be disciplined and rigorous, based on demonstrable erudition, and accessible to the broadest courts of appeal. To make sense of difference in this way is not relativism, and understanding a religion requires neither assent nor dismissal. But without understanding, no judgment of any religion or its values and practices can have intellectual merit or advance knowledge; it is impressionistic, mere prejudice. In all this, the study of religion exhibits precisely the sort of cultural difference we encounter in society and possesses distinctive resources for the educational issues of the contemporary academy.

If there is a contextual resemblance between religion and the new fields of study, there is a procedural one as well. In precisely the sense that these new fields of learning move from experience to conviction to argument, they resemble theology. This similarity should encourage us to rethink the place of theology in the study of religion, particularly in secular institutions. Over the past quarter century, the study of religion has developed a strong tendency to identify theology as mere confessionalism and to place theology — as constructive and analytical discourse — out of academic bounds. It now is commonplace for students to complete a college religion major without having read, or sometimes even encountered, such figures as Barth, Bonhoeffer, Tillich, Niebuhr, Rosenzweig, or Heschel. Few religion departments will insist that their majors need a semester's exposure to theological thinking as a basic part of their orientation in the study of religion. The separation of theology from religion diminishes both.

At the very least, theology is the intellectual elaboration of a religion. It is a kind of thinking about a religion that emerges from within a religion. Though it necessarily reflects the "native'"viewpoint, theology is more than merely expressive. Rather, it is the attempt to articulate and make explicit what a religious intellectual judges to be basic to and implicit in the way a religion is structured and the way it works. Although theology emerges from within a religion, it necessarily entails both criticism and self-criticism, reflection and self-reflection. Religions cannot see themselves and thus can neither develop nor persist, without theological articulation. All religions, albeit in different forms, have a theological discourse, which is as natural to them as is myth, symbol, or ritual.

Because theology is discursive, it is a species of argument. Indeed, theology can be seen as a religion's argument about its convictions, its application of those convictions to the world beyond itself. Theology, therefore, also is a mode of translation. It looks outward in a way that other components of a religion — ritual, for example — do not. Indeed, it often is through theology that outsiders begin the process of understanding the "inside" of a religion, its structure of sense and sensibility. In a cultural period that sometimes seems ready to abandon the complexities of language for the silent essentialism of the body, theology in an academic context will remind us that religion also — powerfully, basically, and necessarily — is a matter for the mind. Confessionalism is no longer a ground for exclusion from academic discourse. The arguments that will justify ethnic studies or gender studies also will justify theology. If we can have feminism in the classroom, we can have theology there too.

Religon as a Model for Difference

Perhaps the most striking irony in the relative absence of religion from academic multiculturalism is that some of our most persistent mental habits and social praxes for dealing with difference derive from religion. In the West, religion has been one of our principal schools for otherness. One of the most enduring western patterns of conceiving and constructing otherness is exemplified in and perhaps generated by the relationship of Judaism and Christianity. For both historical and theological reasons, Christianity must have a theory (or theories) of its difference from Judaism in order to be Christianity. As a result, Judaism has had to develop a reciprocal theory (or theories) of its difference from Christianity.

There are many ways Judaism and Christianity, as religions and as cultures — and Jews and Christians as individuals — have come to represent and conceive one another. All of these have been a major part of the possibilities for pluralism, and the obstacles to it, that have shaped western culture and western attitudes about difference and otherness. These models of difference have been persistent components of the western social order. In what remains, let us focus on one of these models of difference, a model I call "otherness by exclusion." This is a model in which otherness is conceived not in terms of mutuality and reciprocity, but in terms of singularity. It is a model in which difference is cast in terms of negation and denial of the other. It is a model that says, "me, not you," or "us, not them." In its most extreme form, it says, "For me to live, you must die."

This model of otherness is a standard component of biblical, rabbinic, and patristic writings, and it has been a foundation stone — some might say a stumbling block — in religious exchanges between Jews and Christians since the first century. Some forms of the idea of Israel as the chosen people can be said to illustrate the model, and the doctrine of supersession, which holds that Christianity has replaced Judaism — and has done so necessarily — can be said to do so as well. This depiction of difference has become a basic part of western consciousness, so much so that many of us have adjusted to it, absorbed it, and can hear it without flinching. The price of our accommodation to the model of otherness by exclusion — in a wide variety of historical and contemporary contexts — hardly requires spelling out. As the novelist David Grossman writes, in a somewhat different context, "We are social creatures..., and even when we are alone we create internal relationships with different parts of ourselves. And when we accustom ourselves to relations like those between master and slave, that division is stamped within us as well. It suddenly becomes a possible mold for our relations with our friends" (40).

How does the study of religion help us grasp both the origin and persistence of this model in Judaism and Christianity? Equally (perhaps more) important, how should we handle teaching it in a classroom setting? The model of otherness by exclusion as it is manifest historically in the encounter of Judaism and Christianity is one of the most painful and intractable elements of the Jewish-Christian encounter, and educational conversations about it are therefore especially important. Cognition and affect go hand in hand; how students feel about what they study influences the way, and whether, they will learn it. How we teach students to think and speak publicly about this material is an important matter.

To help us gain a sense of the persistence and contemporaneity of the model of otherness by exclusion, consider a recent book by James D.G. Dunn entitled, *The Partings of the Ways between Christianity and Judaism and their Significance for the Character of Christianity*. Dunn's book is a fine example of the genre of scholarship that attempts to understand Christianity against and within its second Temple Jewish context. At the conclusion of his work, Dunn writes that his *"lasting impression of this study must be the enduring Jewish character of Christianity"* (258). One paragraph later he concludes:

> One thought in particular has returned to me again and again during my work in preparing these chapters: *Christianity began as a movement of renewal breaking through the boundaries first within and then round the Judaism of the first century.* At its historic heart Christianity is protest against any and every attempt to claim that God is our God and not yours. Against any and every tendency to designate others as "sinners", as beyond the pale of God's saving grace, or to insist that for sinners to receive forgiveness they must become righteous, that is "righteous" as *we* count "righteousness." Against any and every attempt to mark off some of God's people as more holy than others, as exclusive channels of divine grace over others. At its heart it is a protest against every attempt to pigeon hole and institutionalize the grace of God, to limit that grace in its expression to the safe confines that human minds can cope with and human capacities organize. At its heart is an openness to the unexpectedness of divine grace, to the new thing which God may wish to do, even when it breaks through and leaves behind the familiar paths and forms. At its heart is the conviction that God revealed himself most fully not just in human word but in human person, not just in rational or even inspired propositions but in the human relationships which can never be confined within words and formulae alone.
>
> And it is this character of Christianity which is encapsulated and canonized within our NT writings, and which gives them their distinctive character within the wider "canon" of Jewish and Christian normative texts. (259)

This long conclusion to a book written to celebrate the Jewish character of Christianity shows just how difficult the model of otherness by exclusion is to shake. Despite Dunn's obvious sympathy for Judaism, and a desire to build historical and intellectual bridges between them, his language of opposition, boundary-breaking, protest, and negation show how powerful the model of otherness by exclusion is, and how it can draw even the best of intentions into its wake.

How should teachers of religion in a liberal arts setting treat the model of otherness by exclusion in a college course? It is important to affirm at the outset that we have an intellectual and pedagogical responsibility not to condemn this model, nor to dismiss it, nor to apologize for it. If religion really is at the heart of American pluralism, then it is in the study of religion in particular that the stark barriers of irreconcilable difference must be confronted. Students — whose public education has largely avoided the study of religion altogether — usually prefer to focus on the agreements between religions than on disputes. But our task as teachers in the study of religion must be to work with our students to understand why, as the model appears in scripture and other ancient Jewish and Christian writings, it was, and remains, compelling to so many. We need to work to understand why this way of thinking was and is both rationally powerful and emotionally appealing to the people who adopted it, without offering moral judgments on it, at least initially. That is easier said than done.

One classroom approach to making sense of otherness by exclusion is to focus on the interplay between the categories of religion and politics, between the constancies of culture and the vagaries of power, to pay attention to the context of the origination of the model (as the texts portray it) and the context of its application. Specifically, we can ask what happens when a model of difference that emerges in a setting of powerlessness is applied in a context of power.

A survey of the literature of early Judaism and Christianity suggests that the Persian period — and its contexts of exile, imperialism, and colonialism — is pivotal for understanding basic patterns of thought and action in the model of otherness by exclusion. Although it is commonplace — and correct — to identify the Persian period with the transformation of Israelite religion into Judaism, we often fail to appreciate — though we often acknowledge — the depth and persistence of a colonial situation and the way it has shaped the some of the foundational texts of Western culture. As scholarship has come to identify them, Judaism and Christianity are religions invented and developed by Jews in contexts of political weakness, if not outright powerlessness. With the exception of the brief period of the Maccabees, the Land of Israel was colonized continuously from 587/6 BCE through the production of the Palestinian Talmud. This means that the literature of what became Jewish religion — Scripture and rabbinic literature — were produced, and made sense, in a context in which Jews had circumscribed and limited control over their own destiny and significant portions of their lives.

Though it may have predecessors, the model of otherness by exclusion emerges with clarity in the Persian period, the period of Judaism's founding. The consensus of biblical scholarship is that the Babylonian exile, which began with the destruction of the Jerusalem Temple in 587/6 BCE and forced the upper echelons of Israelite society to migrate from the Land of Israel to Babylon, was a period of decisive transition in which the exiles' social organization, type of leadership, and religious practice underwent significant change. Daniel L. Smith suggests that the exile was a traumatic experience — exilic literature is preoccupied with the theme of suffering — and that the Israelites had to resist or face cultural death. They had three options for resistance: military, political, and cultural. Counseled by their prophets, particularly Jeremiah, the exiles chose to resist culturally but forge useful political relations with the ruling powers. They built strong cultural boundaries between themselves and their non-Israelite neighbors and transformed elements of their pre-exilic heritage into symbols of their identity. In this period, the Sabbath, intermarriage, and purity rules loom large. Smith lucidly explains this dynamic with reference to laws of ritual purity.

> It was not the *formulation* of laws of purity that represented the most creative response to Exile by the priestly writer, for...many of these laws...rest on older traditions. It was rather the *elaboration* of these laws to emphasize the *transfer* of pollution and the association of holiness with *separation*. While the post-exilic community reflected the results of these concerns, the most logical Sitz im Leben for their primary function was the Exile itself. The presence of these ritual elaborations of the meaning of separation lends...weight to our thesis that the Exile represented a threat to the Jewish minority. In sum what we see in the development of purity law is a creative, Priestly mechanism of social survival and maintenance. To dismiss this creativity as "legalism" is to forget, or ignore, the sociopolitical circumstances in which it was formulated. Majority cultures rarely understand, much less appreciate, the actions of minorities to preserve and maintain identity. (149)

The identification of separation with holiness has self-evident and far-reaching consequences for our model. As Smith notes, the strategy of survival devised by the exiles was successful — the Bible is proof of its effectiveness — and it assumes and responds to a circumstance of nearly total political powerlessness. The Israelites' strategy makes resistance to oppression internal rather than external and tries to make the ruling powers work to the advantage of the internal culture.

The next chapter in Israel's history shows what happens when a context shifts. In 538 BCE, nearly a half-century after the exile began, the Persian emperor Cyrus, who had conquered Babylon the year before, issued an edict allowing the Jews to return to their native land to rebuild their destroyed Temple. Under a sequence of leaders — Zerubbabel, Nehemiah, and Ezra — and as clients of the Persian emperor, some Jews returned home, to a land in which most of them had never lived, and they imported the religion of separation and holiness they so brilliantly crafted for an exile of powerlessness.

But now the context has changed, both for them and their religion. First, the cast of characters has changed. The ideology of protection and cultural maintenance that was developed to protect them from real aliens is now applied to their cousins, so to speak, Israelites not taken into exile, who do not share their experience of exile and deprivation, people who, like the returning children of exile, claim to be Israel too. Second, their political situation has changed. They have more power than they did in exile. More power, but not real power. The returning exiles, as well as those left behind, the people of the Land, are still colonized, still dependent on the Persians. In effect there are now two different Israels, each claiming to be the one Israel, and each dependent on the colonial power to legitimate the group's status. The Persians apparently practiced "ethnic collectivization," and membership in "ethnically distinct groups" may have determined possession of land and property (Hoglund). This establishes the setting for the internal application of the model of otherness by exclusion. The following passage from Ezra 4:1-3, whatever the historicity of its specifics, illustrates beautifully:

> When the enemies of Judah and Benjamin heard that the returned exiles were building a temple to the Lord the God of Israel, they approached Zerubbabel and Jeshua and the heads of the families and said to them, "Let us join you in the building, for like you we seek your God, and we have been sacrificing to him ever since the days of Esarhaddon king of Assyria, who brought us here. But Zerubbabel and Jeshua the rest of the heads of families in Israel said to them, "The house which we are building for our God is no concern of yours. We alone will build it, as his majesty Cyrus king of Persia commanded us."[3]

All the elements of the model of otherness by exclusion are here, including the colonial backdrop. The returnees alone will build God's temple, which they do with the imprimatur of the pagan king. Indeed,

---

[3]For a discussion of the translation of this verse, see Blenkinsopp: 45

the passage suggests a direct connection between legitimacy in the Lord's house and the Emperor's support (Blenkinsopp: 39-40; Carroll: 576). Here is otherness by exclusion. It is a response to imperial domination, to uncertain legitimacy, to lack of power, and it is aimed internally, not externally, at, or against, others who claim to be Israel, people who claim to be like "us." This model served to shape intragroup relations within Jewish society under imperial rule. In the early centuries of Judaism and Christianity within a context of political weakness — or perceived weakness — when Jews disagreed with one another religiously, the result tended to be mutual exclusion rather than negotiation

This model is evident in the response of the Dead Sea Scrolls to the defiled priests of the Jerusalem Temple, and in the utterly gratuitous scorn the Gospel of Matthew heaps on its hated "scribes and Pharisees." We also encounter it in Tosefta Hullin 2: 20-21, in a savage rabbinic condemnation of the so-called *minim*, a term translated as "sectarians," which many take to be Christians:

> The sacrifice of a *min* is idolatry. Their bread is the bread of a Samaritan, and their wine is deemed the wine of idolatry, and their produce is deemed wholly untithed, and their books are deemed magical books, and their children are *mamzerim* (illegitimate). People should not sell anything to them or buy anything from them. And they should not take wives from them nor give children in marriage to them. And they should not teach their sons a craft. And they should not seek either financial nor medical assistance from them.

Whether or not the *minim* were Christians is less important than the fact that rabbinic literature describes them as wearing phylacteries, offering sacrifices, and read and write Torah (Green). Early rabbis, like the returned exiles, had to prove their legitimacy, now to Roman imperial power, and drew sharp, exclusionary boundaries around those resembled them too closely.

In exile, the religion of holiness and separation protected the Jews from becoming culturally similar to those who were different. At home, in the Land of Israel, the same religion allowed them to declare themselves different from those who were culturally similar.

Since, after the return, the pattern of otherness by exclusion was a primary mode of intra-Jewish conflict, it hardly can surprise us that it characterizes much of early Christian discourse as well, particularly in the Gospel of Matthew, but also in Paul, Hebrews, and other New Testament writings. Christianity, after all, was a kind of Judaism. The pattern is applied with special vigor in the writings of early Church fathers, particularly Melito of Sardis, who accuses the Jews of deicide, and John Chrysostom. In these two cases in particular, the heat of the polemic is a function of too much political weakness and too much similarity. In Sardis, where Melito wrote, the Jews were politically powerful, the owners of a massive urban synagogue, and members of the town council. Melito was a figure, so far as we can tell, of no import at all. Perhaps his very inconsequence inflamed his rhetoric. Likewise Chrysostom. His sermons reached a feverish and unhealthy pitch largely because he feared the influence of the synagogue on his congregants. To be sure, once the Roman Empire became Christian, the words of Matthew, Melito, and Chrysostom acquired a power their authors perhaps never intended, with ugly consequences for the Jews.

All these examples suggest that in the study of Jewish-Christian relations the similarities between the two religions are more consequential than the differences. As Jonathan Smith has recently written:

> The issue of difference as a mode of both culturally encoding and decoding, of maintaining and relativizing internal as well as external distinctions, raises...the observation that, rather than the remote "other" being perceived as problematic and/or dangerous, it is the proximate "other," the near neighbor, who is most troublesome. That is to say, while difference or "otherness" may be perceived as being LIKE-US or NOT-LIKE-US, it becomes most problematic when it is TOO-MUCH-LIKE-US or when it claims to BE-US. It is here that the urgency of theories of the "other" emerges, called forth not so much by a requirement to place difference, but rather by an effort to situate ourselves. This, then, is not a matter of the "far," but preeminently of the "near." The deepest intellectual issues are not based upon perceptions of alterity, but, rather, of similarity, at times, even, of identity. (13)

To proximity — whether cultural or geographic — we must also add the variable of political power, the power of self-control, for the model of "otherness by exclusion" began in weakness and ended in unequal power relations. This model has been so successful that its patterns of perception and discourse of exclusion have persisted even when the circumstances of origination changed drastically. We know that power and proximity are two key variables in explaining the pattern. We must now search for the rest, and the study of religion will guide us on our way.

Epilogue

Pluralism is not simply a matter of the acceptance of mere difference. It is the tolerance of irreconcilable difference. What makes pluralism plural is the brute fact that, in the end, we are not going to change one another very much. American culture long ago renounced the possibility that irreconcilable differences would lead to social and political divorce.

The study of religion can be a powerful contributor to achieving the pluralistic society the Constitution mandates. American democratic pluralism requires a public that can respect difference. But we cannot respect what we cannot understand, and, more important, we destroy our common bonds as Americans if we judge one another without understanding. And invariably we do judge one another. Respect for difference does not come naturally; it has to be taught and it has to be learned. Genuine tolerance is not only an acquired skill, it is also an acquired taste. Religion is at the core of American pluralism and grounds a rich American heritage of toleration. It therefore stands to reason that the study of religion can be — and should be — basic to an American education.[4]

[4]My gratitude goes to Douglas R. Brooks, Th. Emil Homerin, Ray L. Hart, and Charles Winquist for help and stimulation.

Appiah, K. Anthony "Identity, Authenticity, Survival: Multicultural Societies and Social Reproduction," in Charles Taylor, *Multiculturalism: Examining the Politics of Recognition*. Princeton, 1994: Princeton University Press, pp. 149-163.

Blenkinsopp, Joseph "Temple and Society in Achaemenid Judah, in Philip R. Davies, ed., *Second Temple Studies.: 1. The Persian Period* Sheffield, 1991: Sheffield Academic Press, pp. 22-53.

Carroll, Robert P. "Israel, History of (Post Monarchic Period)," *Anchor Bible Dictionary* New York, 1993: Doubleday, Vol. III, pp. 567-576.

Dunn, James. D.G. *The Partings of the Ways between Christianity and Judaism and their Significance for the Character of Christianity* Philadelphia, 1991: Trinity Press International.

Gitlin, Todd "The Rise of Identity Politics," in Michael Berube and Cary Nelson, eds., *Higher Education Under Fire*. London and New York, 1995: Routledge.

Green, W.S. "Otherness Within: Towards a Theory of Difference in Rabbinic Judaism," in J. Neusner, ed., *To See Ourselves as Others See Us*. Chico, 1985: Scholars Press, pp. 49-70.

Grossman, David *The Yellow Wind*, New York, 1988: Delta.

Hoglund, Kenneth "The Achaemenid Context," in Philip R. Davies, ed., *Second Temple Studies.: 1. The Persian Period* Sheffield, 1991: Sheffield Academic Press, pp. 54-72.

Jenkins, Richard *Pierre Bordieu* London, 1992: Routledge.

Moore, R. Laurence *Selling God: American Religion in the Marketplace of Culture*. Oxford, 1994: Oxford University Press.

Smith, Daniel L. *The Religion of the Landless*. Bloomington, 1989: Meyer-Stone Books.

Jonathan Z. Smith, "Differential Equations: On Constructing the 'Other'," The University Lecture in Religion, 1992, Arizona State University.

II.

RE-IMAGINING THE BIBLE

2

Building Temples Out of Words, Building Temples Out of Stones: Venturing beyond Historical and Literary Reconstructions of Second Temple Israelite Religion

Kent Harold Richards
Illiff School of Theology/University of Denver

Almost 20 years ago the organizer and chairman of this conference wrote that "the point and purpose of tradition is not to pass on historical facts but both to create and to interpret contemporary reality, to intervene in history."[1] Today he has asked, "what kind of lessons does history teach us?" He has asked many more questions, and, I might add, some very ambitious interrogatories. "What do we mean by 'religion and the social order'?" "How do religious systems of the social order impart to a social group that sense of structure and meaning that holds people together and explains to them who they are and what they do together?"

Neusner's observation and his interrogatories today are related. In fact, I would sum up the questions merely by recasting the 20-year-old indicative statement to an interrogative: How might we intervene in history? To answer the question directly, and on the surface somewhat simply, I would say the only way to intervene is to develop, at a

---

[1] Jacob Neusner, "The Study of Religion as the Study of Tradition," in *History of Religions* 14 (1975), p. 195.

minimum, "bifocal vision." Now that is an appealing image to folks my age, but may not be so attractive to university students! Unless we are able to develop some images of preferred futures from our vantage point in the present, we are unlikely to be shapers of any intervention in history. We are likely to become the shaped not the shaper.

Since we are in a university context, I think that I should remind you of the incredible tenacity of universities. It has been reported that

> Taking as a starting point 1530, when the Lutheran Church was founded, some 66 institutions that existed then still exist today in the Western world in recognizable forms...the Catholic Church, the parliaments of Iceland and the Isle of Man, and 62 universities.[2]

Clark Kerr and his associates who discovered this fact went on to say that universities "have come out less changed than almost any segment of their societies." One wonders if this is a sign of distinction or decay. Certainly universities must reflect something of their surrounding culture without yielding to it. The fast forward we are in at the moment makes me wonder if the disciplines of the university and education in general is adaptable enough for the twenty-first century. The date in the sixteenth century that was used for this observation about the staying power of the university also is a date related to the rapid development of a new medium called the printing press. We are certainly on the cusp of the flourishing of a new medium called the computer. It is radically shaping how intervention takes place. We in the university will not be able to rest on the fact that universities have survived the best of all other institutions over the last 500 years. Universities are being challenged and should be challenged. We will need bifocal vision, if we are to meet the challenge.

One of the ways to meet the challenge is to try some diverse methods as we approach issues important to the study of religion and the social order. In order to observe the diverse forms of temples across the religions of the world and to assist each of us in the identification of our images of temple I will show you a series of photographs of temples. Speaking in a more comparativist mode, we will observe a series of images of holy space and place from a variety of religions. The purpose is for us to begin to have something over against which we can gain some contact with our own image of temple. We gain a kind of bifocal vision from seeing our own images beside those of others. Some of the pictures will be familiar to you. I suspect that no one will have seen all of these spaces and places. You will no doubt be puzzled my some of the photographs. Others may evoke in you some immediate attraction,

---

[2]Three Thousand Futures: The Next 20 Years in Higher Education (1980), p. 9.

distraction or some sort of ambivalence or even disinterest.   Another part of the purpose in our observing these 80 slides is to suggest our need as students of religion to use not only the textual images of temples built from words but also 'the temples built out of stones. The slides do not utilize enough of what we are going to need in the teaching of spaces and places of the twenty-first century, but it is a start. As it has been said, we teachers must begin to transform our low tech classrooms to meet more adequately the high tech kids we are seeing in the seminar room and lecture hall.

Second, and against these images of holy place and space I want to play the role of a speaker from the middle of the fifth century B.C.E. I will try to interject comments so that we have some common ground regarding the location out of which this speaker comes in the Persian Period and the Second Temple.

There is a warning label placed on my comments. I have no grand synthesis for you! The disposition of historical, literary and social science methods is part of our discussion over these days. I will not be holding my breath for someone to solve the issues. In fact, should it emerge I can assure you that we will know that we have indeed *not* intervened in history! For intervention is not a finished product, but a continuing and ever novel venture.

Photographs of Sacred Space and Place

The photographs re-present sacred space and place among a variety of religions from across the world.   They do not intend to be comprehensive nor to present a typology of temples. There is no effort to assert that these are the only places religious activities take place. In fact, one segment of the Hindu tradition is expressed by a twelfth century devotionalist poet, Basavanna, who writes, "the rich will make temples for Shiva. What shall I, a poor man, do? My legs are pillars, the body the shrine, the head a cupola of gold."[3] This observation from the Hindu writer will serve as a reminder to us that "it would be a serious error to assume that the study of stone (material) or literary (wordly) temples is the study" of any religion as a whole. To think of the body as a temple helps us to blow open our all-too-narrow conceptualization of holy space and place.

These photographs serve as a reminder that place has at least three dimensions: locales – the physical setting; location – the social, economic and religious effects at large on the locales; and a sense of place – or "structure of feeling." Place "refers to discrete if 'elastic' areas in which

---

[3]C.J. Fuller, "The Hindu Temple and Indian Society" in *Temple in Society* edited by Michael Fox (1988), p. 50.

settings for the constitution of social relations are located and with which people can identify."[4]

These photographs will also help us identify some of our own personal constructions of the places we have named temple, or as is the more common term in the Hebrew tradition "house of God." The photographs serve as a visual text. My words to you are also a text. And in fact your hearing is your construction of a text. The context between each of these texts may make it more possible for us to understand how we might intervene in history, open our eyes to envision new temples that are needed to transform the often dismal social order that surrounds us.[5]

When looking at a set of photographs I can not help but be reminded of Ian McEwan's evocative lines in his novel *Black Dogs.*

> It is photography itself that creates the illusion of innocence. Its ironies of frozen narrative lend to its subjects an apparent unawareness that they will change or die. It is the future they are innocent of. Fifty years on we look at them with the godly knowledge of how they turned out after all....with no thought for who will one day be holding photographs of us.

The extent to which we are able to hold photographs, especially ones of ourselves and the places we frequent, is indicative of our capacity to gain a bifocal vision. As the futurists have told us, we will even be better off if we imagine diverse scenarios of who will be holding our photographs. Think of those who care about us deeply holding those snapshots, but also the stranger and the enemy. What photographs of sacred place are you holding and have those pictures created for you an "illusion of innocence"?

---

[4]John Agnew, "Representing Space" in *Place/Culture/Representation* edited by James Duncan and David Ley (1993), p. 263.
[5]The slides shown at this point in the lecture incorporated images from many sources, and were arranged to juxtapose holy spaces from around the world. It was not intended to create a typology or thematic study. It was a multi-cultural representation of site and religious tradition, but did not include images that might intrude on sacred rituals. Images included sites from Israel (Shechem, Dome of the Rock, Avdat, the Western Wall and others), Burma, Thailand (especially a *pi* or spirit house), Alaska (a youth retreat), Tehuiltcan and other sites in Mexico from a variety of cultures, San Francisco (a Japanese tea house), Greek temples, cathedrals of Europe and China, just to name a few. My student assistant Sherry Nanninga coordinated the collection. Slides courtesy of Kent Harold Richards, Sherry Nanninga, Dr. Fay T. Bresler, Linda Closson, and Diane Kotowski (Curator of Visual Resources, University of Denver School of Art).

Conversation with a Second Temple Figure[6]

You need to let your imaginations run. I am a speaker from the mid-fifth century B.C.E., that is, from the midst of the Persian Period. I live amongst battles between various leaders from within my people in this small province of Judah. The prophetic book of Haggai may even illustrate the suppression of a deep conflict between leaders and people. There are also disagreements between leaders of the Persian Empire and the royal leaders of other empires. And there are challenges among the people themselves. We choose up sides by identifying ourselves as people of the land as opposed to returning exiles. There are even those who are opposed to the building of the temple (Isaiah 66:1-3). Certainly some from Samaria wanted to take part in the building of the temple but were promptly told by those closest to me among the returning exiles that Cyrus had told us, the returnees, to do the rebuilding ourselves (Ezra 4:3). While there are diverse perspectives on the temple found among our prophets, they, too, still seem to accept the new prominence of the Jerusalem temple.

Even the use of the term Jew is ambiguous among my people. Sometimes those closest to me, that is, the returning exiles, are able to group this designation from the others (Ezra 4:12). On other occasions people say Jew refers just to those living in Judah (Ezra 4:23; 5:1; Nehemiah 3:33-34). On still other occasions it names Jews living in other places (Nehemiah 4:6; 5:8). My group of returnees, those who really have the only right to use the distinctive name Jew, are clearly more economically blessed than those who remained in the land. We also have more power in the social fabric of our small region of fewer than 20,000 inhabitants. I remind you that our province of Judah is no larger than half the size of the state of Rhode Island. However, I am reminded of the vastness of the empire in which we reside.

I should also tell you that the legal and social roles of women in my community are considerably more advanced than some of you moderns have led people to believe. I could show you women in the Jewish community who were able to rise from slavery to a position in the temple, to divorce their husbands, hold property, buy and sell daughters who inherit even where there is a son. Now I know your society might not look on all of this as an enormous advantage given the litigenous nature of your society, especially in matters related to the family. However, you might want to examine the way some of us sought to hold

---

[6]The following were used to construct this conversation: Gösta W. Ahlström, D. Boyarin, Phillip R. Davies, Tamara C. Eskenazi (both works), T.C. Eskenazi and K.H. Richards, J.M. Miller and J.H. Hayes, J. Scott and P. Simpson-Housley, and Jonathan Z. Smith (both works).

community and temple together. Inheritance and who one marries makes a difference in very practical matters related to property. We have small enough pieces of property so we need to observe carefully the ways of retaining our sacred place and space. I can't so easily separate religion and the social order like you moderns seem to do.

I come from a group of people closely associated with the writing of the Ezra-Nehemiah book. We have tried to present a more unified perspective by understanding our city and people as the house of God. Despite the variations seen by others we are a people struggling with identity, shaping our place and space, sometimes by chance and other times from design. We are not insulated from the political and economic demands of a massive empire, but seeking amongst those demands a renewed sense of what it meant to worship the Lord in this place we call Judah.

As you can tell by our story in Ezra-Nehemiah we were not frozen in depicting ourselves only as followers of great leaders. Oh yes, we had our Abrahams and Sarahs, our Moses and Aaron and even in my community Ezra and Nehemiah. Their memoirs were used to contrast with the shifting recognition that our triumphs, such as the building of the city-temple, came about from the work of people over time and not just great leaders. If you want the story depicting events in the heroic mode of a revivified David and a heroic Zerubbabel, then we preserved that photograph as well in the I Esdras book. One of your contemporaries said it best, when comparing your Washington Monument and the Viet Nam War Memorial in your nation's capitol. She said, I Esdras's view of the restoration corresponds to the Washington Monument whereas the Viet Nam War Memorial focuses the – central human actor – as Israel.

You moderns, or do you prefer to be called post-modernists, seem to have dated us within the period 539 – 332 B.C.E. For some odd reason you call our age the Persian Period. That seems strange since we find our representatives still around into your time. And well, the Persian designation seems to focus more on the large-scale forgetting of our powerful place. You moderns have a tendency of blocking off periods of time in very neat ways, much as you do with your photographs. You freeze the frame so that you can gain control of it, yet every moment it slips from your grasp.

I am actually quite unimpressed with the range of your photographs of holy places. The Persian Empire in which I have lived is vast. It stretches from Greece, across Turkey just below the Black Sea and Caspian Sea and beyond Afghanistan. Running around the Mediterranean Sea, it includes Syria, Lebanon, Israel, across the delta of the Nile in Egypt and even to the west beyond Libya. Dropping down deeper into Egypt at least as far as Elephantine across the Red Sea including portions of Saudia Arabia, Jordan, Iran, Iraq and beyond the Indus River. I suppose it covers over six or seven time zones, and an area larger than the continental United States.

Even the vast boundaries of my Persian Empire are too small a stage on which to understand those of us who were returning exiles. I reside in a world where two major civilizations, East and West, live. Now, you are big on computers and the Internet has brought some select few of you to imagine cultures and religions across the world meeting. But I live in a world where there was mutual transmutation and an interconnectedness that you are just beginning to sense. A decision in Susa altered the destiny of Athens and reverberated in Jerusalem.

Do not forget that I have read from the scribal libraries of Greece some writers from this period of time whom you might have heard of: Herodotus, Thucydides, Xenophon, Sophocles, Aeschylus, Euripides, Plato, Aristotle, and Demosthenes. I will spare you the time, and not mention the vast Egyptian literature available to me. And you have characterized my period of history as a "dark age"!

I see all these diverse temples in your slides. I recognize them as coming from far reaching places. And you ask me, why is the Second Temple not described anywhere in the literature? You complain that the single description says that it had a height of 90 feet and a width of 90 feet, but no length is mentioned. Nothing. You ask, was it a cube? My retort is twofold. First, you have elaborate descriptions elsewhere in the documents of my people. Go and read in your public gatherings the accounts in 1 Kings 4-6 and 2 Chronicles 2-4. If that is not good enough for you, go to the extensive visionary account of Ezekiel 40-46. If you still say that is not enough, then I suggest that you go to other places in the prophetic corpus where they speak from the standpoint of a finished and rededicated Second Temple.

I heard one of you ask, "When is the temple in the text a real temple and when is it a textual temple?" Well, this aggravates me and leads me to my second retort. You see, you have forgotten that my temples are both material and written. You have forgotten that I and my returning exiles do not read literature for pleasure. Reading is not an act of volition. I can not choose to read or not read. The Torah requires that I should read in it every day of my life and I will thereby learn to fear the Lord my God (Deuteronomy 17:19). I also do not forward the practice you in the West have of reading privately. The privileged social sites for the practice of reading in Europe in Late Antiquity, the Middle Ages, and the Early Modern period are the study and the bedroom. Reading in my tradition in fact has no word that means what you mean by reading a book. What you mean is "essentially private, individual consumption of narrative with the effect of and for the purpose of 'pleasure.'" It almost defies my imagination to think how your view of reading can seek any intervention into history or ability to interpret contemporary reality.

Permit me now to jump out of this character to say more specifically some of the understandings of temple that have emerged in Second Temple studies. Then I will conclude with several comments.

We have learned a fair amount about temples in the ancient Near Eastern world. We know that cities and temples "belong together." We know that during the Persian Period temples functioned as a kind of administrative center, even as banks receiving money and loaning money, working on land transactions. The administrators – often priests – were under the auspices of a distant imperial power. They dealt with the control of personnel, budgetary issues and the oversight of legal issues (Nehemiah 13).

The temples in the Persian Period were at the center of a new sociopolitical organization that flourished. These so-called, civic-temple communities merged temple personnel, so-called religious roles, with the free, property-owning citizens of a particular settlement. The members of this "merger" formed a privileged, self-managing, economic block. In effect citizenship in these civic-temple communities was a function of the relationship to the cult and provided the long arm of the law from the imperial leadership to every corner of the domain.

One of the temple-city case histories from the Persian period is the ancient temple-city of Uruk and its shrine dedicated to Inanna. Thousands of texts show a major temple area; indicate that it had land holdings for farming and grazing; rented these to farmers who produced for the temple. The entire operation was funded by the rents, as well as contributions, both voluntary and mandatory. There was a huge work force including slave labor. Membership in the temple-city was restricted and grouped into ancestral houses (Ezra 2 and the kinship lists are similar) headed up with an "elder" who exercised considerable power (Ezra 10:8, 14, 16).

We know that during this period local temples were cultivated and established to serve the needs of the imperial power. Temples were viewed as "promoters of social cohesion" and "catalysts for economic exchange." It is doubtful that the Cyrus decree (Ezra 1:2 ff) was issued just out of some religious piety or new-found dedication to the Lord. More than likely the focus was on the leadership of returnees to help the imperial power in the outreaches of the kingdom forward stability, and secondarily to build temples that were houses of worship. Judah and Jerusalem were surely no exception to this focus. While the retained photographs of this period do not conceal this broader Persian persuasion, they also unfold a new-found understanding of community. A community gathered in public for the reading of the Torah.

Unfortunately we do not have the archives of the temple in Jerusalem so we must work with data from other civic-temple communities. However, as we look to the biblical literature and the surrounding social, cultural and economic practices of the Persian Period we are able to piece together very similar circumstances and ways of dealing with the necessities of running an empire, as vast as the Persian Empire. While it is easy to understand the perspective of the biblical literature's focus on the "island" of Jerusalem and Judah, we must not forget the sheer mass of the empire's weight.

We have learned that it is as important to look at the surrounding practices of the Persian Empire as it is to look at the linkages intimated in the biblical literature between the First and Second Temples. All indications are that there were significant differences in the social structures of the tenth and the fifth centuries B.C.E. One major difference between the Solomonic Temple and the Second Temple is clear. The difference was generated by the changed social, economic and cultural circumstances. The Solomonic Temple was funded and built by royalty itself. David purchased the land for the temple (2 Samuel 24:18ff) and used his own funds to construct the edifice (1 Kings 5:15ff; 9:10ff). The Second Temple was constructed with funds from the central administration of the civic-temple community and with gifts from Jews in Babylonia (Ezra 1.4,6; 2.68-69). One could say it was the returning exile portion of the community to the exclusion of those who had remained in the land who owned the temple and administered it on behalf of the distant imperial rulers.

In addition to this so-called Second Temple in Jerusalem it is becoming more reasonable to assume that a temple may also have existed in Babylon. The Persian leaders encouraged ethnic minorities to maintain their own collective identity throughout the vast empire. Not only Jews, but other groups were supported in the organization of administrative centers we have referred to as civic-temple communities. It only stands to reason that these exiled Jews with the support of the Persian Empire would have transported the idea when returning to Jerusalem. They had practiced governing themselves this way. They knew how it worked. When they returned to Judah they used the temple as much as a religious place and space, as a reclaiming of place and space in a political and economic sense.

Concluding Remarks

Several brief concluding remarks will suffice. First, as a historian and literary critic I can look back at representations of the Persian Period and the Second Temple written at the end of the nineteenth century C.E. and recognize their distortion of the reality as I see it. I do not doubt that they thought that their representations were accurate. Many of them thought they were giving us a mimetic representation. Examining those representations that we find false can give us the opportunity to "begin to question the representations which we find self-evidently true. Only then will our own sites of representation become visible to us."[7] Hayden White has said this far better than I might.

> When we seek to make sense of such problematical topics as human nature, culture, society, and history, we never say precisely what we wish to say or mean precisely what we say. Our discourse always tends to slip away from our data towards the structures of consciousness with which we are trying to grasp them; or, what amounts to the same thing, the data always resist the coherency of the image which we are trying to fashion of them....[8]

Second, we must dare to reach for different types of bifocal vision. In fact, I am about to say we need trifocals in this business of discovering how to "intervene in history." We need a careful focus on the past without freezing the narrative so that the present is more useful to us. But we also need to imagine the future so that we begin to think about who may be holding our photographs one day. We need to be more playful in order to accomplish that task.

Third, these folks we are learning about in Persian Period Judah, especially the ones who put together the remarkable story of Ezra-Nehemiah, have given us an incredible gift that does not dazzle with the magnificence of the Davidic picture, but it does present an "enduring model, a way of life, that the rabbinic sages assiduously seek to emulate"[9] with their interest in community, city-temple and Torah.

---

[7]James Duncan, "Sites of Representation" in *Place/Culture/Representation*, p. 54.
[8]Tropics of Discourse (1978), p. 1.
[9]Tamara Eskenazi, *In an Age of Prose* (1992), p. 192.

Bibliography

Agnew, John. "Representing Space: Space, Scale and Culture in Social Science," *Place/Culture/Representation*, eds. James Duncan and David Lay. New York: Routledge, 1993.

Ahlström, Gösta W. *The History of Ancient Palestine from the Palacolithic Period to Alexander's Conquest* with contributions by Gary O. Rollefson, ed. Diana Edelman. Journal for the Study of the Old Testament Supplement Series 146, 1993.

Boyarin, Daniel. "Placing Reading: Ancient Israel and Medieval Europe," *The Ethnography of Reading*, ed. Jonathan Boyarin. Berkeley: University of CA Press, 1992.

Davies, Philip R. *Second Temple Studies 1: Persian Period.* Journal for the Study of the Old Testament Supplement Series 117. Sheffield: Sheffield Academic Press, 1991.

Duncan, James. "Sites of Representation: Place, Time, and the Discourse of the Order," pp. 39-56 in *Place/Culture/Representation*, eds. James Duncan and David Ley. London: Routledge, 1993.

Eskenazi, Tamara Cohn. "Out from the Shadows: Biblical Women in the Postexilic Era," *Journal for the Study of the Old Testament* 54 (June 1992) 25-43.

———. *In an Age of Prose. A Literary Approach to Ezra-Nehemiah.* Society of Biblical Literature Monograph Series 36. Atlanta: Scholars Press, 1988.

———. and Kent Harold Richards. *Second Temple Studies 2: Temple and Community in the Persian Period.* Journal for the Study of the Old Testament Supplement Studies 175, 1994.

Fox, Michael V. ed. *Temple Society*, Winona Lake: Eisenbrauns, 1988.

Fuller, C. J. "The Hindu Temple and Indian Society," pp. 49-66 in *Temple in Society*, ed. Michael V. Fox. Winona Lake: Eisenbrauns, 1988.

Jackson, Peter, and Susan J. Smith. *Exploring Social Geography.* London: George Allen and Unwin, 1984.

McEwan, Ian. *Black Dogs.* London: Pan Books Limited, 1992.

Miller, J. Maxwell and John H. Hayes. *A History of Ancient Israel and Judah.* Philadelphia: The Westminster Press, 1986.

Neusner, Jacob. "The Study of Religion as the Study of Tradition," *History of Religions* 14 (1975) 191-206.

Scott, Jamie and Paul Simpson-Housley, eds. *Sacred Places and Profane Spaces. Essays in the Geographies of Judaism, Christianity, and Islam.* Westport, CT: Greenwood Press, 1991.

Smith, Jonathan Z. *Map is Not Territory. Studies in the History of Religions,* Studies in Judaism in Late Antiquity 23. Leiden: E. J. Brill, 1978.

——. *To Take Place.* Chicago: The University of Chicago Press, 1987.

Three Thousand Futures: The Next 20 Years in Higher Education. San Francisco: Jossey-Bass, 1980.

White, Hayden. *Tropics of Discourse. Essays in Cultural Criticism.* Baltimore: Johns Hopkins University Press, 1978.

Response to Kent Harold Richards's "Building Temples Out of Words, Building Temples Out of Stones"

Karl-Johan Illman
Åbo Akademi

I think Kent Richards is right in arguing that we should try to develop a bifocal or even trifocal vision in order to be able to have our "tradition intervene in history." I also think that he has tried to follow the invitation of Jacob Neusner to speculate about what we would know if we had other sources at our disposal besides those that we do have. These sources would be the photographs we have seen, on the one hand, and the fifth-century B.C.E. speaker on the other.

But I am not quite sure that I know where the borderline between then and now would go. If the photographs show me ruins, how can I fill in the missing parts of those temples? By imagination? And the speaker of then will tell me partly what I have read in the ancient sources, partly what I imagine him to tell. So, how will I then get out of my interpretative circle? I think the answer is, I will not. On the other hand, if the snapshots show us modern temples they don't necessarily help us construe this two and a half millennia old Jerusalem temple, from which we do not have any ruins left. Can I use them in reconstructing the second temple? Maybe.

It is entirely appropriate that Kent Richards reminds us about the various textual sources in the Bible and outside which contribute to our understanding of the second temple. They do to a certain degree give us different perspectives on the temple as an institution, not only as a "house of God" but also as a social and political center as well. However, we of course very much miss certain voices: I think of those who remained in the land and who were not permitted to take part in the building of the new temple. I also think about those who did not like to have the temple rebuilt at all. Was it because they did not like to have a temple built at the order of the Persian king who they feared would be a tool of oppression? Or was it because they had lived without a temple for sixty years and didn't think it necessary for prayer? Or was it because they thought that once the new temple was built by the returnees, they would not have a place on the mountain of the Lord?

As you see, I can only speculate here. What I mean to say is that the sources we have always give us the view of a few persons: Ezra, Nehemiah, Haggai and some of the other prophets. We will not know what "The people of the land(s)" thought of the holy business of the temple. Therefore I would have been happier had Kent Richards chosen as his interlocutor not a person closely associated with the writing of the Ezra-Nehemiah book. It seems that what this person is going to give us is an apology for the returnees' policy toward those other people. I would have liked Kent Richards to speculate about what a member of the opposing group would have said. As I said, we don't have the sources, obviously because history is written by the winners. But think about the twenty years delay between Cyrus's edict of 538 and the actual beginning of the rebuilding of the temple.

Why did they hesitate, if the emperor had not only permitted them to rebuild the temple but actually ordered them to do so? The usual answer is, because they didn't have the means to do it immediately. Maybe so. But is it also possible that they who would have liked to start the rebuilding immediately were so few in number that they had to wait for help? Were perhaps the people of the land so much stronger that their opposition towards rebuilding the temple or their unwillingness to give it to the returnees delayed the rebuilding until the newcomers became strong enough to have it their way? What would have happened had the people of the land won this fight? Would they have rebuilt the temple at all, and if they had, what kind of temple? These are questions I would have liked to speculate about.

In conclusion: it is easy for me to concur with Kent Richards's emphasis on the need for even trifocal vision of our sources about the second temple then, our own photographs of our temples and, finally, our way of relating these to one another, if I understand him correctly. But in addition to these there is still room for speculating about those possible sources which are lost to us, but which we so badly would need in order to have a more full view of the Judean religion and society back in the fifth century B.C.E. How will we ever be able to fill in these gaps? I think only by way of imagination – imagination, of course, informed by our extant sources, and I think that this is what we are doing here. If this would be then the outcome of our conference it has helped us quite a bit on the way.

3

Traditio-Historical Criticism and the Study of Jesus

Bruce D. Chilton
Bard College

Introduction

There must be a change in the reading of the New Testament if we are to understand what it is and what it is doing. There is at the moment a consensus among conservatives and liberals, an unwitting conspiracy, to deny the New Testament its place as a religious document.

Conservatives (whether themselves fundamentalists, or influenced by fundamentalists) have protected the Bible from historical criticism. For them it provides a consistent message concerning salvation in Christ, warranted by reliable witnesses. Liberals, rather than banishing history, have preferred to baptize it. They read the Bible in a way which emphasizes its production by individual authors operating under specifiable or imaginable circumstances.

Conservatives and liberals thrive on their contention, in this field as in others. The conservative pastor can ridicule the liberal professor for missing the point of the document under discussion. The liberal professor can pour scorn on the conservative pastor for claiming as God's word a collection of incidental writings. I can name (indeed, I belong to) professional organizations whose purpose is to engage in precisely that sort of polemic. But both sides join in the unstated agreement that what they are arguing about is literature. Literature not simply in the sense of documents written, but literature in the sense of writings produced for the express purpose of being made public. The

39

battle is over what the aim of publication was: Did the authors join to articulate a harmonious message, or to address more local concerns? The myth that the New Testament is literature has crippled our ability to read it. We are constantly looking for what cannot be found, the conservative's eternal truth harmoniously stated, or liberalism's authors of heroic imagination. Culturally, we expect the New Testament either to be a fact or to be a fiction. In that expectation, we are foisting our strictures onto documents which evolved to address quite different concerns. The Gospels (for example) were instruments of teaching disciples long before they were documents for publication. The documents of the New Testament as a whole were generated by churches for churches, in order to define and maintain their identities. The materials the documents contain draw from the riches of earlier instruction. Those materials were spoken before they were written, and believed before they were spoken.

Once we appreciate that the New Testament was produced by faithful communities for their own benefit, we are on the way towards understanding its contents. To be sure, only on the way; not actually there. We do not know those communities directly; we may become familiar with them only through the texts which they produced. And then there is one more complication. The Gospels evolved out of the traditions of several communities quickly overlapping in time, producing, accepting and reforming traditions as they ordered their lives. Reading the Gospels therefore involves making the acquaintance of the communities beneath the text. Our reading must be a function of how we understand the communities and practices which generated traditions.

Traditio-Historical Discussion

Because the New Testament is a collection of documents, it seems natural to treat its contents as what authors produced for an audience. For most of its history, Christianity has accepted the primacy of written communication: texts have been preserved, collected, annotated, translated, expounded, and otherwise interpreted. Once the canon was agreed, between the second and the fourth centuries, recourse to a fixed group of writings was formalized. Even while arguments concerning the canon were pursued, the underlying assumption was that a consensus regarding *written* texts was required.

What, however, of the period which led up to the composition of written texts, and the process of preserving traditions which resulted in the documents of the canon? Just as textual criticism is designed to elucidate the history of texts, so traditio-historical criticism is designed to elucidate the history of the traditions which made up those texts. What was there *before* the time early Christian authors could write for a relatively stable constituency, the formative period during which local churches emerged without the benefit of a published canon?

By definition, the period with which traditio-historical criticism concerns itself is briefer than the period with which textual criticism concerns itself. The Gospels became available as documents in the period between the destruction of the Temple (a probable incentive for the composition of Mark) and around A.D. 100 (in the case of John). But it is obvious that some traditions incorporated within the Gospel are much older. Below, we will consider Paul's teaching concerning Jesus' last supper with his disciples (1 Corinthians 11:23-26), which is comparable to the presentation of the Synoptic Gospels. Paul wrote to the Corinthians c. A.D. 56, and he states in the passage that he received his tradition "from the Lord" (v. 23). How did early Christians such as Paul receive, frame and transmit traditions concerning Jesus? Traditio-historical criticism focuses on the relatively brief period between Jesus and the first documents of the New Testament.

It is as well that the period in question is short, because the analysis involved in traditio-historical work is complex. There are two, related reasons for this necessary complexity. First, because the concern is with what preceded written evidence, we have by definition no external check on the processes which resulted in the writing of the Gospels. Second, we gain access to those processes only by means of our hypotheses regarding how the traditions were formed which are crystallized in the New Testament.

Both those elements of complexity bring with them temptations to reduce the problems they pose by oversimplification. Not infrequently, students (and even some scholars) will invoke a theory of early authorship by eyewitnesses, in order to short-circuit the task of traditio-historical criticism. Sadly, for such theorists, the Gospels themselves refer to earlier traditions and their importance. Luke 1:2 refers to the previous witness of "eyewitnesses and servants of the word," and John 20:30; 21:25 refer to traditions which might have been included in that Gospel, but were not. As early as c. A.D. 53, Paul had warned the Galatians of the dangers of "a different gospel" (Galatians 1:6): evidently, there were distinct, sometimes conflicting strategies of preaching within the early Church. We cannot say from the outset what precisely their contents were, but neither can we critically deny their existence.

Hypothesis regarding how traditions concerning Jesus were shaped is an unavoidable part of our study. Only by understanding the traditions which produced the text can the text in itself be understood. When a document is produced as literature, by a single person, reading the text involves getting to know the author; in the case of the Gospels, the authorships which produced the texts are communities. It is they we become familiar with as we identify the traditions of the Gospels. For that reason, it is misleading to speak of "Matthew," "Mark," "Luke" and "John" as if they were people we knew. The Gospels "according to" those four (as they are designated in Greek titles of the texts) are the triumphal news of God's victory in Christ[1] as promulgated in their various communities. The precise role of those figures "according to" whom a Gospel was written, be it as creators of material, collectors, editors, local historians, etc., is simply unknown.

Gospels are texts of churches, and faith in Christ – a faith which varied greatly in character and definition during the period – is often of greater concern within them than the understanding of Jesus in anything like a historical sense. The Gospels are also in the position of translating the traditions of Jesus, in both linguistic and cultural terms, into a social environment unlike his own. The simple identification of the historical Jesus with the Jesus of the Gospels is not tenable.

Nonetheless, the Gospels do refer back to Jesus as their source. We cannot understand what the texts are saying unless we appreciate the Jesus they refer to, whether or not we conclude in a given instance that their literary Jesus may be identified with the historical Jesus whom we construct. Jesus is the reference of every Gospel as the principal figure of their literary history, whom they point back to. Understanding the traditions which make up the Gospels will put us in a position to evaluate the Jesus of their literary history. The historical Jesus, in other words, only emerges as we infer what Jesus, within the environment of early Judaism, must have said or done so to have produced the traditions of the New Testament as we understand them.

Traditio-historical criticism is an engagement with the text of the New Testament which is designed to uncover the processes and the stages by which that text emerged. Although Jesus and the Gospels have been particular concerns among historians of tradition, the approach is appropriate in respect of any document which is not the product of a single author. In order to emphasize that, our initial example will be drawn from the work of Paul (although comparison with the Synoptic Gospels will naturally come into play). Before we proceed to an exegetical discussion, however, a brief description of the evolution of the approach is in order.

---

[1]The modern fashion of rendering eujaggevlion as "good news" overlooks the military resonance of the Greek term as reflected in the Septuagint.

Martin Dibelius and Rudolf Bultmann[2] are usually, and rightly, identified as the scholars who pioneered inquiry into the roots of the Synoptic tradition. Their concern was not with documents which may or may not have existed before the Gospels were written, but with the forms of oral tradition which fed into the formation of the Gospels. The idea was that, over the course of time, a tradition would be passed on within a community, and the community would shape that tradition into certain well defined forms. For example, a tradition might be used to celebrate the power of a deity or to give point to a particular teaching. Bultmann treated the transfiguration as an instance of the first category, and the dispute over fasting (Mark 2:18-22) as an instance of the second.[3]

Particularly as developed by Bultmann, form criticism has been roundly criticized.[4] Three principal faults have been identified. First, the notion of a community which created definite forms has been attacked. In the development of the Hebrew Bible, institutions such as the Temple, the monarchy, and prophetic schools were in a position to shape traditions, and production of cycles of tradition over the course of generations and even centuries would have been possible. A definite correspondence between the form of traditions and the influence of public institutions is plausible under those conditions. That extensive lapse of the time and (equally important) the formality of social structure are simply not cognate with the situation in which the New Testament emerged. Second, insofar as the development of oral tradition within the culture and period of the New Testament has been attested, the picture of isolated passages (*pericopae*) circulating in a free-floating fashion has not been confirmed. Traditions seem rather, from the outset, to have emerged within cycles, and were often associated with influential teachers and schools within early Christianity. Third and finally, the analogy with tradition as it was emerging within early Judaism confirms the importance of prominent, named teachers in the formation of tradition, and makes it seem apparent – contrary to Bultmann's assumption – that a link between such traditions and what we would call

---

[2]See Dibelius, *From Tradition to Gospel* (tr. B.L. Woolf; Cambridge: Clarke, 1971) and Bultmann, *The History of the Synoptic Tradition* (tr. J. Marsh; New York: Harper and Row, 1971).

[3]Cf. the discussion in Taylor, pp. 63-87 and 142-167.

[4]In addition to Taylor's book, see Thorleif Boman, *Die Jesus-Überlieferung im Lichte der neueren Volkskunde* (Göttingen: Vandenhoeck and Ruprecht, 1967); Birger Gerhardsson, *Memory and Manuscript: Oral Tradition and Written Transmission in Rabbinic Judaism and Early Christianity* (Upsala and Lund: Gleerup, 1964) and *The Origins of the Gospel Traditions* (London: SCM, 1979); Harald Riesenfeld, *The Gospel Tradition* (Philadelphia: Fortress, 1970); Rainer Riesner, *Jesus als Lehrer. Eine Untersuchung zum Ursprung der Evangelien-Überlieferung* (Tübingen: Mohr, 1981).

history is not to be excluded from the outset. Traditions may bear the marks of their historical development, including the people and events which initiated them; however much communities may have influenced the traditions they handed on, there is virtually no evidence that they created them.

Form criticism in its Bultmannian form should be regarded as a method which has been superseded. Since the end of World War II, students of tradition have not been limited by its presuppositions. Increasingly, following the example of Heinz Schürmann,[5] they have seen the process of the formation of the Gospels to have been one in which traditions were formed, collected, and ultimately crystallized in writing in the documents we can read today. Tradition was the foundation upon which redaction, the editorial procedures followed at the stage of writing, could take place.

Because we have evidence only of the last stage, when traditions – whether oral or written (or some combination of the two) – were composed in a documentary form, it is all too easy to fall into the trap of imagining that Gospels were composed in a purely scribal manner. Among documentary theories, the most popular has it that Mark was written first, and that Mark was used in the production of Matthew and Luke. But even that theory supposes an additional source of Jesus' teaching (commonly called "Q"), and is embarrassed by cases in which Matthew and Luke agree in presenting Markan material in a form different from Mark's own wording. So even the most widespread scribal theory of the origins of the Gospels in fact assumes that scribal and oral media were combined in the production of the documents, and acknowledges the limits of our certainty in deciding what was written and what was oral at the time each Gospel was composed. The principal scholar of the most frequently cited documentary theory, B.H. Streeter, openly appreciated the role of non-written sources in the production of the Gospels. Unfortunately, the point of his theory has sometimes been lost in the retelling.[6] We can say with some precision how one Gospel compares with another; but we can only guess how precisely the material

[5]See, for example, *Das Geheimnis Jesu. Versuche zur Jesusfrage:* Die Botschaft Gottes (Leipzig: St. Benno, 1972); Chilton, *God in Strength. Jesus' Announcement of the Kingdom:* The Biblical Seminar (Sheffield: JSOT, 1987); Matti Myllykoski, *Die letzten Tage Jesu. Markus und Johannes, ihre Traditionen und die historische Frage* (Helsinki: Suomalainen Tiedeakatemia, 1991).
[6]Cf. Chilton, *Profiles of a Rabbi. Synoptic Opportunities in Reading about Jesus:* Brown Judaic Studies 177 (Atlanta: Scholars Press, 1989), 34-43. The relevant works of Streeter are three articles in *Studies in the Synoptic Problem* (ed. W. Sanday; Oxford: Clarendon, 1911) and *The Four Gospels* (London: Macmillan, 1924).

within one Gospel came to be known to the community in which another Gospel was produced.

Once it has been appreciated that the writing of each Gospel is a late stage in a process in which traditions were generated, traditio-historical study takes on its proper importance. Although they were composed at different times, the writings of the New Testament were produced at discrete stages within the development of early Christianity. All the documents assume that an initial, usually oral preaching about Jesus has been heard and accepted at some point in the past, whether recently or long ago. That predominantly oral message, the triumphal news or "gospel" (*euanggelion*) of God's victory, is only indirectly attested in the documents of the canon. The term "Gospel" came to be applied to specific documents because they presuppose and build upon the message concerning Jesus.

The first three Gospels represent a second stage, following acceptance of the message of the initial gospel which their audiences had heard. They are written as catechesis (elementary instruction), in order to prepare sympathetic hearers of the gospel of Jesus for genuine membership in their churches, a membership marked by baptism. The Pauline correspondence represents the degree to which baptism was only a beginning in the life of disparate churches. For all their differences, churches of differing communities and places felt an identity with one another, not least because they shared common (although not identical) traditions. The attempt to address common problems and questions as communities in contact with one another made controversy a characteristic feature of primitive Christian history.

In that the first three Gospels emerge from the catechetical stage of the movement, when candidates were prepared for baptism, they provide the best indications of the governing concerns of the movement as it initiated new members. The first three Gospels are commonly called "Synoptic," because they may be viewed together when they are printed in columns. Unfortunately, their obviously literary relationship has caused scholars to presume that they were composed by scribes working in isolation who copied, one from another. A comparative approach, served by an understanding of the development of tradition into documents within both early Judaism and Christianity, has brought us to the point where deviations of one document from another, related document, are not assumed to be purely scribal changes. Rather, agreement and disagreement provide opportunities to grasp accurately the social function and meaning of a given document by referring to the distinct ways it construes material which it shares with comparable documents.

Within such an approach, agreement among the Gospels is no surprise, because documents of early Judaism and Rabbinic Judaism also present synoptic relationships, sometimes with greater verbal similarity, and often with more than three documents involved. What is notable in the synopticity of the first three Gospels is that the orders of passages, one after another, can be compared regularly; that justifies their literary characterization as the "Synoptics" in a distinctive sense. Once their function within catechesis is appreciated, the cause of their agreements (including a commonly programmatic order) and their deviations becomes evident: what we see in the first three Gospels are the methods of baptismal initiation followed in three influential, nearly contemporaneous, but separate churches. There is a reasonable degree of consensus that Mark was the first of the Gospels to be written, around A.D. 71 in the environs of Rome. As convention has it, Matthew was subsequently composed, near A.D. 80, perhaps in Damascus (or elsewhere in Syria), while Luke came later, say in A.D. 90, perhaps in Antioch.

For reasons which have been explained, the cycles of tradition which fed the Gospels, and the relationships of the cycles to early teachers such as Paul, must be matters of inference and hypothesis. The strength of any traditio-critical theory is both its inclusion of the available evidence, and its power to explain the texts as they may be read today. Certain figures within the early Church are named repeatedly in those texts as bearers of authoritative tradition: Peter (or Cephas, the original, Aramaic form of his cognomen), James (the brother of Jesus), and the Twelve. Only one example of a complex of tradition which they (and Paul) influenced will be discussed here, but as we proceed it will be helpful to bear in mind some of the cycles of tradition which scholars have often identified.

The Petrine cycle must have been available in Aramaic by c. A.D. 35, in time for Paul to be informed of it at the time of his visit to Jerusalem (see Galatians 1:18). But the very name "Peter" attests early translation into Greek, in association with the wider field of preaching for which that apostle accepted responsibility. The Petrine cycle within the Synoptics may be identified by the appearance within its stories of Peter, James, and John, in which group Peter is the chief representative; the cycle substantially included the initial call of the first disciples, the healing of Jairus's daughter, the confession at Caesarea Philippi, the transfiguration, the eucharist, and the struggle in Gethsemane. By design and in fact, the Petrine usage of narrative for the purpose of catechesis established a paradigm in the primitive Church; the Synoptic Gospels are a monument to that narrative strategy. The genesis of the Gospels was a function of a uniquely Christian program: baptism in the name of Jesus.[7]

In its earliest phase, "Q" was a collection of sayings in the nature of a mishnah which a rabbi's disciples might learn, virtually contemporaneous with the Petrine cycle. From its origins in Jesus' movement as instruction of the Twelve, the proverbial source known as "Q" developed in the environment of Galilee and Syria in a markedly apocalyptic direction. The cycle is generally held to have focused on rules of discipleship, which were generalized in order to regulate communities, and it is widely held to have been developed by around A.D. 50.[8]

The cycle of James was in the nature of a version of the Petrine cycle and "Q" for the apostolic group around Jesus' brother which was centered in Jerusalem. Both the Petrine cycle and the Jacobean revision of that cycle were known in Antioch prior to the council in Jerusalem which took place c. A.D. 49 (see Galatians 2). The Jacobean revision itself may be dated c. A.D. 40, since it went through some development before Paul became acquainted with it in Antioch, although he was not apprised of it at the time of his visit with Peter c. A.D. 35. The Jacobean revision of the Petrine cycle would have included the insistence that the Twelve alone could provide the sense of the parables, a collection of such parables, a note of Jesus' rejection by his own neighbors, a commissioning of the Twelve, and (as we shall see) the paschal interpretation of the eucharist within a more detailed story of the passion than the Petrine cycle had offered. Apocalyptic addenda (most prominently, the discourse in Mark 13) were included at a later stage.

The primitive cycles or revisions of tradition (Petrine, Jacobean, instructional ["Q"]) were amalgamated into the Hellenistic catechesis reflected in the Synoptic Gospels, probably first of all in Antioch. The relationship among the sources of the catechesis is represented schematically in figure 1 *(not shown here)*. The most likely exponent of the unified catechesis is Barnabas. His standing is consistent with the wide acceptance of the Synoptic tradition, and the greater accommodation to Jacobean influence in the Synoptics as compared to Paul would be characteristic of Barnabas (see Galatians 2:13).

The Synoptic catechesis was a paradigm which was then developed and published in Rome (Mark), Damascus (Matthew), and Antioch itself (Luke). The spine of each Gospel is the narrative catechesis of the Petrine cycle, supplemented by Jacobean revision of that catechesis, and the

---

[7]Cf. also Acts 10:34-43, and the reflection of a baptismal setting in vv. 44-48.
[8]Cf. John S. Kloppenborg with Leif E. Vaage (eds.), *Early Christianity, Q and Jesus: Semeia 55* (Atlanta: Scholars Press, 1992).

instruction of the Twelve ("Q"). Their similarities and differences are best understood as functions of the particular sort of catechesis (preparation of catechumens for baptism) which was current in each community. No Gospel is simply a copy of another; rather, each represents the choices among varying traditions, written and/or oral, and the development of those traditions which had taken place in a given locality, as represented in figure 2 *(not shown here)*.

Paul's Symposial Strategy and the Last Supper

The times and places of his activity, his contacts, and the vehemence of his opinions all make Paul a vital key to the generation of traditions in the Gospels. Paul himself reports his conflict with representatives of the circle of James (Galatians 2:11-13). Paul advocated fellowship at table among Jews and Gentiles, and Peter fell in with the practice. But when the Jacobeans arrived, the Jews of the community – including Peter and even Barnabas – began to separate from the others.

That policy of separation included the eucharist, in that the cycle of James represented Jesus' last supper as a Seder, the meal of Passover. The chronology of John excludes such an understanding (see 18:28; 19:14, 31), since Jesus dies on the day of the preparation. Even in the Synoptics, the authorities decide to deal with Jesus *before* the feast (Mark 14:1- 2; Matthew 26:1-5). (Luke 22:15 [possibly from "Q"] may similarly be taken as the expression of an *unfulfilled* desire to eat the Passover.) In any case, the lamb, the unleavened bread, the bitter herbs required for a Seder (see Exodus 12:8) are notable only for their absence from any primitive account of the last supper.

What makes the last supper into a Seder is a single passage, from the circle of James, in which Jesus is depicted as arranging for the paschal celebration (Matthew 26:17-20/Mark 14:12-17/Luke 22:7-14); the passage presses the action into an improbably cramped space of time, but makes the paschal setting of Jesus' meal – and therefore the eucharist – incontestable. Such an extension of the Torah to the last supper as a Seder meant that "no uncircumcised person shall eat of it" (Exodus 12:48). Eucharists modeled on Jesus' meal would therefore be exclusively Jewish, as well as tied to the liturgical practice of Judaism.

The Jacobean program as a whole did not go unchallenged in Antioch, as Paul's correspondence attests. Paul, we have already seen, reports his own resistance to James's program in regard to purity. A few years later (c. A.D. 56), in the course of writing to the Corinthians concerning appropriate behavior during the Lord's supper, he also develops a line of resistance to the Jacobean understanding of eucharist (1 Corinthians 11:17-34).

It is well known that Paul's overall concern in the passage is with the practical good order of the congregation during fellowship at meals (1 Corinthians 11:17-22, 33, 34). In light of that purpose, the solemn assurance towards the beginning of the passage, that he is passing on the tradition he received (1 Corinthians 11:23), has seemed somewhat out of place.[9] The insistence upon precision in regard to what Jesus did and said is not obviously in keeping with the simple purpose of maintaining decorum at the "dominical supper" (κυριακὸν δεῖπνον, v. 20). But in the context of the success of the Jacobean program, Paul's valiant effort to resist any paschal restriction becomes explicable.

Paul insists upon the older, Petrine tradition in opposition to the paschal program of the Jacobean tradition. Paul's own reference in Galatians 1:18 to a period of fifteen days during which he visited with Cephas in Jerusalem confirms what his language in 1 Corinthians 11:23 attests: he indeed "received from the Lord" (1 Corinthians 11:23), through Cephas (Galatians 1:18), what he "handed over" (1 Corinthians 11:23) to his hearers, the Petrine model of eucharist. In writing to the Corinthians some seven years after the meeting in Jerusalem which agree his sphere of interest in the relation to the "pillars" (Galatians 2:1-10),[10] Paul resisted the emerging influence of the annual Passover ritual upon eucharist which was a hallmark of the Jacobean tradition. In Pauline teaching, frequent repetition was a commandment: "do this, as often as you drink, for my memorial" (τοῦτο ποιεῖτε ὁσάκις ἐὰν πίνητε εἰς τὴν ἐμὴν ἀνάμνησιν, 1 Corinthians 11:25c). The plain meaning of Paul's clause is softened by the habit of adding "it" in translations. But taken at face value, Paul's paradigm involves the recognition that any festive meal is an appropriate occasion of the "memorial."

Paul resists the Jacobean paradigm of eucharist in 1 Corinthians as much as he deplores the Jacobean program of purity in Galatians. He confirms the Petrine teaching, because that tradition permits of the accessibility and the repetition of eucharist.[11] He reminds his hearers of

---

[9]For discussion, and a suggestion which anticipates the present treatment, cf. Oscar Cullmann, "The Lord's Supper and the Death of Christ," *Essays on the Lord's Supper:* Ecumenical Studies in Worship 1 (with F.J. Leenhardt, tr. J.G. Davies; Richmond: John Knox, 1958), 17-20.

[10]For a plausible reconstruction of Paul's relationship to James, Peter, Barnabas, and the communities they represented, cf. Nicholas Taylor, Paul, Antioch and Jerusalem. *A Study in Relationship and Authority in Earliest Christianity:* Journal for the Study of the New Testament Supplements 66 (Sheffield: Sheffield Academic Press, 1992).

[11]Xavier Lwon-Dufour, *Le partage du pain eucharistique selon le Nouveau Testament* (Paris: Editions du Seuil, 1982), 118, 119 also acknowledges the possibility of Paul's familiarity with what he calls the Markan and I call the Petrine tradition.

what he already had taught as authoritative, a teaching "from the Lord" and presumably warranted by the earliest witness: in that sense, what he hands on is not his own, but derives from his highest authority, "the Lord" (11:23). The meaning of the eucharist is not to be found in any limitation to Passover, but in all believers' solidarity in the memory of the Lord's death "until he comes" (1 Corinthians 11:26-29).

Within the Petrine tradition itself, Jesus' last meal began with the Judaic custom of blessing bread (cf. m. Berakhoth 6:5-8; b. Berakhoth 42a-46a), and its meaning was conveyed by the wording that Jesus' blood was "of the covenant" (Matthew 26:26-29/Mark 14:22-25/Luke 22:19-20). The blood poured out is deliberately reminiscent of the sacrifice of the covenant in Exodus 24 (vv. 6-8) which Moses offered: Jesus is strongly associated with Moses in the Petrine tradition (cf. Matthew 17:1-9/Mark 9:2-10/Luke 9:28-36).

Paul prefaced the identification of the wine in 1 Corinthians 11:25a with what seems a clumsy introduction:

"In the same way he took the cup also, after supper..."
ὡσαύτως καὶ τὸ ποτήριον μετὰ τὸ δειπνῆσαι....

The identification of the bread by Jesus is said simply to have taken place "on the night when he was betrayed" (v. 23b). The statement that the cup came "in the same way" at first appears equally vague, but then the phrase "after supper" seems to insist upon a particular moment. If the actions indeed unfolded "in the same way," both the bread and the cup were identified by Jesus "after supper."[12] Whenever exactly Paul understood the bread to have been eaten in relation to other foods, his abstraction of the "dominical supper" from an actual meal by means of his rendering of the Petrine tradition is evident.

The effect of the introduction concerning the cup is to distinguish the drinking of wine from a single cup – and perhaps even the eating of bread – from any meal which might occasion the "dominical supper." Indiscriminate eating and drinking were practices which particularly concerned Paul (11:21, 22); by emphasizing the Petrine order, he could address local abuses at Corinth, and at the same time claim unity with the practice within the primitive Church warranted by Petrine authority. The price of Paul's formulation was to abstract the "supper" from the sorts of meals which had inspired it within the ministry of Jesus.

Cf. the translation of his work, *Sharing the Eucharistic Bread: the Witness of the New Testament* (tr. M.J. O'Connell; New York: Paulist, 1987).
[12]The wording of Luke 22:20a, which employs the same phrase, is within a better defined narrative context, which distinguishes the cup after the meal from what precedes; Paul's presentation is less lucid.

The abstraction of the eucharist from communal meals was attractive within Hellenistic Christianity. Eucharist became sensible and commendable within the practice of philosophical symposia. Such symposia were distinguished from others by a formal transition from meal to the proper, or "drinking party,"[13] and an avoidance of less than philosophical entertainments.[14] Philo attests the extent to which the institution needed to be protected from abuse (cf. *De Continentia* 57, 64). The Pauline phrase, "after supper," coordinates the supper with a well-ordered and comparatively sober philosophical symposium.

The generally Synoptic portrayal of the "last supper" implies a similar degree of sobriety, and the Lukan presentation expressly limits the consumption of wine that may take place in connection with any commemoration of the meal. In Matthew and Mark, the action unfolds "while they were eating" (Matthew 26:26/Mark 14:22), and presumably drinking as well. The present form of the Lukan text manages to reduce the amount of drinking that may be imagined in connection with the meal by means of a more specific order of events: reference to the Passover (22:15, 16), sharing of wine with reference to the kingdom (vv. 17, 18), eating bread in remembrance (v. 19), and drinking again "after supper" (meta; to; deipnh`sai) in view of the new covenant and the kingdom (v. 20).[15] Two cups, and two cups only, are associated with the meal in Luke. With varying degrees of rigor, Paul and the Synoptics mandate sobriety at the dominical symposium.

---

[13]See Dennis E. Smith, "Table Fellowship as a Literary Motif in the Gospel of Luke," *Journal of Biblical Literature* 106 (1987), 613-638, 630 (citing Plato, *Symposium* 176A; Xenophon, *Symposium* 2.1; Athenaeus, *Deipnosophists* 11.462c-d). The passage from Xenophon also refers to more popular entertainments, involving a female flute player, a female dancer/acrobat, and a young man who both played the zither and danced. The passage from Athenaeus shows how the usage of sumpovsion differs from that of dei`pnon, and 462f. attests to the extent to which drinking much was held to be a virtue. For further discussion of the symposium, see Baruch M. Bokser, *The Origins of the Seder. The Passover Rite and Early Rabbinic Judaism* (Berkeley: University of California Press, 1984), 50-66.

[14]Smith, p. 621, citing Plato, *Symposium* 176E; Athenaeus, *Deipnosophists* 5.186a. The former passage (immediately prior to the reference Smith has in mind) also attests the greater attention to the consumption of wine which should distinguish a philosophical symposium from others. Likewise, Athenaeus' observations may be gathered better, in their criticism of drinking too much, by reading from 5.179e until 5.190a.

[15]Smith, p. 628, argues that a "short version" of the Lukan eucharistic text (vv. 15-19a) better suits the Gospel's theology than the inclusion of the longer reading. What he fails to consider is (1) that his proposal results in reversing symposial order in relation to the meal, and (2) that the control of the consumption of wine was of concern within the Hellenistic world generally, and the early Church in particular.

Hellenistic innovations within the Petrine teaching which Paul handed on went further. First, the phrase "this is my blood of the covenant" became "This cup is the new covenant in my blood" (1 Corinthians 11:25, τοῦτο τὸ ποτήριον ἡ καίνη διαθήκη ἐστίν ἐν τῷ ἐμῷ αἵματι). The linguistic changes involve several substantive consequences. The fuller phrase, simply in terms of its structure, is more stately. The thought is more developed than the direct metaphor, "This (is) my blood;" the assertion is explicated so as to avoid misunderstanding Jesus' actual blood as a repeated offering. That misunderstanding, in turn, can only have arisen after the "supper" had ceased to be viewed as comparable to the sacrifice of Exodus 24. Instead, Jesus' blood was sometimes seen within Hellenistic Christianity as comparable to that of the heroic martyrs, in the manner of 4 Maccabees 6:28-29; 17:21-22 (see Hebrews 9:11-14). The notion of the necessary repetition of human bloodshed was therefore an inference to be avoided, and the new wording precludes just that inference.

At the same time, the correctly taken cup is now made a covenant in the sense of a rite to be replicated correctly. Zechariah 9:11 provides a key to the grammatical structure and the sense of the Hellenistic version of Petrine tradition which Paul hands on in 1 Corinthians 11:25. God in Zechariah had promised to rescue the captives of Zion "by the blood of your covenant" (בְּדַם־בְּרִיתֵךְ])[16]: the older, Petrine emphasis upon covenant (in association with Exodus 24) is now linked to the salvific value of blood in the new wording. Most strikingly, the covenant itself is now "new." The usage of language from Jeremiah 31:31 is less important for its biblical pedigree than for its insistence, within the innovative grammatical form of the statement, that Jesus' act amounts to a *covenantal requirement* which is to be discharged "as often as you drink, in remembrance of me" (1 Corinthians 11:25). Unlike the Jacobean limitation to Passover, Paul's appropriation of the Petrine tradition envisages frequent celebration by all those who could eat together. As far as Paul was concerned, *pace* James, that included all baptized persons.

The repetition which is enjoined in 1 Corinthians 11:25 is, then, by no means incidental for Paul. "As often as you drink" within the tradition of the Petrine circle is used as a bulwark against the limitations implicit within the association of eucharist with Passover, and especially the paschal chronology, of Jacobean tradition. Paul's assumption is that Jesus' last meal, the paradigm of the Lord's supper, was of covenantal significance, a sacrificial "memorial" which was associated with the death of Jesus in particular. The wording of that later version of Petrine

---

[16]The sense of the phrase is, "my covenant with you," as in the New Revised Standard Version. The Septuagint omits the pronoun altogether.

tradition agrees most closely with Luke, the Synoptic Gospel which has the strongest associations with Antioch. It is likely that Paul's version of the Petrine tradition derived from his period in Antioch, his primary base by his own testimony (in Galatians 2) until his break with Barnabas.

"The cup" by the Antiochene phase of the Petrine tradition is doubly symbolic. It stands for the new covenant which Jesus mediates by his death, and it also takes the place of the blood which seals Jesus' death. Neither transfer of meaning would have been possible, without the previous understandings that the wine within the cup was in some sense Jesus' blood, and that the blood was of covenantal significance. In both those aspects, 1 Corinthians 11:25 and Luke 22:20 give the appearance of being developed forms of Petrine tradition, the usage which developed in Antioch. Paul's symposial strategy is to apply the authority of eucharistic practice in Antioch, prior to the influence of James's circle, against the influence of the Jacobean identification with Passover and its attendant (in Paul's view, limited) insistence upon purity.

The perspective of Antioch, attested in the symbolism of the cup in both Paul and Luke, involves a fresh conception of the place of "blood" in eucharist. The earlier form of the Petrine tradition (which was closely related to Jesus' practice) simply had it that the wine was blood, a surrogate of covenantal sacrifice. In the Hellenistic environment of Antioch, such a meaning could easily be confused with the notion of drinking a deity's blood in one of the Mysteries. The association of Jesus' last meal with his execution, which was already a feature of the Petrine tradition, would have further encouraged the confusion. The Antiochene wording avoided any confusion of that kind, by making the cup the point of comparison with the new covenant, and describing the covenant as achieved "in" or "by" (ἐν) Jesus' blood.

Although the phrase "in my blood" (1 Corinthians 11:25; Luke 22:20) excludes a possible misunderstanding of the Petrine eucharist, it also conveys a positive appraisal of Jesus' own "blood," that is, his death. The offering commemorated in the bread and wine is not simply a covenantal sacrifice in the general sense established within the Petrine cycle, but the particular form of the sacrifice known as the sacrifice for sin, or *ḥaṭa'at* (cf. Leviticus 4). When Paul conceives of Jesus' death sacrificially, he does so as such a sacrifice ("to deal with sin," or "as a sin offering," περὶ ἁμαρτίας, Romans 8:3). Indeed, by the time he came to compose Romans, he had been referring to Jesus' death in that way for some five years; in Galatians 1:4, Jesus is also described as having given himself for our sins.

In sum, by reading Paul from a traditio-historical point of view, together with the Synoptic Gospels, several models of eucharist become apparent, all in the form of narratives of Jesus' last meal with his disciples. For the Petrine tradition, the meal was a form of blessing and breaking bread which established Jesus' Mosaic stature in mediating the covenant. The circle of James developed the paschal associations of the meal, in order to insist upon its strict limitation to the circumcised, that is, to Christian Jews. Paul insisted upon the authority of Peter/Cephas over James's, and accepted the characterization of the meal in Antioch as a form of symposial solidarity with a heroic martyr.

Jesus' Meals and His Occupation of the Temple

The sacrificial associations of Jesus' last meal – with the covenant in the Petrine cycle, with Passover in the Jacobean, with Jesus' personal and atoning death in the catechesis of Antioch – point back towards the generative meaning of Jesus' act, the meaning which produced such conceptions. If we proceed with the traditional reading, which sees the "body" and "blood" as Jesus' own in a biographical sense, it is virtually impossible to understand the development of the traditions within their Judaic contexts.

The Mishnah, in an effort to conceive of a heinous defect on the part of a priest involved in slaughtering the red heifer, pictures him as intending to eat the flesh or drink the blood (Parah 4:3). Because people had no share of blood, which belonged only to God, even the thought of drinking it was blasphemous. To imagine drinking human blood, consumed with human flesh, could only make the blasphemy worse. So if Jesus' words are taken with their traditional, autobiographical meaning, his last supper can only be understood as a deliberate break from Judaism. Either Jesus himself promulgated a new religion, or his followers did so in his name, and invented the last supper themselves. Both those alternatives find adherents today among scholars, and the debate between those who see the Gospels as literally true reports and those who see them as literary fictions shows little sign of progress. But in either case, the question remains: If the generative act was anti-sacrificial, how did the cycles of traditions and the texts as they stand come to their sacrificial constructions?

There is another, more historical way of understanding how eucharist emerged in earliest Christianity, an approach which takes account of the cultural changes which the development of the movement involved. Interest in the social world of early Judaism, and in how Christianity as a social movement emerged within Judaism and then became distinct from it, has been growing for most of this century. The result is that we are no longer limited to the old dichotomy, between the "conservative" position that the Gospels are literal reports and the "liberal" position that they are literary fictions. Critical study has revealed that the Gospels are composite products of the various social groups which were part of Jesus' movement from its days within Judaism to the emergence of Christianity as a distinct religion. When we place eucharistic practices within the social constituencies which made the Gospels into the texts we can read today, we can understand the original meaning Jesus gave to the last supper, and how his meaning generated others.

The last supper was not the only supper, just the last one.[17] In fact, the last supper would have had no meaning apart from Jesus' well established custom of eating with people socially. There was nothing unusual about a rabbi making social eating an instrument of his instruction, and it was part of Jesus' method from the first days of his movement in Galilee.

Meals within Judaism were regular expressions of social solidarity, and of common identity as the people of God. Many sorts of meal are attested in the literature of early Judaism. From Qumran we learn of banquets at which the community convened in order of hierarchy; from the Pharisees we learn of collegial meals shared within fellowships (*haburoth*) at which like-minded fellows (*haberim*) would share the foods and the company they considered pure. Ordinary households might welcome the coming the Sabbath with a prayer of sanctification (*kiddush*) over a cup of wine, and open a family occasion with a blessing (*berakhah*) over bread and wine.

Jesus' meals were similar in some ways to several of these meals, but they were also distinctive. He had a characteristic understanding of what the meals meant and of who should participate in them. For him, eating socially with others in Israel was a parable of the feast in the kingdom which was to come. The idea that God would offer festivity for all peoples on his holy mountain (see Isaiah 2:2-4) was a key feature in the fervent expectations of Judaism during the first century, and Jesus shared that hope, as may be seen in a saying from the source of his teaching known "Q:"

> Many shall come from east and west,
> and feast with Abraham, Isaac, and Jacob
> in the kingdom of God (see Matthew 8:11/Luke 13:28, 29).[18]

Eating was a way of enacting the kingdom of God, of practicing the generous rule of the divine king. As a result, Jesus avoided exclusive

---

[17]I owe the phrasing to Hershel Shanks, who in a personal conversation used it to help summarize my position.

[18]Because my interest here is in the traditional form of the saying, before changes introduced in Matthew and Luke, I give a reconstructed form, see *God in Strength*, pp. 179-201.

practices, which divided the people of God from one another; he was willing to accept as companions people such as tax agents and other suspicious characters, and to receive notorious sinners at table. The meal for him was a sign of the kingdom of God, and all the people of God, assuming they sought forgiveness, were to have access to it.

Jesus' practice of fellowship at meals caused opposition from those whose understanding of Israel was exclusive. To them, he seemed profligate, willing to eat and drink with anyone, as Jesus himself observed in a saying also from "Q:"

> A man came eating and drinking, and they complain:
> Look, a glutton and drunkard,
> a fellow of tax agents and sinners (see Matthew 11:19/Luke 7:34).

Some of Jesus' opponents saw the purity of Israel as something which could only be guarded by separating from others, as in the meals of their fellowships (*ḥavuroth*). Jesus' view of purity was different. He held that a son or daughter of Israel, by virtue of being of Israel, could approach his table, or even worship in the Temple. Where necessary, repentance beforehand could be demanded, and Jesus taught his followers to pray for forgiveness daily, but his understanding was that Israelites as such were pure, and were fit to offer purely of their own within the sacrificial worship of Israel.

As long as Jesus' activity was limited to Galilee, he was involved in active disputes, but essentially inconsequential ones. Slightly deviant rabbis in Galilee were far from uncommon. But Jesus also brought his teaching into the Temple, where he insisted on his own teaching (or *halakhah*) of purity. The incident which reflects the resulting dispute is usually called the cleansing of the Temple (Matthew 21:12-13/Mark 11:15-17/Luke 19:45-46/John 2:13-17). From the point of view of the authorities there, what Jesus was after was the opposite of cleansing. He objected to the presence of merchants who had been given permission to sell sacrificial animals in the vast, outer court of the Temple. His objection was based on his own, peasant's view of purity: Israel should offer, not priest's produce which they handed over money for, but their own sacrifices which they brought into the Temple. He believed so vehemently what he taught that he and his followers drove the animals and the sellers out of the great court, no doubt with the use of force.[19]

Jesus' interference in the ordinary worship of the Temple might have been sufficient by itself to bring about his execution. After all, the Temple was the center of Judaism for as long as it stood. Roman officials

---

[19]For a full discussion, see Chilton, *The Temple of Jesus. His Sacrificial Program Within a Cultural History of Sacrifice* (University Park: Pennsylvania State University Press, 1992).

were so interested in its smooth functioning at the hands of the priests they appointed that they were known to sanction the penalty of death for sacrilege. Yet there is no indication that Jesus was arrested immediately. Instead, he remained at liberty for some time, and was finally taken into custody just after one of his meals, the last supper. The decision of the authorities of the Temple to move against Jesus when they did is what made the last supper last.

Why did the authorities wait, and why did they act when they did? The Gospels portray them as fearful of the popular backing which Jesus enjoyed, and his inclusive teaching of purity probably did bring enthusiastic followers into the Temple with him. But in addition, there was another factor: Jesus could not simply be dispatched as a cultic criminal. He was not attempting an onslaught upon the Temple as such; his dispute with the authorities concerned purity within the Temple. Other rabbis of his period also engaged in physical demonstrations of the purity they required in the conduct of worship. One of them, for example, is said once to have driven thousands of sheep *into* the Temple, so that people could offer sacrifice in the manner he approved of (in the Babylonian Talmud, see Beza 20a, b). Jesus' action was extreme, but not totally without precedent, even in the use of force.

The delay of the authorities, then, was understandable. We could also say it was commendable, reflecting continued controversy over the merits of Jesus' teaching and whether his occupation of the great court should be condemned out of hand. But why did they finally arrest Jesus? The last supper provides the key; something about Jesus' meals after his occupation of the Temple caused Judas to inform on Jesus. Of course, "Judas" is the only name which the traditions of the New Testament have left us. We cannot say who or how many of the disciples became disaffected by Jesus' behavior after his occupation of the Temple.

However they learned of Jesus' new interpretation of his meals of fellowship, the authorities arrested him just after the supper we call last. Jesus continued to celebrate fellowship at table as a foretaste of the kingdom, just as he had before. But he also added a new and scandalous dimension of meaning. His occupation of the Temple having failed, Jesus said over the wine, "This is my blood," and over the bread "This is my flesh" (Matthew 26:26, 28/Mark 14:22, 24/Luke 22:19-20/1 Corinthians 11:24-25/Justin, *Apology* I.66.3).

In Jesus' context, the context of his confrontation with the authorities of the Temple, his words can have had only one meaning. He cannot have meant, "Here are my personal body and blood;" that is an interpretation which only makes sense at a later stage. Jesus' point was rather that, in the absence of a Temple which permitted his view of purity to be practiced, wine was his blood of sacrifice, and bread was his flesh of sacrifice. In Aramaic, "blood" (*d^e ma*) and "flesh" (*bisra*, which may also be rendered as "body") can carry such a sacrificial meaning, and in Jesus' context, that is the most natural meaning.

The meaning of "the last supper," then, actually evolved over a series of meals after Jesus' occupation of the Temple. During that period, Jesus claimed that wine and bread were a better sacrifice than what was offered in the Temple: at least wine and bread were Israel's own, not tokens of priestly dominance. No wonder the opposition to him, even among the Twelve (in the shape of Judas, according to the Gospels) became deadly. In essence, Jesus made his meals into a rival altar, and we may call such a reading of his words a ritual or cultic interpretation.

The cultic interpretation has two advantages over the traditional, autobiographical interpretation as the meaning Jesus attributed to his own final meals. The first advantage is contextual: the cultic interpretation places Jesus firmly with the Judaism of his period, and at the same time accounts for the opposition of the authorities to him. The second advantage is its explanatory power: the cultic interpretation enables us to explain sequentially subsequent developments in the understanding of eucharist within early Christianity. The cultic sense of Jesus' last meals with his disciples is the generative meaning which permits us to explain its later meanings as eucharistic covenant, Passover, and heroic symposium.

Conclusion

The New Testament defies the conservative and the liberal mythology, because it refuses to be literature. Instead, it insists upon the meanings which generated it, each meaning with its own integrity. In the case of eucharist, all the types are present. The meal as attested in our documents was and remains a meal of purity in anticipation of the kingdom, a surrogate of sacrifice, a covenantal occasion, a true Passover, solidarity with a martyr, and miraculous food (at the stage of the fourth Gospel, see John 6, where Jesus is himself the bread of heaven). Those are the meanings, embedded within practices which we can imagine, which produced the texts we read today.

Our old ideologies want to put us on a diet, as if to protect us from so much meaning. The conservative ideology, patroned by Joachim Jeremias, wants us to eat only the fiber of eucharist as Passover, with no deviation through the tradition. The liberal ideology, patroned by Burton Mack, wants us to eat only the whipped cream of the eucharist as imagined symposium, with no tradition to be deviated from.

There is a reason for which American ideologies are more sclerotic than most. We have just won a war. A cold one, but a war nonetheless.

Our conservatives have insisted upon a free market everywhere (which we have never had here); our liberals have urged the wisdom of accommodation (while being unwilling to change themselves). Both sides can be thanked for winning the war, but can now be buried under the monument of their own victory. Burial is the only decent thing to do with them, because they are not calibrated to the land of the living.

Eucharist is neither a conservative fixed datum nor a liberal dream. (For saying that, conservatives will call me a relativist, and liberals will call me a fundamentalist; their voices have survived their brain waves.) In its origin and through its tradition, it is generated by practices and practical meanings. That is also how it survives today, a specifically religious force, identifiable by means of a generative exegesis, untamable by the forces of ideology.

Bibliography

For an accessible introduction to traditio-historical criticism in the hands of a masterful exegete, the student may well consult C.H. Dodd, *The Apostolic Preaching and Its Developments* (New York: Harper, 1960). Although form criticism as a method has been superseded in many ways, the traditio-historical insights of Martin Dibelius and Rudolf Bultmann remain both valuable and fundamental. Of the two, Dibelius is more lucid and discursive (see *From Tradition to Gospel* [tr. B.L. Woolf; Cambridge: Clarke, 1971]) while Bultmann is more detailed and analytic (some might say dogmatic, see *The History of the Synoptic Tradition* [tr. J. Marsh; New York: Harper and Row, 1971]). A critical appraisal which remains useful is offered by Vincent Taylor, *The Formation of the Gospel Tradition* (London; Macmillan, 1945). A more philosophical consideration is available in Erhardt Guttgemanns, *Candid Questions Concerning Gospel Form Criticism:* Pittsburgh Theological Monograph Series 26 (Pittsburgh: Pickwick, 1979).

Several scholars have moved beyond a critique of form criticism, into the development of alternative portraits of primitive Christian traditions. Among them are Birger Gerhardsson, *Memory and Manuscript: Oral Tradition and Written Transmission in Rabbinic Judaism and Early Christianity* (Upsala and Lund: Gleerup, 1964) and *The Origins of the Gospel Traditions* (London: SCM, 1979); Harald Riesenfeld, *The Gospel Tradition* (Philadelphia: Fortress, 1970); Rainer Riesner, *Jesus als Lehrer. Eine Untersuchung zum Ursprung der Evangelien-Überleiferung* (Tübingen: Mohr, 1981). In varying ways, all three scholars have been justly criticized for imagining that rabbinic rules of handing on tradition were normative during the first century. Once allowance is made for the greater pluralism of early Judaism, many of their insights remain useful.

The task of relating the Synoptic Gospels to the pattern of oral and written tradition within the early Church was already recognized by B.H. Streeter, whose *The Four Gospels* (London: Macmillan, 1924) should still be consulted from that angle. More recent attempts to explain the emergence of the Synoptics from the point of view of traditio-historical criticism are Bo Reicke, *The Roots of the Synoptic Gospels* (Fortress: Philadelphia, 1986) and Chilton, *Profiles of a Rabbi. Synoptic Opportunities in Reading about Jesus:* Brown Judaic Studies 177 (Atlanta: Scholars Press, 1989). A range of representative positions in the discussion of "Q" may be found in John S. Kloppenborg with Leif E. Vaage (eds.), *Early Christianity, Q and Jesus:* Semeia 55 (Atlanta: Scholars Press, 1992).

The most recent phase in the investigation of traditions of Jesus' last meal in their relationship to eucharistic practice is investigated in Xavier Lwon-Dufour, *Sharing the Eucharistic Bread: the Witness of the New Testament* (tr. M.J. O'Connell; New York: Paulist, 1987) and Chilton, *A Feast of Meanings: Eucharistic Theologies from Jesus through Johannine Circles:* Supplements to *Novum Testamentum* (Leiden: Brill, 1994).

Hermeneutic and Epistemology of the Traditio-Historical Method: A Response to Bruce Chilton's "Traditio-Historical Criticism and the Study of Jesus"

Michel Machado
University of South Florida

Professor Chilton's article, *Traditio-Historical Criticism and the Study of Jesus,* provides us with an excellent opportunity to examine the difficulty involved in any reconstruction of the past, for historical studies in general and New Testament studies in particular. This article emphasizes the primacy of a hypothetical orality over evidence provided by written texts. When orality becomes the hermeneutical framework by which the written text is interpreted, the evidence as such disappears. This could easily lead to a circular reasoning that seems to strengthen the hypothesis, without proving it to be true. Our task is to test the usefulness of the traditio-historical method in a hermeneutic task and to consider the basis of its epistemology.

The concepts of communities and cycles are the fundamental points of the method. The traditio-historical method attributes the authorship of the gospels to various communities. So even if the gospel of "Luke" and the book of Acts do claim that the author and the recipient of the books are individuals and not communities, a single, individual authorship of these books is passed over. How does the traditio-historical method dispense itself with such evidence? The answer to this question can be rightly appreciated when addressing the problem of cycles. The concept of cycles provides scholarship with an easy way to eliminate such evidence.

Consider the notion of the Seder as pertaining to the cycle of James. The traditio-historical method declares that the Seder which appears in each Synoptic gospel pertains to the cycle of James. Since the cycle of James pertains to the first stage of the tradition, the gospels being the second stage, there is no possibility that the gospel's evidence can be used to falsify the theory of this article. Cycles become an easy way to exorcise evidence by relocating these into a primal tradition-building stage, creating for these a new context and shifting such evidence to a new paradigm. Following this procedure, the gospel as an entity with intentionality or historical credential loses all validity apart from a concatenation of cycles. The second stage of the tradition, the gospels, becomes a product of the amalgamation of these cycles and bears no meaning outside a careful discrimination of pericopae pertaining to different cycles.

The Seder example evidences the precariousness of the methodology used in this article. Labeling the mention of the Seder in the gospels as part of the Jacobean revision disregards that the author of Luke is a first century apologist of Paul. Further, it appears improbable in view of Paul's opposition to Jacobean revisionism and in view of the universalism of the author of Luke that "Luke" would include in his gospel a discriminatory thesis minted by the Jacobean ideology against the Gentile element of the Christian communities.

This leads to another question, accepting the ideological shift of the article: how could those same communities as creator of the genre Gospel have agreed to include such divisive points as the Seder as well as other issues, in their religious production? Are we to believe that the Jacobean revision was so powerful that it could impose its point of view on all communities? The partisans of Paul and all Gentile believers would hardly have agreed to this.

Other related problems arise with the epistemology of the method. For example, the approach taken by the article takes the absence of the mention of the lamb, the unleavened bread, the bitter herbs as being proof that the hypothetical primitive account did not know of a Seder. To this, it can be answered that if the Gospels already spoke of a Seder, these elements were understood to be essential to the ritual, further, since the emphasis of the text is upon the cup and the bread, these "missing" elements would naturally not be mentioned. Here is a good example of technical language used in the proper way for the proper time. In addition, the problem of the time of the Seder has always been puzzling.

The Gospels have no qualms about opposing the Seder of Jesus' group and the official Seder: It is quite possible that this particular group followed a different, solar calendar and would have made a point to eat it at the "right" time in opposition to the official one. Annie Jaubert (first, but with others after her) has published a monograph on this subject.[1] These questions could never be resolved if such a methodology should become prevalent in New Testament studies.

Following the traditio-historical method seems to imply the discarding of a document's evidence, and a disregard for the information given by those very documents. Moreover, the example of the dual Seder alerts us to the possibility that the real problem lies in the constraints imposed on this article by the scholarly consensus of the day. This consensus considers the followers of Jesus as a new *aventuriste* group in the story of Judaism. Is it possible to step out of this consensus and avoid the either/or solution in treating the Gospels' relationships with each other? Why not avoid so much frustration and consider a better paradigm and one which could interpret the dual Seder theory by considering the followers of Jesus as a Judaism, at least until Pentecost and what it represents, with its own tradition and understanding of Judaism.[2] This paradigm would replace the followers of Jesus in their context and avoid the anachronistic dichotomy between them and a version of "official" Judaism that was established after the post-Constantinian era and patterned after normative Judaism.

---

[1]*La date de la derniere Cene*, RHR, 146 (1954), pp. 140-173; *La Date de la Cene* (1957): *Jesus et le calendrier de Qumran*, NTS, 7 (1960), pp. 1-30.
The hypothesis of a solar calendar has the advantage to harmonize rather than to oppose the witness of the Gospels about a dual Seder. Since we know that "heterodox" communities used this calendar, it is possible that this problem could only be solved by Annie Jaubert's hypothesis. The adversaries of this hypothesis have discarded it because of lack of certainty about the inner workings of this calendar, not because of having settled the matter definitively and to their advantage. We must credit the Gospels with consistency; we need to adapt our interpretation to their framework of understanding the dual Seder, not the contrary. Evidence presented by the Gospels has the advantage of being part of the narrative unity of the work and should be favored above divergent theoretical constructions.
[2]Professor Jacob Neusner has published *Parallel Histories of Early Christianity and Judaism*, BR, (spring 1987) pp.42-55, a seminal article bearing on this question.

III.

THE USE OF LITERARY EVIDENCE OF A HISTORICAL CHARACTER TO RECREATE A RELIGIOUS CONCEPTION OF THE SOCIAL ORDER

4

What the Sources Do Not Say: The Judaism We Must Imagine

Jacob Neusner
University of South Florida

Gaining perspective on the subject of our work – the study of the lessons of history as these concern the interplay of religion and the social order – requires that we find an illuminating analogy: To what is the doing of our work to be compared? For through the right analogy, imagination is stimulated, and a new way of seeing things nurtured.

Take my problem, for instance, which is to remember that the goal of studying the sources vastly transcends the sense and meaning of the sources. For my work in the study of the religion, Judaism, focuses exclusively on written evidence, and it is easy to end my work at what should be its starting point. That is, having described, analyzed, and interpreted the documents, I may well lose sight of the reason why. So, to remind myself, I have to ask, exactly to what does the written evidence testify? But answering that question in a concrete way proves not so easy.

But a metaphor then allows me to find the answer. Where to find such a metaphor? It is to be located in the careful framing of this task of comparison and contrast, the work of making a parable for learning. I frame my issue in these words: When people wrote down the books that constitute the principal statement of Judaism in its formative age, what was it that they were putting into words and sentences for tradition to the ages? The question for two hundred years has elicited answers of a single type: people were writing down what they wished to remember as

67

authoritative and true. But in the time and place that witnessed the formation of these documents, among the sages responsible for them, did people write things down as an act of historical memory?

The answer to that question, which will dictate the character of the metaphor I seek, first of all depends on whether people then supposed that because something happened and was accurately recorded, those who are informed of what happened come under the obligation to accept the truth that history has handed down. But in ancient times, while people wrote narratives, they did so to teach lessons that enjoyed authority not by reason of historicity, not at all. They wrote down what happened because they believed that, in what happened, God spoke to them. But they believed, further, that God spoke to them in other, and more consequential ways, through prophecy, for example. And it is no wonder that the historical writings of the Hebrew Scriptures, Joshua, Judges, Samuel, and Kings, are classified as prophecy, not history at all. That is not because people doubted the historicity of the information they contained, but because they wrote and preserved history for an other-than-historical purpose. For them, it followed, to read these writings as history misses the point and purpose of what is read; it is like missing the point of a novel by criticizing not characterization or narrative but the typefaces or page layout; or it is like imputing a sustained narrative plot to a page-by-page reading of the St. Petersburg, Florida, telephone book.

But if authority derived from some source other than the accurate account of what had really happened, had really been said or done, then what point was there in writing the books that ancient Judaism set forth and that Judaism from that time onward deemed authoritative and holy? The answer was and remains, they wrote down what they knew of God and God's will for humanity in general, and for them in particular. That intention accounts for the Pentateuch, for Prophecy, for the Writings, that all together form the written part of the Torah, that is, the Hebrew Scriptures that Christianity calls "the Old Testament." And it also explains why we have the documents of the other part of the Torah, the oral part, comprising the Mishnah, a law code, the two Talmuds, commentaries on the Mishnah, and the Midrash compilations, commentaries on the Hebrew Scriptures. So we wonder, when people wrote down the documents of the Torah, oral and written, that they handed on to coming generations, what precisely did they think they were writing down? If not history, then religion, But what does it mean to write down religion? That is the question that, from my perspective, responds to the task of identifying some of the lessons that history – meaning, writing down or otherwise preserving what has been, what has happened to people and what they have learned – conveys concerning religion within the social order.

Asked in that way, the question invites a metaphor for what we do when we deal with religion, written down into words to be handed on from past to present and onward into the long future. To what may we compare the documents that contain those words? My answer is to invoke as my governing metaphor the art of the dance. Writing down the knowledge of, the encounter with, God is to be compared to dancing out music, that is, I compare the books that convey religious knowledge and experience to the dance as the physicalization of music, a conception I heard from Martha Graham. What did Miss Graham mean when she said, "the dance is the physicalization of music"? What she explained was, when she heard music, it would be in movement and gesture that she embodied what she heard. When in Chicago she saw for the first time the painting of the girl with the scarlet sash, she wanted immediately to dance the painting. And she knew just what she would do. Her limbs told her.

Now, in the context of the religion, Judaism, which identifies God's revelation with words written down in a book, and in the context of the kindred religions that identify book writing as a principal medium for conveying knowledge of God, Islam and Christianity, a book is the writing down of religion, that is to say, the encounter with God in time and in the present moment. I work on the writing down of religious experience, specifically on books the very study of which later on was itself deemed to bring about two religious events. First, study itself would form a religious experience. And second, and more urgent, the books themselves would make accessible to me the encounter with the holy God that the framers of the books preserved in them. For the holy books in the view of those who made, valued, and later preserved them as authoritative and true, record and preserve what it means to know God – as much as the dance records and preserves what it means to embody music. The metaphor then compares "know" to "embody." Encounter with God is not philosophical, that is, the mere factual knowledge that God exists, any more than the melody is the (mere) dance. Encounter with God is religious, that is, meeting with the living and very particular God who creates, commands, is concerned with Israel. But the knowledge of the encounter, recorded in words and in writing, makes possible our encounter afresh (so Judaism maintains concerning the Torah), just as the dance of the music makes possible the fresh re-presentation in physical ways of the melody.

True, the sages did not confuse map with territory, encounter through learning with the actuality of encounter itself, any more than Martha Graham conceived that the physicalization of music took the place of the music. The ballet would always begin with the notes of the orchestra (or the silent beat before the sound began), and the study of the

Torah would always commence with the prior knowledge of God present in the Torah. The Torah is not God, the ballet is not the music. The encounter with God, for religion, the music itself, for the dance – these remain always other, but no longer, wholly other and inaccessible, and that is what Torah learning promises for Judaism's knowledge of and encounter with God made manifest in the Torah, as much as it is what the ballet promises for the realization of music. These are, then, remarkable and noteworthy writings, not to be reduced to trivial dimensions.

The "Judaism" we must imagine finds its definition in the metaphor that has, I hope, stimulated us to see things in a different way from before. What imagination must supply, which learning cannot, concerns the human experience of God in a particular context: how through these books these sages recorded what they knew about God out of the Torah's record of God's presence and God's imperative. We study books, but our imagination must then transform the words into the issues that the words mean to record, and transcend those issues, too. For books represent the writing down of religious experience, and it must follow, what is important about those books is the religious experience that is realized, given concrete form, in them. Can we use our imagination to gain access, then, to not only what the books say, but what they meant to those who wrote them down in this way, rather than in some other, to make this statement in particular, rather than any other in general?

Framed in that way, the question draws upon the truth that God lives in the details. The issue then is, where and how we are to see in the mind of the writers people working their way from the details to the God that dwells therein. (In other contexts, the dancers or the storytellers or the composers or those who say prayers have to be viewed in the same perspective.) In seeing matters in this way, I follow in the path explored by Andrew M. Greeley in his *Religion as Poetry*,[1] who states matters in this language:

> ...religion does not end in experience, image, story, ritual and community but it begins with such phenomena – and takes its raw power from them. Reflected religion is derivative of experiential religion, prose religion is derivative of poetic religion....One's relationship to the transcendent...is a template for other human relationships....

Greeley underscores that, in religion, the medium conveys the message, but the medium by no means forms the message. Religion claims to

---

[1]Andrew M. Greeley, *Religion as Poetry: An Empirical Model*. Unpublished MS, dated 6/8/93, p. 299.

begin with the encounter with God and to present for coming ages through all time the consequences of that encounter.[2]

Now that observation of Greeley forms the starting point for my observation that, in Judaism, people wrote down in writing of a particular character precisely what they knew about God, as much as, in Christianity, they told the stories of what they knew about God or engaged in philosophically defined theological argument and analysis to formulate that knowledge; as much as in Islam, they revered in the Quran the record of God's exact words to the Prophet. And so, too, in Judaism sages meet God in the pages of the Torah, inclusive of its originally oral formulation in the Mishnah, Talmuds, and Midrash compilations, so that the encounter with God takes place in learning; as much as in Indonesia it is through theater and through dance; as much as in Islam it is through state building; as much as in Christianity, it is in the miracle of the Eucharist (for Catholics) or in the offering of song and sermon (for Reformation Protestants) or in the experience of direct encounter and rebirth (for Evangelical Protestants), and so on and so forth. But I need hardly observe that when we study these religions we cannot do more than examine the record. In the nature of things, it is simpler to focus upon the record than what the record records and represents, so far as writing down and re-presentation prove at all feasible, given what is at stake in religion.

That is why the task in studying religion in history begins when we realize what we study is not religion but only the record of religion; religion is to the sources, the data, the permanent record of religion as dance is to music. Just as dance re-presents music in the form of gesture, so religion re-presents the encounter with God in enduring, this-worldly forms. Just as we cannot touch music but we can respond to it in gesture, so, in religion, we respond to what is ineffable and sublime, the other-worldly in the context of the here and now of social being. In that context, appreciating our documents, deeming the knowledge of them to form an end in itself – these perfectly natural responses to sublime writings obscure what is captured, imperfectly to be sure, in those

---

[2]The formulation, "religion claims to...," makes it unnecessary to enter the question of whether religion, or a particular religion, sets forth the record of an authentic encounter with the one God or with a God or (more to the point) even whether there really is a god for religion or a religion to know. Studying religion as an activity of humanity in society imposes its own intellectual discipline and program. The starting point is that religion exists in the world that we can study, and in studying that world, we deal with the facts of human conviction, conscience, and conduct. Surely the facticity of religion in the here and now requires no demonstration. That premise then forms the starting point for all academic study of religion.

writings. Drawn onward and inward as we are by the intellectual power and beauty of written sources that have stood the test of time and even defined the social order for many generations, we who describe a Judaism attested solely in writing lose perspective on the context and character of our composition. We look in one direction only, toward the analysis of the interiority of our sources. Our account of that Judaism then takes for granted that these stand for the data, the exclusive, exhaustive data, for the Judaism we undertake to describe, analyze, and interpret.

We therefore forget that even the documents before us record by indirection, inference, and oversight a transcendent experience embodied in the social world that lies beyond their own horizons but defines their boundaries, too. These same documents, like the actors' hands in an Indonesian show of light and shadow, may be made to form shadows against a screen, so that, on the other side, we may see the movements of what is both reflected in light and shadow, and also hidden, by the screen. The sources form that screen, revealing but also obscuring at one and the same moment. So we devote our best energies to the analysis of what we know, which is what the documents record, when we should do well to reserve space for the use of imagination. I insist that what we cannot show we do not know. But I also wish to argue, we can show very well things that our sources do not mean to say but tell us anyhow.

That is not to suggest we make things up as we go along, committing acts of anachronism or uncontrolled fabrication against the writings that for late antiquity comprise Judaism's sole evidence for the transcendent. To explain what I do not mean, I note that a critic calls me to task for a massive failure of imagination. Let me quote the language, since it has a bearing upon the point I wish to make: "Neusner, in fact, has proposed that this was true of the early rabbis. This shows a lack of imagination and a failure to consider the accident of survival. If we had a collection of private Pharisaic prayers, we would find them as deeply devotional as are the hymns from Qumran."[3] Once more I am accused of failure of imagination in the first degree. Now we need not be detained by the details of the matter; what is striking is the critic's certainty concerning the character of evidence we do not have. He knows not only what has survived, but also what ought to have survived but has not. It is one thing to move from the known to the unknown; it is quite another to dictate the character of evidence and then condemn third parties for not sharing one's own pipe dreams. That kind of "imagination" has no bearing upon imagining Judaism. For who can predict the contours of an

---

[3]E.P. Sanders, *Judaism. Practices and Beliefs, 63 B.C.E.-67 C.E.* (Philadelphia, 1992: Trinity Press International), p. 414.

accident that has not happened? And how are we to know if we are wrong? I cannot think up a test of falsification for a proposition concerning evidence we do not have. This critic recommends precisely the kind of imagination that substitutes for rigorous thought and serves as a kind of labor saving device for self-assured but lazy scholars. It is, after all, much easier to make things up as we go along, then attributing the result to our very personal surmise, than rigorously to explore the outer limits of actual evidence. But that is what I propose to learn how to do. .

What if? why? and why not? – these are the questions that stimulate imagination. All invoke the premise that we can know from our sources more than they wish to tell us, and that that kind of knowledge can be subjected to the same controls of testing for falsification, then extension for analysis and interpretation, that govern our use of the facts that the sources do convey. We undertake, then, not fantasy but a mental experiment. How to proceed? Moving from the known to the unknown, the first step is to know precisely what we know. That sounds easier to define than it is in fact. For it means stepping back, backward to the known, rather than freely forward, into the unknown. For at stake in the use of imagination is the reading of the sources we do have: how can we make still better use of them than we already do? Any other question yields that process of undisciplined fabrication that shades over into fiction, on the one side, or charlatanism, on the other. And at this point, I find myself obligated to turn from the abstract to the concrete.

Let me specify, then, what I study and why it matters. I study a religion out of one kind of sources. What I want to know is the relationship between the religion people hold and the world they inhabit: Why does a religion serve when it does and lose plausibility when it no longer serves? Religion as a human activity carried out in community forms the center of my interest, and, as I shall explain, my sources are ideal for such a study, all of them deriving from a collectivity and standing for a textual community.[4] I have now to imagine other kinds of sources to tell me about the same religious system.

What do I mean by religion, and what are the sources for the study of religion? I find in a statement by Andrew M. Greeley guidance in answering both questions and gaining perspective on my task:

> Religion is story, story before it is anything else, story after it is everything else, story born from experience, coded in symbol, and reinforced in the self and shared with others to explain life and death, death and life.

---

[4]To borrow Brian Stock's fine phrase in his *The Implications of Literacy* (Princeton, 1987: Princeton University Press).

> In its nuances and resonances, its shadings and allusions, its suggestions and its hints, its density and its ambiguities, its many levels and its multiplicity of messages, the story appeals to and discloses the total human person, soul and body, intelligence and senses, reason and intuition, reasoning and instinct....[5]

Lest Greeley be wrongly interpreted to speak of what is personal but not social, I point to his stress on the social context of religious storytelling: stories constitute a storytelling community, defined by those who grasp and respond to what is meant in the story:

> Religious heritages constitute storytelling communities...or a congeries of storytelling communities...a group of humans who share a common repertory of symbols and a sufficiently common interpretation of these symbols so that it is relatively easy to tell them the story and relatively reasonable to expect that they will 'get it'....[6]

That is the context in which we address the Judaism of late antiquity that is portrayed in the documents produced in a continuous and coherent trajectory by "our sages of blessed memory," that is, the rabbis of the Land of Israel and Babylonia from ca. 200 through ca. 600 C.E. [=A.D.].

When Greeley says that religion is a story, he argues that through gestures of a symbolic character, stories are evoked even when not told in so many words; he does not reduce religion to its personal dimension nor deprive it of that dimension, but his stress on the religious community as a "storytelling community" points us toward our problem: What stories did other Jews in the same time and place tell, what stories did "our sages of blessed memory" tell that did not survive, what should we know about this same Judaism that we do not now know if our evidence extended to writings of another kind, or to evidence of another classification besides the written?

When we study a religion represented for us only in writing of the rather arcane kind before us, we lose sight of a variety of other representations of religion that we have a right to anticipate and should contemplate in our mind's eye. Let me give five ways in which religion, including Israelite religion, expressed itself: through [1] dance, [2] song, [3] theater, [4] processions and other forms of communal re-presentation, and [5] craft and art, inclusive of the creation of holy objects. If a sage were to plan a museum of his Judaic system, what would he include, and how would he set up his display? In that question commences that act of imagination that I wish to set forth. What are the things that the sage

---

[5]Andrew M. Greeley, *Religion as Poetry: An Empirical Model.* Unpublished MS, dated 6/8/93, p. 90.
[6]*ibid*, p. 93.

would put in a single display case? What are the combinations he would make?

His religion came to expression, as do many religions, not only or mainly in words lacking passion but in prayer; not in random movements but in choreographed ones; not in prose but in poetry; not in routine happening but in drama. So we ask, if a sage were to write down the dances he did or had done for him, the songs he sang or the songs he taught people to sing, the rites of reenactment in the enchantment of theater, the rituals of communal celebration in the streets, the making and manipulation of holy object – knots, amulets, kinds of garments for instance – what kind of writing should we anticipate he would write? And what if he made up people and things that happened to him – wrote fiction, meaning it to be fiction?

What do I maintain forms the principal medium of expression of religious encounter that served the ancient Judaic sages? It encompasses but is not principally in dance or music, knot tying or dietary abstinence, sexual activity or inactivity, though all of these matters came within the circle of sanctification conceived by those sages. Since they wrote books, they must be encountered first of all as intellectuals, by which I mean, people who receive the world through the media of intellect, thought, reflection, puzzlement and criticism; people who form their response to the world through the media of proposition, argument, evidence, and analysis. Intellectuals will ask questions, like Moses before the burning bush: What is this strange phenomenon? I think I shall take a closer look – and find out the reason why for what I am observing. Now, what Judaism records Moses did with what he learned involves a variety of activities, political in nation building, prophetic in the laying down of prophetic commandments, but, above all, book writing. God was then known, and to be known, not only in the thin voice of silence, but in the full throated, public commandments to define the kingdom of priests and the holy people: the rules of sanctification.

Having set forth the proposition and argument that there is a "Judaism" – an encounter with God through the Torah – that we know through use of imagination in the reading of sources, I face a further, and, for the present, final task. It is to ask, at what point and quite how the sages of the Torah used their imagination to make a statement upon the nature of the encounter with God in the Torah. That is, just as I claim it is my task to use my imagination to make a statement upon their encounter with God through the Torah, so I must find in their processes of thought a model for myself, a validation and a standard of authenticity. If I claim to interpret, then I must show that my mode of interpretation corresponds to the character of what is interpreted. The task is reciprocal and mutual: what do I think they did, which forms the model of what I must do in studying what they did. This somewhat abstract statement immediately becomes more concrete when I define what it is that I think forms the raw materials for imagination, by which I mean: What told them the questions they were to confront, what entry into the processes of intellect and argument did they define for themselves? The answer to that question tells us what sages would have selected for their Judaism museum, and which items they would have put in the same display case.

I choose as the sages whose imagination governs the framers of the single authoritative document of the Torah ("Judaism"), which is, the Talmud of Babylonia, the summa of the labor of Torah study carried on from Sinai to the seventh century of the Common Era, and the constitution and by-laws of holy Israel from then to the present day. Now, as a matter of fact, most of what the sages who wrote the compositions that form the Talmud set forth is a simple explanation of the sense and meaning of the Mishnah, a second-century philosophical law code. Of the Mishnah's sixty-three tractates, they wrote commentaries to thirty-seven. And a close reading of those thirty-seven tractates that comprise the Talmud of Babylonia shows that the bulk of the writing consists in Mishnah exegesis. Where sages met God in Mishnah exegesis forms a problem for exposition in its own terms. For the present task – an exposition of the power of imagination – a single point suffices.

Where sages in the Talmud spoke for themselves and only for themselves, and not in behalf of the Mishnah's earlier writers, some three or four centuries earlier, is in a single point. Time and again, in laying out the meaning of a given Mishnah tractate, the framers of the Talmud introduced huge composites that in no way serve the task of Mishnah exegesis – explaining words and phrases and implications of rules of the Mishnah. Rather, these composites set forth sustained expositions of a given topic or proposition completely separate from the Mishnah passage at which said composites are situated. And the jarring juxtaposition – the Mishnah's rule, an exposition thereof, and then a vast treatise on something absolutely separate from the Mishnah's rule – represents the point at which the sages who compiled the Talmud made a statement of their own. The substance of that statement, I contend, when properly grasped gives us entry into the religious encounter that sages wished to make accessible. It is not the comment they wished to make on the subject at hand but the meeting with the mind of God exposed in the authentic context in which the subject at hand is to be expounded.

These altogether too abstract formulations may be illustrated by the Talmud's treatment of two subjects set forth in the Mishnah. The first is the Mishnah's presentation of rules of conduct on the intermediate days of festivals, in Mishnah-tractate Moed Qatan. The law is that, during the days between the first and final days of the festival of Tabernacles (Sukkot), celebrating the first full moon after the autumnal equinox, and similarly the first and final days of the festival of Passover (Pessah), celebrating the first full moon after the vernal equinox, people are not to perform acts of servile labor. Those intermediate festival days are not full fledged holy days, but they also are not ordinary workdays. Now in that setting, we find a sustained and extensive exposition of a topic that the issue at hand – the sanctification of holy days – scarcely would lead us to introduce at all, and that topic is so jarring as to leave a dreadful impression: Is the Talmud incapable of rational thought at all? I shall spell it out in a moment. My second case is the Mishnah's presentation of the rules of self-affliction on the Day of Atonement, in line with the commandment of Leviticus Chapter Sixteen that, on the Day of Atonement, along with the rites in the Holy of Holies of the Temple, people are to refrain from eating, drinking, and various other everyday pleasures, in an act of self-affliction in atonement from sin. Here, once more, the Talmud introduces, in the context of fasting from food and drink, a topic that on the surface violates the simplest rules of logic: that a context govern the contents of whatever is offered for discussion in that context. Both cases, we shall see now, make us wonder whether there is any rhyme or reason for the topical program of the Talmud in general, and eminent expositors of the Talmud even now tell large audiences that the Talmud follows no rational principle of organization at all.

Now to the two cases. The first introduces into the exposition of the laws of conduct on intermediate days of the festival the prohibition of mourning (Bavli-tractate Moed Qatan).[7] And once we are told that

---

[7]In my outline of the Talmud to Mishnah-tractate Moed Qatan, the relevant points are as follows: XV.C, D, E: Here is the point at which the framers of the Talmud have made a statement that is entirely their own, reshaping the topic of the Mishnah in ways that the Mishnah tractate cannot have led us to anticipate in any way. The set of composites takes up the rules governing the mourner on the intermediate days of the festival, and this shades over into a systematic presentation of the rules of mourning in their own terms. Then, E, others who are comparable to the mourner in their status – not permitted to conduct themselves in ordinary society in accord with the rules that otherwise govern uniformly – are introduced. The net effect is to transform the re-presentation of the Mishnah tractate by introducing a topic that the Mishnah tractate scarcely touches. XVIII.B, C, D, E, F, G, I: The topic of mourning is once more treated in its own terms, out of all relationship to the Mishnah tractate's interest in it. Here again, we have what amounts to a small tractate on mourning, a range of general rules, special problems, and then the inevitable case of the sage produced in this context as in many others now carrying us far beyond the limits of the Mishnah tractate.

mourning does not take place on the festival's intermediate days, we are given a long exposition on the general theme of death, mourning, and burial. Precisely what has death to do with the intermediate days of the festival? To answer that question, we must understand the rules of thought that govern in the Mishnah and beyond, which are familiar, philosophical ones of comparison and contrast. That is to say, the principal mode of thought of the Mishnah is that of comparison and contrast. Something is like something else, therefore follows its rule; or unlike, therefore follows the opposite of the rule governing the something else. So as a matter of hypothesis, let us assume that the framers of Talmud-tractate Moed Qatan found self-evidently valid the modes of thought that they learned from the Mishnah and so made connections between things that were alike, on the one side, or things that were opposite, on the other. How do death and mourning compare to the intermediate days of the festival? The point of opposition – the contrastive part of the equation – then proves blatant. Death is the opposite of the celebration of the festival. The one brings mourning, the other, joy. And the Mishnah's inclusion of the mourner on its list of those whose special situation must be taken into account then precipitates thought about the item on the list – the mourner – that most clearly embodies the special circumstance of all items on the list.

But if the contrast proves obvious, the point of comparison – how are these things similar, and what rule pertains to both – emerges with equal facility. Extremes of emotion – mourning, rejoicing – come together in the normal cycle of life and the passage of time. Each takes its place on a continuum with the other, whether from the perspective of the passage of time in nature or the passage of life, also in nature; whether from the perspective of the sacred or from the standpoint of uncleanness. The natural rhythm of the year brings Passover and Tabernacles, the celebration of the first full moon after the vernal and autumnal equinoxes, respectively. The natural rhythm of life brings its moments of

---

XIX.B, C, D, F: The topic of mourning for sages, the death of sages, and the like, along with further comments on mourning rites, predominates once more. Here again, the Mishnah tractate in a tangential way has introduced a topic in the context of the Mishnah tractate's program. Then the Talmud composite treats the topic in terms not to be predicted out of the way in which the Mishnah tractate has introduced said topic. Now the topic takes on a life of its own. XX.C, E, F: Forms of lamentation take over, and the matter of the intermediate days of the festival falls by the way. Once more the result is the same. The essay shades over from mourning to death: dying suddenly, the angel of death, and the angel of death and sages. XXI.B, C, D: Not surprisingly, the free-standing composite pursues its own interest, which is [1] rules of mourning with [2] special interest in sages. It is hardly surprising that D ends with the condition of sages in the world to come, that is, after death.

intense emotion, too. But death and the festival also form moments of a single continuum, one of uncleanness yielding to its polar opposite, sanctification, sanctification yielding to uncleanness. Death, we must not forget, also serves as a principal source of uncleanness, the festival, the occasion for sanctification beginning with the removal of cultic uncleanness and the entry into a state of cultic cleanness. These opposites also take their place on a single continuum of being.

So in establishing the connection, through treating the categories as equivalent and counterpart to one another, between death and the festival's intermediate days, what have our sages in Talmud-tractate Moed Qatan said in their own behalf, not about the Mishnah but through their re-presentation of the Mishnah? They make the connection between the one and the other – death and the festival's intermediate days – so as to yield a conclusion concerning the everyday and the here and now. These are neither permanently sanctified nor definitively unclean, neither wholly the occasion for rejoicing without restriction as to acts of labor nor entirely the occasion of common ventures without restriction as to attitudes of exaltation. The days between festivals, like ordinary life, after birth but before death – these are to be seen as sanctified but not wholly so, just as life forms the realm of the angel of death, but only for a while. The festival comes – and so does the resurrection of the dead and the life of the world to come, of which the festival, like the Sabbath, gives us a foretaste.

The second (Bavli-tractate Yoma),[8] concerns a still more jarring juxtaposition. It involves fasting on the Day of Atonement in expiation

---

[8]In its reading of the presentation of the Day of Atonement by Mishnah-tractate Yoma 8:1-2, the Talmud introduces the matter of manna at just the point at which the rules of fasting are expounded by the Mishnah. An outline of the treatment of the subject shows how the Talmud makes its statement through its re-presentation of the Mishnah.

B. COMPOSITE ON THE AFFLICTION OF SOULS ON THE DAY OF ATONEMENT, IN PARTICULAR, THROUGH FASTING

1. I:4: Tannaite complement: "You shall afflict your souls" (Lev. 16:29) – might one suppose that a person should therefore sit in the sun or in the cold so as to suffer anguish? Just as the prohibition of work means, sit and do nothing, so the commandment to afflict one's soul means, sit and do nothing by abstinence.

2. I:5: Tannaite complement as above, with the resolution: Just as the prohibition of work covers a matter for which in another context one would incur liability on the Sabbath in particular, so the affliction of the soul covers something for which in another context one would incur liability. And what might that be? This would refer to eating meat of a

sacrifice that has been subjected by the officiating priest to an improper intention or eating meat that has been left over and not burned at the required time.

3.   I:6: "You shall afflict your souls" (Lev. 16:29) – here we find a reference to affliction, and elsewhere we find a reference to the same matter. Just as elsewhere, the affliction concerns hunger, so here the affliction must concern hunger.

C.   APPENDIX ON THE AFFLICTION THAT INVOLVES EATING: THE CASE OF MANNA

1.   I:7: "Who fed you in the wilderness with manna...that he might afflict you" (Deut. 8:16) – R. Ammi and R. Assi – One said, "One who has a loaf of bread in his basket is not the same as one who has no loaf of bread in his basket. And one said, "One who sees what he is eating is not the same as one who does not see while he is eating."

   a.   I:8: Continuation of Ammi and Assi composite; an interpolated proposition tangential in the foregoing.

   b.   I:9: Continuation of Ammi and Assi composite.

   c.   I:10: Continuation of Ammi and Assi composite.

      I.   I:11: Thematic add-on.

2.   I:12: "We remember the fish that we used to eat in Egypt for nothing" (Num. 11:5) – Rab and Samuel: "Real fish" vs. "A euphemism for sexual relations."

3.   I:13: "The cucumbers and the melons" (Ex. 11:5) – "In the manna they tasted every sort of food but not the taste of the five specified items, cucumbers, melons, leeks, onions, and garlic."

4.   I:14: "Now the manna was like coriander seed" (Num. 11:7) – "It was round like coriander seed and white like pearl."

   a.   I:15: Tannaite complement: "Now the manna was like coriander seed" (Num. 11:7): – the letters for the word for coriander bear the meaning that the manna was like flax seed in its capsules.

   b.   I:16: Tannaite complement: The letters for the word for coriander bear the meaning that the manna told the Israelites whether an infant was born at nine months, after intercourse with the first husband, or at seven months, after intercourse with the second husband.

      I.   I:17: Just as the prophet told the Israelites what was to be found in clefts or holes, so manna would reveal to Israelites what was in the clefts and holes.

5.   I:18: "And when the dew fell upon the camp in the night, the manna fell upon it" (Num. 11:9). "And the people shall go and gather" (Ex. 16:4). "The people went about and gathered it" (Num. 11:8) – how so?

6.   I:19: It is written "bread" and also "dough of cakes" and "they ground it" (Num. 11:8) – how so?

7.   I:20: "...or beat it in mortars" (Num. 11:8) – This teaches that with the man there descended for the Israelites women's cosmetics, that is, things that are ground in a mortar.

8. I:21: "And boiled it in pots" (Num. 11:8) – This teaches that with the manna there descended for the Israelites the makings of a pudding.

9. I:22: "And they brought yet to him freewill-offerings every morning" (Ex. 36:3) – What is the meaning of every morning? Precious stones and jewels descended from heaven and were given by the people as freewill-offerings.

10. I:23: "And the taste of it was like the taste of a cake baked with oil" (Num. 11:8) – Just as the infant tastes at the breast any number of tastes, so for the manna, whenever the Israelites ate it, they found in it a whole variety of flavors.

11. I:24: "And Moses said, This shall be when the Lord shall give you in the evening meat to eat and in the morning bread to the full" (Ex. 16:8) – Meat, for which they asked not in the right way, was given to them at the wrong time. Bread, for which they asked in the right way, was given to them at the right time.

12. I:25: "While the meat was yet between their teeth" (Num. 11:33). And it is written, "But a whole month" (Num. 11:20) – how so? The middling folk died on the spot, the wicked suffered pain for a whole month.

13. I:26: "And they spread them all abroad" (Num. 11:32) – "Don't read, 'they spread abroad' but read the same letters with the vowels that yield, 'they were slaughtered.' This teaches that the Israelites incurred the penalty of being slaughtered."

14. I:27: "And they spread them all abroad" (Num. 11:32) –

15. I:28: It is written, "bread," and also "oil," and also "honey" (Ex. 16:29, 31, Num. 11:8). Which was it? Said R. Yosé b. R. Hanina, "For the young, bread; for the old, oil; for the children, honey."

16. I:29: The word for quail is written to be pronounced shlaw but we pronounce it as slaw. What does this mean? Said R. Hanina, "When the righteous eat it, it is at ease, but when the wicked eat it, it is like thorns for them."

     a. I:30: Said R. Hanan bar Raba, "There are four kinds of quail, and these are they: thrush, partridge, pheasant, and quail."

18. I:31: It is written, said R. Yosé b. R. Hanina, "Dew on top, dew on the bottom; it looked like something put in a box."

19. I:32: "A fine scale-like thing" (Num. 11:9) – Said R. Simeon b. Laqish, "It is something that melts on the palm of the hand." R. Yohanan said, "It is something that is absorbed by the two hundred and forty-eight parts of the human body."

20. I:33: Tannaite complement: "Man did eat the bread of the mighty" (Ps. 78:25) – "It is the bread that the ministering angels eat," the words of R. Aqiba.

21. I:34: "But now our soul is dried away, there is nothing at all" (Num. 11:6) – They said, "This manna is going to dry up

of sin, and, on the other hand, God's nourishing Israel in the wilderness with manna. The propositions prominent in the exposition of the theme of the manna treats the manna as Heaven's response to self-affliction for sin. Thus "Who fed you in the wilderness with manna...that he might afflict you" (Deut. 8:16): Just as the prophet told the Israelites what was to be found in clefts or holes, so manna would reveal to Israelites what was in the clefts and holes. Meat, for which they asked not in the right way, was given to them at the wrong time. Bread, for which they asked in the right way, was given to them at the right time. "While the meat was yet between their teeth" (Num. 11:33). And it is written, "But a whole month" (Num. 11:20) – The middling folk died on the spot, the wicked suffered pain for a whole month. When the righteous eat the quail, it is at ease, but when the wicked eat it, it is like thorns for them. "Man did eat the bread of the mighty" (Ps. 78:25) – "It is the bread that the ministering angels eat." The manna marked Israel as supernatural – and so does its fasting.

These important additions, in the form of large-scale composites, introduce into the representation of the theme of the Day of Atonement conceptions and considerations of which the Mishnah scarcely takes cognizance. While the conception of heaven's response to afflicting oneself by fasting is providing manna in the wilderness – the bread that the angels eat! – strikes me as the single most remarkable initiative, the other propositions before us prove equally striking. Seen as a group, they yield the following proposition: the Day of Atonement, which the Torah lays out as principally a Temple occasion, overspreads the world. That is not a merely moral statement but one of cultic consequence, since we see the rite itself as one affecting the world beyond the Temple walls in the way in which the one analogous in its careful concern for the high priest's purification, the burning of the red cow, does. Israel's sin in the

---

　　　　　their bowels. For is there any born of woman who takes in
　　　　　but doesn't excrete?" the words of R. Aqiba.
22.　I:35: His disciples asked R. Simeon b. Yohai, "How come the
　　　　　manna came down to the Israelites only once a year?"
23.　I:36: Now R. Tarfon and R. Ishmael and sages were in
　　　　　session, dealing with the passage on manna, and R. Eleazar
　　　　　the Modite was in session among them. R. Eleazar the
　　　　　Modite responded and say, "The manna that came down for
　　　　　Israel was sixty cubits high."
　　a.　I:37: Issi b. Judah says, "The manna that came down for
　　　　　　Israel kept ascending until all the kings of the east and
　　　　　　west saw it, as it is said, 'You prepare a table before me
　　　　　　in the presence of my enemies, my cup runs over' (Ps.
　　　　　　23:5, 6)."
24.　I:38: Continuation of I:36.

world intrudes into the cult, because the Temple, the mark of divine favor, was lost on account of Israel's sin. But Israel's virtue, the virtue of self-affliction through fasting, can win heaven's cordial response, analogous to the provision of manna in the wilderness. That is because Israel's ordinary life compares with the Temple's sanctification; even as the Temple space is sanctified, so Israel's space is marked off by signs of the holy. Just as the Temple's priests display their riches in the ample cult, so Israel's sages display their resources of virtue and intellect in the service of the mind and heart, study of the Torah. And, it must follow, the righteousness represented by a life fearful of sin and rich in repentance, which comes to its climax on the Day of Atonement, infuses the entire people of Israel, not only the priesthood in the Temple on that same holy day.

The upshot is, the Mishnah's presentation of the Day of Atonement, its recapitulation of the themes of Leviticus Chapter Sixteen in the proportions of Scripture's treatment of that topic, is both replicated and revised. What for Leviticus and Mishnah-tractate Yoma forms a cultic occasion, in which Israel participates as bystanders, emerges in Bavli-tractate Yoma as an event in the life of holy Israel, in which all Israel bears tasks of the weight and consequence that, on that holy day, the High Priest uniquely carries out. On the Day of Atonement, holy Israel joins the high priest in the Holy of Holies; this they do on that day by afflicting themselves through fasting and other forms of abstinence, recalling how with heaven's favor they would eat the bread of angels; this they do on the other days of the year by entering into the disciplines of the Torah; this they do through their lives of virtue. The Day of Atonement, the occasion on which the high priest conducts the rite in the privacy of the Holy of Holies, emerges transformed: the rites are private, but the event is public; the liturgy is conducted in the holy Temple, with sins sent forth through the scapegoat, but the event bears its consequences in holy Israel, where sins are atoned for in the setting of the everyday and the here and now. What is singular and distinct – the rites of atonement on the holiest day of the year in the holiest place in the world – now makes its statement about what takes place on every day of the year in the ordinary life of holy Israel.

And that is how the Day of Atonement would make its way through time, not the sacrificial rite of the high priest in the Temple, but the atonement celebration of all Israel in the world. What mattered to the compilers of Leviticus and the Mishnah alike was the timeless rite of atonement through the bloody rites of the Temple What captured the attention of the framers of the Bavli tractate, by contrast, was the personal discipline of atonement through repentance on the Day of Atonement and a life of virtue and Torah learning on the rest of the days of the year. They took out of the Holy of Holies and brought into the homes and streets of the holy people that very mysterious rite of atonement that the Day of Atonement called forth. When the compilers of our Talmud moved beyond the limits of the Mishnah tractate, they transformed the presentation of the day and its meaning, transcending its cultic limits. And it was their vision, and not the vision of Leviticus Sixteen and the Mishnah's tractate, that would prove definitive. The upshot is then obvious: when sages wrote down what their encounter with God had taught them, what they wrote down was what they knew about God in the here and now of a life of penitence and atonement lived in the details of workaday life. They transformed the Torah's presentation of the Day of Atonement into the comparison and contrast of fasting and of divine nourishment and explained how the two meet in the encounter with God.

These two examples of how in formulating the re-presentation of entire Mishnah tractates, the framers of the Talmud made a statement of religious encounter show where and how imagination, first theirs, then ours, wins its point of entry. No received text dictated to sages that when discussing the intermediate days of the festival, they should juxtapose mourning to rejoicing; nor did any instruct them that the right theme for clarifying the full meaning of fasting on the Day of Atonement must be, how God nourishes Israel from heaven. I find it difficult to imagine less likely candidates for introduction into the exposition of just these topics, and that is why I credit imagination – sages' imagination in compiling the Talmud – with the power to transform a topic and so to transcend it at a deeper layer of meaning altogether.

It was their imagination that produced the astonishing, the jarring, but the illuminating juxtaposition of opposites that the Talmud tractates under discussion lay out. And seeing one thing in the setting of something utterly opposite, sages produced a message of their own, one that, I think, allowed them to say something they had learned about God in the Torah. That is, it is something they had learned and wished to teach – not the framers of the Oral Torah written down in the Mishnah, not the framers of the Written Torah of ancient Israel's holy Scriptures. It is the product of their imagination. And by imagination I mean, their capacity to think beyond the bounds of the already thought, their courage to take risks in ranging into the unknown, and their conviction that, in the Torah, they encountered not only what God had said long ago, but what God is saying in the here and now of their own intellect. The Judaism we must imagine in our labor of describing, analyzing, and interpreting an ancient, living faith then takes shape within our venture of trying to imagine what stimulated someone else's imagination. That is to say, we must undertake the exegesis of exegesis,[9] or, in simpler language, we must try to explain the connections that someone else found compelling: the obvious.

---

[9] I refer to the conception of the study of religion as the exegesis of exegesis that is put forward by Jonathan Z. Smith, who has made us aware of the critical issue of the recombinancy of a fixed canon of "things" in his discussion of sacred persistence, that is, "the rethinking of each little detail in a text, the obsession with the significance and perfection of each little action." In the canonical literature of Judaism, these minima are worked and reworked, rethought and recast in some other way or order or combination – but always held to be the same thing throughout. In this context I find important guidance in Smith's statement:

> An almost limitless horizon of possibilities that are at hand...is arbitrarily reduced...to a set of basic elements....Then a most intense ingenuity is exercised to overcome the reduction...to introduce interest and variety. This ingenuity is usually accompanied by a complex set of rules ["Sacred Persistence: Towards a Redescription of Canon," in William Scott Green, ed., *Approaches to Ancient Judaism* 1978, 1:11-28. Quotation: p. 15}.

Smith observes:

> the radical and arbitrary reduction represented by the notion of canon and the ingenuity represented by the rule-governed exegetical enterprise to apply the canon to every dimension of human life is that most characteristic, persistent, and obsessive religious activity....The task of application as well as the judgment of the relative adequacy of particular applications to a community's life situation remains the indigenous theologian's task; but the study of the process, particularly the study of comparative systematics and exegesis, ought to be a major preoccupation of the historian of religions (op. cit., p. 18).

Smith speaks of religion as an "enterprise of exegetical totalization." Smith invokes the metaphor of a diviner's basket of the Ndembu, as Smith describes that divinatory situation:

> Among the Ndembu there are two features of the divinatory situation that are crucial to our concern: the diviner's basket and his process of interrogating his client. The chief mode of divination consists of shaking a basket in which some twenty-four fixed objects are deposited (a cock's claw, a piece of hoof, a bit of grooved wood,...withered fruit, etc.). These are shaken in order to winnow out' truth from falsehood' in such a way that few of the objects end up on top of the heap. These are 'read' by the diviner both with respect to their individual meanings and their combinations with other objects and the configurations that result (op. cit., p. 25).

The examples I have given show that in Judaism, combining topics that we should not "ordinarily" see as related at all forms the counterpart to a cock's claw in the Ndembu culture. Both will be fixed, but will combine and recombine in a large number of different ways.

To conclude by stepping beyond the boundaries of the academic and descriptive study of religion and into the circle of theological exposition of norms, I may make a simple statement of what I take to be the consequence of these facts. It is that religious experience – God's address to us, our encounter with God – takes place, also, when we think the unthinkable and imagine what lies beyond all reasoned reflection, how things are like one another, or how they are unlike one another, when it is we, in our own minds, who initiate the comparison or contrast. Speaking within the religion that calls itself "the Torah" and that the world calls "Judaism," I say very simply: God works through us when we imitate God through our mastery of God's thoughts, in God's own wording of those thoughts, in the Torah: "for my thoughts are not like your thoughts," the prophet sets, and in the Talmud we learn, but in the moment of unearned insight, unanticipated simile, inconceivable metaphor, ours can become like God's. For, after all, before creation, who but God can have imagined heaven and earth – not to mention humanity.

Language is Religion: Response to Jacob Neusner "What the Sources Do Not Say: The Judaism We Must Imagine"

Stein-Atle Vere
University of South Florida

The Judaism of the Dual Torah is a textual religion; it becomes aware of the divine by reading the literary evidence of its ancestral religion. As such it acknowledges language to be at the very center of the religious experience. Dr. Neusner, now, divides Judaism's sacred texts from Judaism's religion, and poses the question: Where does the religion take place – in the record of the language or in the mind of the language user? Inky letters on parchment do not have divine encounters, people do. It is precisely each Jew's encounter with the transcendent God that makes Judaism religious. To study a religion like Judaism, one must not ask what the sacred texts mean – that is only the beginning – one must ask how they accomplish an awareness of God. There is a process at work within language that allows a person to experience the divine when dialoguing over the sacred records.

The Religious Energy of Language

If language is the capacity to create meaning, and religion is a search for meaning, religion is most likely an aspect of language. Moreover, religion shares language's personal and social dimensions, by being both an experience of symbols and a communication of that experience to others through those symbols. Arguably, language is itself the religious experience.

The Judaism of the Dual Torah is peculiarly aware of the religious nature of language. Its cosmology therefore suggests a useful map for understanding it: the world, the Torah and the imageless God correspond to the *cosmic*, the *transcendent* and the *divine* levels of language. Humans dialogue at the cosmic level of language, but in doing so they can engage in powerfully meaningful experiences of the transcendent and the divine. They tell narratives to metaphorically describe their experiences to others. The communication of these narratives then socializes a group to share the experience of these levels of meaning, and thus completes the religious process of language. To put it in other words, religion is language becoming aware of itself and transforming human relationships in that awareness.

Dr. Neusner's definition of religion, adapted from Dr. Greeley, is persuasive: a religion is a group's shared narratives to metaphorically articulate a widely experienced transcendent. Nevertheless, the explicit concept of narrative is far too passive, either being a description or an accidental receptacle of the transcendental experience. Narrative, rather, is a tremendous characteristic. Not only does it communicate an idea but it compels the listener to approximately re-experience it. When narrating religiously, it has the power to force the hand of God, to seize God and expose God's presence to the entire audience. Or, to snatch the audience unaware and catapult them up into the thrones of heaven. Dr. Neusner touched on the narrative's power throughout his paper and concluded the following, "God works through us when we imitate...God's thoughts, in God's own wording of those thoughts, in the Torah...In the moments of...unanticipated simile...[our thoughts] can become like God's."

Every person carries on the daily exercise of sorting out and living out all the narratives that govern the operation of her or his world. Sometimes in a flash of surprise those narratives align themselves "wrongly" and the whole system collapses. A glaring fracture then exposes the salient presence of what or who is infinite – the personal unity founding the universe that we normally experience only in its particulars. The brief numinous quality then silhouettes and imprints whatever narrative we were focusing on at the time. Apparently this fracture occurs most dramatically in a narrative of comfort juxtaposing narratives that spell out danger.

The person tries to share that numinous narrative within its special context to convey the inexplicable happening to others. The listeners may not really understand what the teller is saying, but they know to look out for something unusual when engaging this special narrative. Sometimes, however, the listeners empathize well and similarly reconstruct the alignment of narratives, and *re-experience a similar transcendent* even as the teller is speaking. Sometimes, the listeners at a much later date accidentally stumble into a similar alignment by themselves.

Narratives are the active energizers of religion, not its passive medium. Understanding how religious narratives function within language gives powerful insight into the nature of language, religion and the human experience itself.

The Meaning of Language

Applying the Jewish cosmology as a model for language teases out three levels of meaning: the cosmic, the transcendent and the divine. "Meaning" is simply the experience of a symbol within a narrative context, thus the three levels offer qualitatively different contexts to determine its own way of understanding a symbol. The cosmic level of meaning defines a symbol by its narrative context. The transcendent level synthesizes the narratives into holistic paradoxes. In the divine level, a symbol's context opens out into the "emptiness" where symbols freely associate for any and every possibility of meaning. A discussion of symbols and their operation within the cosmic, transcendent and divine contexts, follows below.

A symbol is any unit of phenomena. It is the basic unit of language, but alone without a context it has no meaning. The visual symbol of green, for example, is meaningless. Only seeing green makes the mind blind, and it does not even notice the visual symbol, unless a contrasting one accompanies it. But the visual stimuli still has no "useful" meaning without a narrative context to indicate its behavior. What does this green light *do*? It "flutters all over the place," or in contradistinction, "it just sits there." A narrative is a collection of symbols, including symbols of action, that constitute a context. It serves as the basic unit of meaning. Meaning is therefore entirely arbitrary. To rearrange the constellations of symbols is to rearrange each symbol's meaning relative to its position among the others. The flexibility is fortunate for it provides humans with a powerful tool for accommodating an endless variety of responses to their environment.

The Narrative Cosmos: the Cosmic Level of Language

The cosmic level of meaning is the mind's representation of its environment – the way all of its "pieces" fit together. The mind associates symbols into narratives, and then the narratives into a supernarrative. Contradictory narratives like "humans die" versus "humans give birth to humans" separate themselves into different locations in the cosmic story. The mind also constructs narratives to fashion its own self-identity, from whose point of view it will relate to the constructs representing other persons. Some narratives evolve into powerful paradigms that organize very diverse kinds of phenomena. These reusable narratives make the cosmos very coherent, and the mind experiences them as very convincing. All the narratives together function organically as a single context that provides meaning for each and every narrative relative to the others.

Yet there are many narratives that cannot integrate into the cosmic order. They fall by the wayside into the peripheral chaos surrounding the cosmos. Nevertheless the borders between the linguistic realms of cosmos and chaos are as fluid as language. The narratives that once were meaningless may start to make sense and work their way towards the center of the cosmos. As these new narratives start to reorganize the other narratives, the old narratives explode. Occasionally, the defunct of narratives sap the cosmic foundation. The cosmos then collapses into ashes, and like the phoenix reborn, new narratives worm their way upwards through the debris to coalesce into a new universe once again. As language inexorably evolves, societies and world rise and fall.

Religion: the Transcendent Level of Language

In the cosmic level of meaning, the focus is on the narratives. The mind reuses the same symbol in association with various others to form many different narrative contexts. Usually it concentrates on just one narrative at a time to specify the symbol's meaning, and ignores the other possibilities. When the mind perceives a familiar symbol in a new ambiguous way, however, it opens up all of its learned contexts to rummage through them one by one. If it finds a context to match the ambiguous one well enough, it then understands the symbol.

The following circumstances will forge a transcendent level of meaning. A symbol happens to associate with two or more contradictory narratives. If the symbol dominates the narratives, its prominence causes them to strongly associate with each other, and actually forge a new composite narrative, called a paradox. The new narrative is autonomous, yet it only makes sense when the original ones are present as part of its context. The paradox therefore unifies the original narratives into a single comprehensive context, that the mind experiences as meaningful. The kind of meaning that a paradoxical narrative achieves is holistic and diffuses the particularities of the conflicting elements. This is the transcendent level of meaning.

Dr. Neusner points out an excellent example of a transcendental narrative within the Talmud, where two contradictory narratives generate a paradox because of their common symbol. The producers of the Mishnah set the requirements for fulfilling the rite of fasting on the Day of Atonement. Fasting helped a person receive the atonement necessary for rectifying past sins. It was thus an expression of God's restorative compassion. The producers of the Talmud, who read the Mishnah, however, interpreted the text in the light of another narrative in the Hebrew Bible because both texts were part of the one sacred corpus: God fed Israel "manna from heaven" when Israel was hungry in the wilderness. Here, too, God displayed restorative compassion while liberating Israel from the bondage of Egypt. The two texts overlap at the implicit symbol of God's restorative compassion. The contradictory symbols are hunger and nourishment. The Talmudic sages "imagined" how these symbols worked together to accomplish a comprehensive understanding of their disparate texts. They employed the common symbol of divine restorative compassion to pull the conflicting symbols into a novel paradox: fasting from physical nourishment is synonymous with feasting on spiritual nourishment.

The paradoxical narrative transcends the original two but does not escape them. Indeed, the paradox is meaningless unless one already knows that God commanded a fast and also fed the hungry food from heaven. The paradox unites the other narratives into a single ambiguous context where fasting and feasting resonate together while participating in the transcendent meaning: God's restorative compassion. This is what religious narratives are all about.

The Transcendent and the Sacred

The transcendent meaning serves a critical role in the wellbeing of the mental life. The mind carries out its allotted narratives to function within its cosmos. They are meaningful in their place but the "meaning of life" stays void. Religious narratives employ transcendental meaning to fuse these fragmentary narratives into a single holistic context that offers total fulfillment for those members whom the cosmos includes. If the mind experiences someone die or someone being born, religious narratives allow the mind to assuage these negative and positive traumas within the whole experience of life.

The humanities, the arts, humor, dreams and religion all operate at the transcendent level of language. The humanities, the arts and humor tend to focus on critiquing individual narratives. Dreams are much more comprehensive but only introspective. Religion is distinct in that it struggles to construct a transcendental *social reality* through transcendental narratives. It synthesizes all human relationships, whether to each other or to the shared cosmos, so that when its participants engage in them in the light of the religious narratives, they will immediately feel a full sense of purpose and a total meaning of life that owns the entire cosmos.

The transcendental narratives of religion are disturbing because they are ambiguous, and compelling because they are holistic. They make cosmic narratives fully meaningful, but their close association with the cosmic narratives also threatens to pull them into the paradox. There the necessary distinctions that allow the cosmos to function will diffuse into an unworkable hodgepodge of symbols. Religious narratives therefore can both empower and undermine the cosmic order. Humans therefore screen off the religious narratives. In this way they can look at it from a distance to experience their mundane narratives within the presence of the whole, while at the same time separating their mundane narratives from its disruptive influence. This process of "sanctification" or separation is the formation of the sacred.

The sacred is an inevitable and necessary aspect of society, but it smuggles within it a terrible darkness as well, what Dr. Fasching names "the demonic irrationality of every finite sacred order." Religious narratives make the cosmic order appear ultimately meaningful, leaving every attempt to criticize them menacingly chaotic. Religious advocates can take a violently conservative stance. The reflex is irrational because they oppose the relentless fluidity of language. The cosmos being a construct of language necessarily evolves as the mind learns about new narratives. Every rigid construct will collapse. To borrow a morale from the biblical Tower of Babel: the bigger they are the harder they fall! Reactionaries can only "protect" their cosmos by extinguishing the presence of people who cannot integrate into their subjective understanding. Ironically, the anti-language sacred is demonic for it speeds its own destruction and instead demonizes the victims whose contributions could have helped the sacred readapt and survive. Only evil arises when the sacred itself has become a static idolatry.

Divine Communion: The Divine Level of Language

The only way to escape the grip of the sacred, Dr. Fasching insists, is to focus on the holy. The holy – as opposed to the sacred – is religion operating at the divine level of meaning. Attention to the whole of the sacred order reveals that it is itself evolving as its symbols associate and disassociate without any fixed narrative reference. The mind indirectly experiences an endless celestial vacuum where dazzling starlike symbols freely orbit into narrative constellations. The context for understanding each symbol opens out into the emptiness to determine a meaning that acknowledges every possible narrative construct simultaneously. Each symbol can represent all that was, that is and that will be. The mind cannot perceive the emptiness directly, but it knows its presence from the unbound behavior of its symbols and their narratives. Infinity becomes meaningful in such a powerful way that it undermines the awe of the idolatrous sacred order, and frees it up. The sacred transcendent becomes a holistic medium for encountering the level of language that exists outside of symbolic experience. As the transcendent engages in dialogue with the infinite, it appears to be in communion with a wholly other. An iconoclastic presence who empowers us to understand every permutation of narratives as meaningful even when they cannot integrate into the cosmic order. The divine level of language makes it possible for human beings to personally relate with the infinite.

The philosophies of postmodernism insist that learning symbols within narrative contexts – or "texts" – arbitrarily determines all human meaning. There is no fixed reference point. There is nothing behind the text to safeguard permanent meaning. This seems to be true except for one qualification. There is "nothingness" behind the text. When the immutable emptiness becomes a meaningful context for understanding the symbols of the text, the mind knows eternity. It is not an eternity where a single narrative stays fast, but a dynamic eternity unflinchingly open to the flux of change. It is an eternity that is open to dialogue.

Nothingness is the most perplexing feature of human language. It is an iconoclastic presence that seems like a rupture forbidding our comprehension to rest. Nothingness is a destroyer that inescapably guarantees freedom. The philosophy of existentialism pays homage to its invincibility, leaping through the absurdity of the transcendent to plummet headlong into the abyss – because only there is the human truly human.

Entry Into Language

The mind is simultaneously aware of the three levels of language, even if they are meaningless. Narratives at the edge of our cosmos may just make no sense. If the narratives do make sense, they may seem fragmentary, and leave the transcendental hunger unabated. Or, doubt may simply cripple transcendental confidence inexplicably, as the mind unknowingly brushes against the divine level of meaning. Humans try to fulfill their existential hunger for meaning, but it is the hunger itself that makes humans human.

Religious narratives are the food of existential hunger. They are paradoxes that synthesize the available cosmic narratives into a comprehensive whole. Because the cosmos evolves, the transcendental paradoxes that ride on top of it evolve, too. The flux of the holistic opens itself to an infinity of change. Thus the divine gains meaning, and the religion survives by readapting cosmic and transcendent narratives to stay in harmony in the intuition of the divine.

The Jewish response to the divine level of meaning is to embrace it with confident risk taking (perhaps *ḥutzbah* in Hebrew). For Judaism the divine level of language is love, itself, moving outside itself to dialogue with another. Its infinity of meaning is at the center of all religious experience. The eyes of the Talmudic sages were watching God as they read their sacred texts. These texts appeared as the variegated components of the worldly Torah. The sages strove to ferret out its transcendental unity that appeared as the mystic Torah. They dialogued among each other to comprehend its meanings. As applicable narratives turned up, they accommodated them into their own working context that allowed the meanings of the fixed sacred words to change! Their understanding was open to the freedom of the divine. By continually resynthesizing their sacred texts within the context of their evolving cosmos, they kept their sacred texts relevant. They also wrote down their dialogues for future discussion. These texts form the two Talmuds. Though the Talmudic texts are again empty of religion, its future readers can carry on the discussion reworking their meanings to expose the presence of the divine. Dr. Neusner calls the writing of texts as the "physicalization" of the dance with the imageless God. No frozen moment in time can capture this dance, but any reader can begin the dance again where the recorded predecessors left off. In the Judaism of the Dual Torah, dialogue is itself sacred; therefore because this sacred is necessarily open to the changing awareness of the divine, the sacred and the holy are identical for this form of Judaism.

Language is Religion

Language is not something we use, really. Language is something we are. As language has three contexts for relating symbols – the cosmic narrative, the transcendent paradox and the divine dissolution – we experience three levels of meaning. We learn and teach narratives to construct our own personal cosmos and to share it with the others in our group. Narrative constructs represent ourselves, the people around us, our expected roles with each other, and how we as a society relate to the cosmos. Dotted within our narrative landscape are the religious narratives that we set aside from our daily affairs. We contemplate their sacred paradoxes to sanctify our cosmic experience with holistic meaning. Their compelling power, however, can scramble our cosmic narratives within their paradox, so we assert discrete thresholds to bind them in. As the cosmic narratives evolve through exploration, we transform our religious narratives to maintain their relevancy as synthesizers of our contemporary cosmic experience. The transformations are terrifying. We experience our whole as groundless, and the cosmos itself as artificial. Courageously we enter the unknown, and our holistic religion enters into dialogue with the infinite. Divine meaning permeates all knowledge, and boundless freedom enters our way of being human. Our religious narratives synthesize our awareness of the divine, and we communicate these narratives to those others who have constructed a similar cosmos. They experience how the narratives align themselves to rupture the cosmic constraints and to peer out into the whole without image. The religious narratives socialize entire groups into the divine level of fulfillment. We also come across many people who do not share our cosmos. We eagerly learn to speak their language, so that we may try to relive their cosmos. We find some narratives very useful, and some not so useful or even damaging. In the process of dialogue we feel our own cosmos become fuzzy and shift. In the moments of cosmic realignment we are the most conscious of the divine level of language, encompassing both the purest love and our humanity.

As humans live, their language employs language to explore its own depths, and the mysteries of the human being manifest themselves in the experience of communication. The human birthing of religion is language becoming aware of itself and transforming its communities of language in that awareness. Religion is healthy, awesome and inextinguishable within the human condition. Religion is language, and language is religion.

IV.

UNCONVENTIONAL EVIDENCE PERTAINING TO TIMES PAST AND ITS LESSONS FOR CONTEMPORARY SENSIBILITY

5

The Study of Modern Muslim Societies: Where Did We Go Wrong?

John L. Esposito
Georgetown University

For contemporary observers and students of the Muslim world to say that Islam is a force in Muslim societies would seem an obvious truism. The Iranian revolution of 1978-79 and subsequent events in the Muslim world, from hostage taking in Lebanon to the Ayatollah Khomeini's condemnation of Salman Rushdie and Saddam Hussein's call for a holy war against the West, have reinforced a fear of "radical Islamic fundamentalism" that has become part and parcel of our contemporary consciousness. Few remember that only two decades ago awareness and knowledge of Islam were minimal both in the academy and among the general public. Most Americans knew virtually nothing about the world's second largest religion, not even its most rudimentary beliefs. Thus, Tom Brokaw on the Today show felt it necessary in the midst of a report on the status of American hostages in Iran to inform his audience that Islam was a world religion with a scripture called the Quran and a prophet named Muhammed. How many in the West would expect that any "civilized" person, even if he/she knew nothing about Christianity, would not have heard the words Jesus Christ and Bible or New Testament?

Academia was part of the problem not the solution. The 1960s saw religion departments and graduate programs open up beyond their traditional focus solely on Christianity and Judaism. However, this usually meant coverage of Hinduism and Buddhism or Chinese and

Japanese religions. Islam remained on the periphery. It fell between the cracks. Students of Christianity knew something of Judaism and vice versa. Students of Hinduism or Buddhism often felt competent enough to teach the other alternative tradition. Virtually, none had any exposure to Islam in their studies and graduate training. I can not count the number of colleagues, experts in the History of Religions, who would admit that they omitted coverage of Islam in their World Religions courses because they knew nothing about it. Others would ask for bibliographic help and suggestions for course syllabi. As religion or religious studies departments expanded, Islamicists (scholars of Islam) were, if anything at all, the last hired and the first fired. Lack of graduate programs in Islamic studies was reflected in the fact that most Islamicists were trained in history programs. With the exception of one or two programs, there were no religion departments in the United States that offered a doctorate in Islamic studies.

The study of modern Islam was particularly "retarded", and I use this word deliberately. Scholars of Islam tended to be historical and textual in orientation – in the best tradition of orientalism; I use the term here in a non-pejorative sense although I agree with much of Edward Said's critique of orientalism. Review most books, especially introductions to Islam. They focused on the pre-modern period; the modern period (eighteenth to twentieth centuries) was covered in the final chapter of the volume, usually the shortest chapter of the book. However excellent H.A.R. Gibb's *Mohammedanism*, the fact that it remained a major text for more than thirty years was testimony not only to the timeless value of much of what Gibb had to say but also to the fact that few believed that much had changed or would change in Islam. It was commonplace when covering Islamic modernism to end with Muhammad Abduh who died in Egypt in 1905 and Muhammad Iqbal who died in Pakistan in 1937! Even here the study of modern Islam focused more on individuals than on changing social realities. Thus, the study of Islam tended to be textual and historical, with an emphasis on scripturalist or the high Great Tradition rather than popular Islam or the Little Tradition. A review of many major journals, *Journal of the American Oriental Society, Muslim World, Journal of the American Academy of Religions, History of Religions,* and *Studia Islamica* as well as the coverage in the internationally recognized *Encyclopedia of Islam* reflect this orientation as well. There were of course individual scholars whose work transcended these limitations. The work of Wilfred Cantwell Smith on modern Islam or of J.N.D. Anderson and N.J. Coulson on Islamic law come to mind.[1] However, they were a clear minority. A study of the training (course work and mentors) and of dissertation topics and subsequent publication topics of the majority of Islamicists reveal a pre-modern, orientalist profile.

Our ability to understand modern Islam and the religious dimension and dynamics of modern Muslim societies was not advanced substantially by the social sciences. Social science, area studies, comparative and international studies were rooted in an understanding of modernization and development based upon and permeated by an evolutionary, western secular bias whose credo seemed to be "every day in every way things should get more and more secular if societies were to come into the twentieth century." Therefore, religion was not taken seriously other than as an historical and cultural legacy which tended to be an obstacle to change.[2] Change was implicitly understood to mean modern (Western inspired or copied) change. As a result, in most graduate programs of Middle East studies or Southeast Asian studies, Islam did not receive separate or substantive coverage but was simply covered as part of the historical or cultural background. A review of major graduate programs reveals few Islamicists or courses on Islam as such. Indeed those historians or social scientists who did do some writing on the Islamic dimension doubled as Islamicists. Thus, without reference to a rigorous and fixed curriculum in Islamics, it was entirely possible for graduate students who majored in Middle East politics to write a dissertation on an Islamic aspect of the Middle East and thus qualify as someone who majored in Islamic Studies.

Publishers had long had minimal interest in books on Islam, seeing little market for them. Few professional journals or annual association meetings provided much coverage of what was happening "on the ground" in Muslim societies in contrast to more textual and historical studies. All of these factors contributed to a climate which discouraged rather than encouraged the pursuit of Islamic studies. When I decided to

---

[1]See, for example, Wilfred Cantwell Smith, *Islam in Modern History* (Princeton: Princeton University Press, 1957), Noel J. Coulson, *A History of Islamic Law* (Edinburgh: Edinburgh University Press, 1964) and *Conflicts and Tensions in Islamic Jurisprudence* (Chicago: University of Chicago Press, 1969), and J.N.D. Anderson, *Islamic Law in the Modern World* (New York: New York University Press, 1959).

[2]See, for example, Daniel Lerner, *The Passing of Traditional Society: Modernizing the Middle East* (New York: The Free Press, 1958), Manfred Halpern, *The Politics of Social Change in the Middle East and North Africa* (Princeton, N.J.: Princeton University Press, 1963), Donald Eugene Smith, *Religion and Political Development* (Boston: Little, Brown, 1970). For an analysis of the factors which influenced the development of modernization theory, see Fred R. von der Mehden, *Religion and Modernization in Southeast Asia* (Syracuse, N.Y.: Syracuse University Press, 1988).

switch my major to Islamic Studies, many colleagues asked why I was going to study that "Abra Kadabra stuff". Most warned that I would not be able to find a job, let alone publish. Initially their concerns seemed well placed. When I took my first position, it was to teach world religions not Islam; indeed the incoming chair made it clear that his preference was for someone who taught Chinese or Japanese religions. A mailing of book proposals to some one hundred publishers yielded few responses. Those that did respond noted that unfortunately there was no market for such projects as an anthology of modern Muslim writings, later published by Oxford University Press with the title, *Islam in Transition: Muslim Perspectives*.[3] The climate changed suddenly and dramatically in 1980. With the Iranian revolution, in a five-week period I was offered contracts for three books. A review of bibliographical materials will demonstrate the extent to which 1980 proved a turning point, unleashing a flood or explosion of publications on Islam and in particular modern Islamic politics and movements.[4]

Too often prior to 1980 there was a pervasive sense of the other-worldly timelessness of Islam rather than the timeliness and contemporary relevance of this dynamic religion. Given the western secular ideological bias of the academy, minimal coverage of religion in the training of area specialists, and the paucity of positions and experts in Islamic studies, it was no wonder that most experts were completely caught off guard by the Iranian revolution and by the emergence of Islamic revivalism and with it the proliferation of modern Islamic movements. Few anticipated, noticed, or knew what to make of them. Many initially declared that the Iranian revolution and the reassertion of Islam in Muslim politics and public life were an epiphenomenon. They were incapable of fathoming how a mighty, modern Shah could be dethroned by a movement whose leader and symbol was the bearded cleric, the Ayatollah Khomeini, living in exile outside of Paris. Their consternation continued as subsequently they saw that it was indeed the more modern "western oriented" states, not the less developed traditionalist states, that were the most vulnerable to political Islam: Iran, Egypt, Lebanon, the Switzerland of the Middle East, and more recently Tunisia, Algeria, and Turkey.

Lack of interest and awareness of modern Islam and its impact on Muslim societies is demonstrated by the state of our knowledge and

---

[3]John J. Donohue and John L. Esposito (eds.) *Islam in Transition: Muslim Perspectives* (New York: Oxford University Press, 1982).
[4]Yvonne Y. Haddad, John O. Voll, and John L. Esposito (eds.) *The Contemporary Islamic Revival: A Critical Survey and Bibliography* (New York: Greenwood Press, 1991).

coverage prior to 1980. With very few exceptions, neither academic experts nor policymakers took note of Islam's role in politics and society. It was not something that their secular orientation and professional training and methodologies valued or prepared them to look for or even see. It is useful to recall that the Iranian revolution shed a light on a reassertion of Islam in personal and public life in the Muslim world, on events in Libya, Egypt, Pakistan, and Malaysia that had been occurring but had gone unnoticed for more than a decade. Throughout the 1970s Qaddafi had turned to Islam to buttress his Arab nationalism and socialism. Zulfikar Ali Bhutto had come to power in 1971 in the wake of the Pakistan civil war which saw East Pakistan transformed into Bangladesh. By the mid 1970s, Bhutto, a secular socialist, had moved Islam from the periphery to the center of Pakistani politics, introducing Islamic laws, hosting international Islamic conferences, appealing to Islam as a source of popular mobilization and a rationale for Arab oil money and obtaining jobs for Pakistani military and laborers in the Arab world. Egypt's Anwar Sadat had come to power in the early 1970s and increasingly appealed to Islam, casting the 1973 Egyptian-Israeli war as a jihad, supported student Islamic organizations to counter the influence of leftists, employed Islamic rhetoric and symbols to enhance his legitimacy. In Malaysia, in the aftermath of Chinese-Malay riots, government policies and social forces combined to generate a reemphasis and reassertion of Malay Muslim identity and the growth of Islamic social and political activism, yielding such new movements as ABIM (the Malaysian Islamic Youth Movement), whose former leader is currently the Deputy Prime Minister and Minister of Finance.[5] The seeming explosion of Islam on the scene was matched very quickly by an explosion of interest and of publications and media coverage.

The study of modern Islam has changed significantly since the Iranian revolution. Introductions to Islam now address not only the Islamic tradition and its legacy but also the implementation of Islam in Muslim life in its rich diversity.[6] Thus the essentialist approach is complemented by acknowledgment of the diversity of the Islamic experience today; the ideal is counterbalanced by a perspective on the real. While for the believer there may be one Islam, it is equally true and

---

[5]For studies of these developments, see John L. Esposito, *Islam and Politics,* 3rd ed. (Syracuse, N.Y.: Syracuse University Press, 1991), John O. Voll, *Islam: Continuity and Change in the Modern World,* 2nd ed. (Syracuse, N.Y.: Syracuse University Press, 1994), and James P. Piscatori (ed.) *Islam in the Political Process* (Cambridge: Cambridge University Press, 1983).
[6]Frederick M. Denny, *An Introduction to Islam* (New York: MacMillan, 1985), John L. Esposito, *Islam: The Straight Path* (New York: Oxford University Press, 1991), Malise Ruthven, *Islam in the World* (London: Penguin, 1984).

useful to recognize that there are many interpretations of Islam. What has this meant in practice in terms of methodology and focus?

The Study of Contemporary Islam

The contemporary resurgence of Islam has revealed the extent to which religion was not just of critical importance in the past but remains a formative influence in personal and social life, a critical issue for the present and future of Muslim societies. Islam has of course always been acknowledged as a continued presence in Muslim societies but it was usually identified with the more traditional sectors. Due to the presuppositions of Western development theories and a tendency to focus on westernized elites, its role as a social and political force was overlooked. From the late 1960s, this approach and understanding has been challenged as Islam has reemerged as a major force both in personal and public life. In personal life, in urban areas in particular though not exclusively, there has been greater emphasis on religious observances (prayer, fasting during Ramadan, dress, family values), a proliferation and dissemination of the message of Islam through publishing, audio and video cassettes. The communications media and the harnessing of its technology has meant both the dissemination of an "international Islam," that is, ability of Muslim preachers and intellectuals to reach an audience far beyond the confines of their locations and thus access of individuals to interpretations of Islam and to events in the Muslim world that take them far beyond the limits of their village, country, or city. The Friday sermon of an Egyptian religious preacher like Shaykh Muhammad Mutawalli can be seen on television in the Gulf. The South African Ahmad Deedat's message and debates with Christian evangelists like Jimmy Swaggart can be the object of admiration among Muslims throughout the world who have seen his many videos. The writings of Islamic activist leaders/ideologues can be distributed in translation in the major Muslim languages throughout the world and be found in pamphlet and book form in cities and villages. Muslim leaders in exile, from Iran's Ayatollah Khomeini to Tunisia's Rashid Ghannoushi can stay in contact with their followers through the distribution of audio cassettes and faxes.

It is the political resurgence of Islam that has commanded the most attention and generated fears of Islamic fundamentalism or a clash of civilizations. Islam for almost two decades served to be a two-edged sword, capable of legitimating as well as de-legitimating, to be used by governments as well as opposition movements. In Egypt not only Anwar Sadat but also his assassins claimed the mantle of Islam. In Pakistan, both Zulfikar Ali Bhutto and the man who overthrew him,

General Zia ul-Haq, used and implemented Islam. In Iran and Pakistan, opposition movements or coalitions that spanned the religious and political spectrum – religious and secular, right and left, arrayed themselves under the umbrella of Islam to topple incumbent governments. At the same time, Islam emerged as a major sociopolitical force when a proliferation of Islamic movements and organizations increasingly provided much needed educational and social services: schools, hospitals, clinics, legal aid societies, and youth groups. Some were merely social service agencies; for others social services were an extension of their political movement and ambitions. All of these activities were rooted in new interpretations of Islam, often incorrectly termed "fundamentalism" and thus deceptively equated with a literalist return to the past.

Because of a liberal secular orientation and bias, the greater emphasis on Islam in Muslim society, in particular politics, led many to apply a pejorative western Christian term or category to the Muslim experience. The term fundamentalism proved inadequate though attractive to the media, many in the academy, and policymakers, for it described what they simply perceived as a retrogressive retreat to the past. As an analytical category, "fundamentalism" fails on many fronts. To begin with, all Muslims are of course fundamentalists in that the Quran and Sunnah (practice) of the Prophet are the foundations of their faith. Furthermore, the term which has been used to describe initially Qaddafi's Libya, Khomeini's Iran, Saudi Arabia, and Zia ul-Haq's Pakistan contributes to the image of a monolithic Islam and a global Islamic threat. It tells us nothing about the nature of their respective governments, their Islamic character, individual leadership styles, or relations with the West. Saudi Arabia is a conservative monarchy in contrast to Libya's radical populist state; Qaddafi's promotes a revisionist interpretation of Islam while the House of Saud is wedded to a more rigorous, puritanical Wahhabi tradition. Iran under Khomeini was a clerically run state while Pakistan's Zia ul-Haq implemented a military guided martial law regime. Both Saudi Arabia and Pakistan have been regarded as allies of the United States while Libya and Iran are characterized as anti-western, radical terrorist states.

The resurgence of Islam has required a combination of methodologies in Islamic studies (that is, language, textual and historical analysis) which seeks to understand the more scripturalist and scholarly (ulama) tradition of Islam with its emphasis on Quran, traditions of the Prophet, law, and Islamic history, as well as the approach with those of social science which studies the social construction and dynamics of Muslim societies. However, both approaches have had to move beyond their tendencies to focus on elites, the former's emphasis on the ulama-generated tradition and the latter's primary concern with the ruling establishment. Because of their worldview, modern historians and social scientists too often focused solely on the political establishment and its western oriented elites rather than populist movements and a new emerging alternative, modern educated but Islamically oriented elite. A dominant scholarly worldview provided a framework of understanding that determined both the objects of study and inquiry as well as the questions that conditioned and determined what was looked for, seen (and not seen) and thus generated conclusions that were limited and inadequate. To paraphrase the New Testament, too often they had eyes to see but did not see and ears to hear but did not hear. Few realized their conclusions were based in fact upon a minority experience – upon the 5 percent elite sector of society.

The challenge was to expand and broaden their horizons, be more inclusive rather than exclusive, more broad-based in the study of Muslim politics and society, and thus to appreciate the diversity of social forces and actors that exist in the contemporary Muslim world. In the process, secular presuppositions that presumed the separation of religion and politics were put to the test – or, to put it more accurately, were discredited. In fact, Muslim activist/ideologues were providing interpretations of Islam that reasserted the centrality of Islam in Muslim life, but they did so not simply by retreating to the past but by responding to the issues of the present. They did so not by withdrawal or literal emulation of the early Islamic community but by utilizing modern technology from printing to audio and video cassettes, from the telephone to the computer.

The tendency to categorize that which deviates from a more liberal secular worldview and model of development as fundamentalist with its connotations of literalism and extremism blinded many to the reality and variety of Islamic activism or revivalism. The shock of Iran and the subsequent tendency to view Islam and events in the Muslim world through the lens of Iran/Khomeini was exacerbated by then President Reagan's projection of Islamic radicalism, Qaddafi's Libya and Khomeini's Iran, as an alternative threat to that of the evil "empire". Thus when the President spoke to the nation the night that the United States bombed Libya, he spoke of Qaddafi, terrorism, and the worldwide Islamic fundamentalist movement. These sentiments were reiterated by Vice President Dan Quayle's identification of radical Islamic fundamentalism with Nazism and Communism when charging Annapolis graduates with the task of defending the United States against future threats to it. The situation was compounded by the propensity of the media and government analysts to emphasize a headline/crisis approach. The hot spots came to define the broader reality and landscape of the Muslim world. Attacks on western embassies, the slaying of Anwar Sadat, and other acts by violent extremists were often equated with Islam itself and with the broader phenomenon of Islamic social and political activism. Thus whereas the acts of radical Christian or Jewish groups have been readily distinguished from the mainstream community, acts of religious extremism and terrorism have been readily ascribed to Islam rather than to misguided fanatics.

Few Islamicists or social scientists focused on contemporary Islamic social and political movements. Few in the 1970s and 80s were prepared to effectively frame and interpret the dynamics of contemporary Islam. Only one scholar had identified the Ayatollah Khomeini, then a rather junior ayatollah living in exile, as a potential political force.[7] Most experts had accepted the received wisdom that Gamal Abdel Nasser's suppression of the Muslim Brotherhood and the execution of several of its leaders had crushed the movement.[8] American diplomats had virtually no contact with Iran's religious leaders.[9] The same could be said for many other countries. Long after Iran, crises in the Muslim world often demonstrated the extent to which we possessed little detailed knowledge about Islamic activist leaders and movements. However, this situation has changed in recent years. The challenge to understand the breadth and diversity of the Islamic movement has required the combination of language, literature, and history with anthropology, sociology, and politics. Expertise in classical textual sources proved insufficient for understanding contemporary activist movements. Knowledge of revealed and classical Islamic sources has had to be combined with analysis of contemporary voices of a resurgent Islam whose interpretations have had a formative influence on the way in which many Muslims understand both their past and present.[10] Thus, the work of Mawlana Abul Ala Mawdudi, Hasan al-Banna, and Sayyid Qutb become essential because of their international impact on Islamic movements as do more recent voices like Hasan al-Turabi, leader of Sudan's Islamic Front and Rashid Ghannoushi of Tunisia's Renaissance

---

[7]Hamid Algar, "The Oppositional Role of the Ulama in Twentieth Century Iran," *Sufi, Saints and Scholars* ed. Nikki R. Keddie (Berkeley, CA: University of California Press, 1972), pp. 231-255.

[8]Even Richard Mitchell's classic study of the Brotherhood tends to this conclusion. See Richard P. Mitchell, *The Society of the Muslim Brothers* (New York: Oxford University Press, 1969; repr., 1993), ch. 11.

[9]For a remarkable case study of the failures of academic experts and government officials alike, see James A. Bill, *The Eagle and the Lion* (New Haven: Yale University Press, 1988).

[10]Yvonne Y. Haddad, *Contemporary Islam and the Challenge of History* (Albany, N.Y.: SUNY Press, 1988) and John L. Esposito (ed.) *Voices of Resurgent Islam* (New York: Oxford University Press, 1983).

Party (previously called the Islamic Tendency Movement). Moreover, prolific authors like Mawdudi have imperceptibly shaped modern Muslim discourse so that many of those who might reject his politics and that of his organization, the Jamaat-i-Islami, would knowingly or, in many cases unknowingly, understand Islam through his vision and interpretation.

The study of contemporary movements has required then work not only in the library but also in the field, knowledge of history and literature of course and sustained contact with leaders and members of Islamic movements that develops the ability to know what Islamic activists say as well as what they do. The pitfalls can be seen in the way in which some have been content to merely conclude from their study of tracts and their commitment to a common Islamic alternative that a "predictable" reality exists and thus overlook the extent to which movements, conditioned by diverse local contexts, vary in their agenda, methods, and goals. Such approaches reinforce the tendency of many in the 1980s to project a monolithic Islamic fundamentalism much as others have espoused an essentialist Islam, forgetting that while for the believer there may be one Islam (One God, one book, one final Prophet), there have also been many interpretations and applications of Islam.

The tendency to deal in fundamentalist caricatures and stereotypes led to further distortions and miscalculations. While many equated Islamic activism with Khalishnikov-carrying mullahs, the majority of Islamic organizations and activists are lay-, not clerical-led, the products not of seminaries but of universities. Rather than clerics, the bulk of activists have been scientists, engineers, doctors, and lawyers. Thus while unemployed and poor youth have been ready recruits for movements so have lower middle and middle class professionals. If political economy is essential to understand the nature and force of Islamic activism so is faith and religious ideology.

The ideological worldview of activists is one which rejects western political and cultural dependency, but not modern science and technology. It regards both European colonialism and the perpetuation of colonialism by an indigenous western-oriented elite as major causes for the political and religiocultural crises of Muslim societies. If Muslims are weak, they believe it is not because of Islam but because Muslims have neglected their Islamic heritage and instead become dependent upon the West. Dependence upon the West, what some have called Westoxification or Weststruckness, threatens the identity and values of society.[11] If the problem is departure from Islam, the cure is a return to Islam. Islam is reasserted as an indigenous alternative to the West and to

---

[11]Jalal Al-e-Ahmad, *Garbzadegi* (Lexington, Ky.: Mazda, 1982).

the East (the former Soviet Union). In the words of the Iranian revolutionary slogan, "Neither East nor West" but instead Allah or Islam. Contemporary activists assert the self-sufficiency of an Islamic alternative for modern Muslims. Islam, they maintain, is a total way of life, a comprehensive blueprint for the good society. Activists in effect remind us of what Wilfred Cantwell Smith pointed out in *The Meaning and End of Religion* – that our understanding of religion is a modern construct that obscures the extent to which world religions provided a way of life.[12] Post-enlightenment definitions or more accurately redefinitions of the nature and meaning of religion set forth a new, modern western understanding. An extension of this argument when applied to contemporary Islam would be that what we are seeing in Islamic revivalism is the assertion that there is no sharp dichotomy between sacred and profane, between the realm of God and that of human beings as well as the preeminence of a God-centered rather than a human-centered universe. This reassertion of the centrality of divine sovereignty is accomplished for Muslim activists through the reimplementation of the Shariah, Islamic law, a comprehensive code for life.

Islamic activists thus assert the importance of this life as well as the next. Implementation of God's rule and law become the basis for Muslim life and for Muslim society. Dawa, the call to Islam, becomes a central concern. The objective is not simply to call non-Muslims to Islam but to call those who were born Muslim to become more self-conscious and observant Muslims. Like liberation theology in Central America, religious principles and values are applied to the here and now. Religious education and awareness are joined to social welfare to implement a more just, Islamic society. Emphasis on the importance of social justice, of Islam as the religion of the oppressed, has become a major theme of contemporary Islamic revivalism. If some have compared the Islamic modernist movement of the late nineteenth and twentieth centuries with the Protestant work ethic, activism today would by analogy be a combination of the Protestant work ethic and social gospel. One can find parallels today between Islamic and Christian social movements. Like Christian base communities of liberation theology, Islamic organizations see themselves as constituting a dynamic nucleus within the broader society called to transform their societies.

The study of contemporary Islamic movements has raised many questions that continue to constitute our research agenda. Both the implementation of Islam by governments and the track record of Islamic

---

[12]Wilfred Cantwell Smith, *The Meaning and End of Religion* (San Francisco: Harper and Row, 1978).

movements have raised many questions about the use or manipulation of religion for political purposes as well as the nature and direction of Islamic reform – "Whose Islam?" and "What Islam?" While the ulama still assert their role as the primary interpreters of Islam, the guardians of Islamic law, both Muslim rulers and an educated lay Islamic leadership have threatened the ulama's domain. Libya's Muammar Qaddafi has ignored and even denounced the ulama. The Saudi monarchy, while usually careful to cultivate strong ties with Saudi Arabia's religious establishment, has in the 1990s increasingly encountered opposition from more independent ulama. Pakistan's Zia ul-Haq, despite a sensitivity to ulama authority and concerns, ultimately was the final arbiter of Pakistan's Islamic experiment. Only Shii Iran has seen the ulama in power. Many Muslims increasingly call for greater political participation and democratization, more consensual (parliamentary or assembly) forms of government. If Islamic governments or more Islamically oriented societies are to be created, Muslims will need to determine who shall define the Islamic character of state and society – rulers (kings, military men, ex-military), the ulama, or elected parliaments.

At the same time, in the latter half of the twentieth century, the proliferation and growth of Islamic movements has witnessed the emergence of a lay Islamic leadership – modern educated, Islamically oriented professionals who have been the founders and key leaders of Islamic movements and organizations. Their role as Islamic actors and their professional expertise have challenged the traditional monopoly of the ulama (the learned) as religious leaders and interpreters of Islam. While Islam in theory knows no clergy and while the right of personal interpretation (*ijtihad*) technically belongs to all qualified Muslims, historically the ulama did constitute themselves as a professional class, the guardians and interpreters of Islam. As such, they were the teachers, scholars, and legal experts in traditional Muslim society. The complex nature and the multiple disciplines necessary to address many modern political, economic, and social issues which are beyond the traditional areas of competence of most ulama, have raised the question of the need to broaden the definition of what constitutes a qualified scholar (*alim*, pl. ulama). Is there now a need for new ulama, or a new class of ulama, experts in the disciplines necessary to address the major social, economic, and ethical questions and issues faced by contemporary Muslim societies?

Regarding "What Islam?" does the reassertion of Islam in Muslim public life mean a process of restoration or reformation? Does the creation of more Islamically oriented societies require the wholesale reintroduction of classical Islamic law, developed in the early centuries of Islam, or will it require a substantial reformulation of Islam? At the heart of contemporary Islamic revivalism are a series of key issues which concern the nature and development of Islam. Whether it be issues of marriage and divorce, the nature of the state and political participation, or the role of women and minorities, the issue of change in Islam and the role of traditional concepts such as personal interpretation (*ijtihad*), community consensus (*ijma*), and consultation (*shura*) have become pivotal.

While some believe that the Islamic paradigm is fixed in classical Islamic law, others distinguish between the *shariah*, God's divinely revealed law, and *fiqh*, human understanding, interpretation, and application of that law. The latter would argue that Muslims must distinguish between those elements of Islamic law which are immutable and those that are the product of human interpretation and thus are capable of change and reform in light of new historical circumstances and social conditions. Similarly, while community consensus traditionally was reduced to the opinion or consensus of the ulama and consultation referred to the ruler's consultation with political and religious elites, today many, though certainly not all Muslims, support the transformation or reconceptualization of these concepts to support parliamentary systems of government and decision making.

Public perceptions, heavily influenced by academic analysts and political commentators in America, Europe, and Israel, have increasingly feared the global threat of Islamic fundamentalism to the West.[13] This outlook fosters an anti-fundamentalist policy to thwart the danger of fundamentalists whose participation in the electoral process is regarded as a duplicitous strategy designed to hijack democracy and subsequently seize power. Articles with titles like "Roots of Muslim Rage," "Rising Islam May Overwhelm the West," and "The Global Intifada," have been followed most recently by: "Beware of Religious Stalinists,"[14] "By Peace or the Sword,"[15] "Wishful Thinking About Islamic Fundamentalism,"[16] and "Islam vs. Democracy."[17] They present Islam as a demographic (Europe and America), global political, and civilizational threat. Focus on "Islamic fundamentalism" as a global threat has reinforced a tendency to equate violence with Islam, to fail to distinguish between illegitimate

---

[13]John L. Esposito, *The Islamic Threat: Myth or Reality?* (New York: Oxford University Press, 1992).

[14]Morton Zuckerman, "Beware of Religious Stalinist," *U.S. News and World Report,* March 22, 1993, p. 80.

[15]E. McQuaid, "By Peace or the Sword," *The Jerusalem Post,* December 16, 1992.

[16]Amos Perlmutter, Wishful Thinking about Islamic Fundamentalism," *The Washington Post,* January 19, 1991, p. 16.

[17]Martin Kramer, "Islam vs. Democracy," *Commentary* Vol. 95, No 1, (January 1993).

use of religion by individuals and the faith and practice of the majority of the world's Muslims who, like believers in other religious traditions, wish to live in peace. In the wake of the World Trade Center bombing, many continue to fail to distinguish between the actions of individuals or a radical minority and the mainstream majority, a distinction made so easily as the world watched the Branch Davidian sect, an extremist "Christian" group in Waco, Texas, led by David Koresh, kill FBI agents and hold off federal authorities for weeks.

Religious extremism remains a threat today as in the past, but it is not restricted to nor inherent in any one religion. The specter of attacks by terrorists motivated by ethnic, religious, or ideological beliefs and grievances is real. The challenge today, as in the past, is to avoid the easy answers yielded by stereotyping or the projection of a monolithic threat, to distinguish between the beliefs and activities of the majority (whether they be Hindus, Muslims, and Sikhs, Christians and Jews, Arabs and Israelis, Tamils and Buddhists) and a minority of extremists who justify their aggression and violence in the name of religion, ethnicity, or political ideology. It is equally important to distinguish between the aspirations and demands of legitimate political opposition (religious as well as secular) groups and extremist groups. Failure to do so leads to the silence of many academic experts and government officials that followed the military's termination of Algeria's experiment with democracy. Fear of fundamentalists prevented many at the time of the military takeover from asking who has really hijacked democracy in Algeria. As with the Cold War attitude toward communism, in a context in which a new threat is projected upon the horizon, the lesson can seem to be that the certainty of dealing with secular authoritarian regimes is preferable to the uncertainties of an Islamic government. There is often a clash of worldviews and values – a religiously informed worldview facilely dubbed "Islamic fundamentalism" and an equally self-assertive secular liberalism of the West and many Muslim elites, whose sense of certitude and righteousness constitutes a "secular fundamentalism".

Extremism is alive and active in the Muslim world as recent events in Egypt demonstrate. It is a threat but more to Muslim societies and populations than to the outside world. However, if we are to understand the current dynamic in many Muslim societies, we need more studies to appreciate the extent to which in the 1990s Islamic revivalism has become institutionalized, part of mainstream society not simply limited to an alienated, marginalized sector on the periphery of society. A broad spectrum of modern educated, Islamically oriented professionals and organizations exist from Egypt to Indonesia offering social and political alternatives: schools, hospitals, clinics, legal aid societies, banks, publishing houses, youth centers, and political parties. Though appealing to Islam or under the banner of Islam, they are equally diverse in their leadership, methods, and agenda. Moreover, we need to recognize that they are motivated not only by political and socioeconomic failures but also by issues of faith, identity, and values.

There are lessons to be learned from a past in which fear of a monolithic Soviet threat often blinded us to the diversity and aspirations of the majority of people; led to uncritical support for anti-communist dictatorships; enabled the suppression of legitimate dissent and massive human rights violations by any whose governments and security forces labeled the opposition communist or socialist.

The risk today is that fear based upon the equation Islam=Islamic fundamentalism=extremism/terrorism will result in exaggerated fears which lead to a double standard in the promotion of democracy and human rights, democracy or political participation for some but not for others. Witness the volume of Western democratic concern and action applied to the former Soviet Union and Eastern Europe but the muted or ineffective response with regard to democratization in the Middle East or the genocide in Bosnia-Herzegovinia. Moreover, fear of fundamentalism creates a climate in which Muslims and Islamic organizations are guilty until proven innocent. If Muslims commit an act, however heinous, they are labeled Muslim fundamentalists. The action is attributed to Islam rather than to a twisted or distorted interpretation of Islam.

The Muslim world like many parts of the world is diverse and in a period of transformation. The reassertion of Islam in public life challenges many of our secular presuppositions. If we are to understand and respond to the challenge of political Islam, its diverse manifestations must be seen within the multiplicity of intellectual and political contexts in which it occurs. Toward that end, our scholarship on Islam must continue to become more integrated in marshaling the insights of multiple disciplines and perspectives. We must broaden as well as deepen our perspectives. In addition, scholarship on Islam too often continues to be Arab-centered and Sunni-dominated. There are of course good reasons for this: the Quran was revealed in Arabic to an Arab in Arabia. The Arab world in a real sense can be seen as the earthly homeland and center of Islam. Yet, the Arab-centered state of scholarship was such that it belied the realities of the Muslim world, the fact that the vast majority of Muslims are non-Arabs (Asians and Africans), and that while Arabic is the language of the Quran and early Islam, the languages of the Islamic community and of Islamic civilization are many. Arab-centeredness was accompanied by the virtual equation of Islam with Sunni Islam and thus, the virtual omission of serious, substantive attention to Shii Islam.

Another concern in contemporary scholarship on Islam is that more often than not, Islamic movements continue to be lumped together as if they were all the same; conclusions are drawn, based more on stereotyping or expectations than empirical research. This problem is due less to the secrecy of individuals and organizations than to more mundane factors: (1) the less we know, the more we tend to generalize or deductively conclude from that which we do know; (2) most Islamicists tend to be trained in and work on the past; (3) many scholars who are non-specialists on Islam have had a more limited training and interest in Islamic movements and even less actual contact with activists. Finally, there is the more pervasive problem which all of us face to some degree. Because of the dearth of scholars in Middle East Studies in general and Islamic Studies in particular, most of us cover vast areas in our research and writing. (I might add that the real problem is when we forget this fact.) A Middle East expert will be called upon and feel free to range over many "different" countries and societies, to speak and write on issues of politics, law, history, society, oil, etc. Yet, analysis of modern Islamic movements and organizations require more than guess work, generalizations, reliance solely on newspaper reports or movement-issued documents. Observation and interaction are particularly important since many activists often write comparatively little and their writings can often be little more than public relations documents. Because of a combination of limited access and interest and a tendency to respond to market (government and media) demands, the breadth, character, and activities of the moderate majority of contemporary organizations go relatively unnoticed.

Significant developments have occurred in our scholarship on Islam and Muslim societies. Extensive coverage of revivalism, its causes, ideologues, implementation by governments and organizations have appeared. These studies were conducted both by non-Muslim and Muslim scholars alike: Americans, Europeans, Asians, Africans, and Middle Easterners. We have witnessed the publication of excellent social and political histories which have demonstrated the desirability of combining textual analysis and empirical data. Greater emphasis on the social sciences has produced excellent studies of peasant organizations and associations which too often do not earn the attention they deserve. These studies forcefully demonstrate the advantages of combining social realities with those ideals and values of the broader Islamic experience, that is, the ideal religio-social blueprint which, though often imperfectly known or quietly circumvented by custom, provides the ultimate authoritative source of Islamic identity, a reference point or framework of meaning for Muslim societies.

A major part of our agenda for the future should be greater emphasis on empirically based studies and in particular comparative studies of Islamic societies. I am not overlooking what has been done in recent years; however, there is much more that needs to be done. To begin with, collaborative efforts which combine the best of textual criticism and social science methodology must be encouraged. Both the big picture and the little picture, the Great Tradition and the folk tradition, are required to truly understand the dynamics of Muslim societies. To focus solely on the Great Tradition to the exclusion of the little or popular tradition is to seriously distort the religio-social reality. Thus, it is important to ask: "What does Islamization mean to the average person in urban areas, to inhabitants of the countryside?" At the same time, we must remember that it is the Great Tradition/official Islam which provides the normative worldview within which may exist or co-exist different and contradictory practices. Whatever the view from the village in terms of local belief and practice, official Islam, like official Christianity and Buddhism, constitutes the norm which unites members of a worldwide religious community across local boundaries and cultural differences and thus provides the criteria for measuring orthodoxy or orthopraxy. To ignore one part of the equation or to pretend to have mastered it all as individual scholars would be to settle for far less than we are capable of. From a scholarly point of view, it is possible to assert simultaneously that there is one Islam and there are many Islams or, to put it more accurately, many interpretations of Islam. We need to hold the two, the one Islam and the many interpretations, in dialectical tension as we analyze Muslim institutions and societies.

There are many areas of investigation worthy of our attention. Let me underscore a few. We need to extend some of the fine studies that have come out in recent years on the ulama. Though the religious establishment has often been closely related to governments and discredited in the eyes of some, the ulama – in particular non-government ulama and mosques – remain important arbiters of social opinion and reflect political realities in Muslim societies. While we know a fair amount about the ulama of Iran and their differences of opinion, how much do we really know about the ulama of Saudi Arabia or Pakistan, both nations where Islam and the ulama play an important role?

Of equal importance in the history of contemporary Islam are the non-traditional ulama or perhaps better, the new interpreters of Islam and leaders of the Islamic community. As is strikingly obvious, the leadership of many Islamic movements and organizations consist of those who by traditional standards do not qualify as ulama. Many modern Muslim leaders are lay intellectuals or activists rather than traditional ulama. Alongside familiar names of the recent past like the Muslim Brotherhood's Hasan al-Banna and Sayyid Qutb or the Jamaat-i-Islami's Mawlana Mawdudi, we find today Sadiq al-Mahdi, Dr. Hasan al-Turabi, Rashid Ghannoushi, Mehdi Bazargan, Khurshid Ahmad, Ismail al-Shatti, Zaynab al-Ghazzali, Maryam Jameelah, Khalijah Sallah, Anwar Ibrahim and many others. They are often individuals who provide fresh interpretations of Islam and exercise important positions of leadership both in the Islamic movement and in government cabinets, parliaments, and ministries, universities, and social service organizations. Yet, how much do we know about most of these individuals, their ideas, and the relationship of their ideas to their actions? When Hasan Turabi, leader of the Sudanese Muslim Brotherhood, first became Attorney General of the Sudan and the Brotherhood filled many important positions in government, few really knew who they were. Even more so, when Tunisia's Habib Bourghiba imprisoned many of the Islamic Tendency Movement leadership and accused them of being Iranian-backed revolutionaries, how many experts really knew who Rashid Ghannoushi was or what the Islamic Tendency Movement represented? There is much to be done to understand this emerging alternative leadership in the Muslim world. They are as important to the history of Islamic belief and thought as to Muslim politics.

    These new Islamically oriented and committed leaders and the organizations to which most belong will require careful studies that combine analysis of textual sources and empirical data. The collection of manifestos and publications must be complimented by in-depth interviews and field research. Islamicists have often been too content with written texts while social scientists have emphasized field studies and statistics. Yet all too often studies of Islamic activists and organizations have found both groups of scholars too reliant on newspaper reports, selected texts, and second-hand information or conjecture. As academics we emphasize the importance of empirical research; however, sometimes it is astonishing to see how often studies of Islamic leaders and organizations are based solely on religious tracts and newspaper accounts and not informed by first-hand experience and interviews. This approach is particularly problematic in an area where textual sources are limited, where key individuals are often too busy to write or too monitored to be frank in public contexts. Moreover, often narrow perceptions of what we do not know are supported by (1) citing indigenous secular-oriented academics or government elites who to protect their own power and prestige are prone to merely reinforce stereotyping by dismissing religiously oriented individuals and groups as naive, fanatic, fundamentalists; (2) relying upon the few (same) empirical studies available on a particular topic even though the data may come from a study of a completely different group and from another country or context.

We have spilled more ink on groups that have occasionally disrupted a society than upon those that are contributing constructively to the transformation of their societies. We have to guard against a media/marketing approach to the study of Islamic movements which emphasizes violent extremists (Egypt's al-Jihad or Gamaa Islamiyya) and underestimates or ignores the influence and activities of moderate leaders and organizations (the Muslim Brotherhoods of Egypt and Jordan, Tunisia's Ennahda).

This is a particularly opportune time to focus more on the comparative study of Muslim societies. There has been a widescale impact of Islam on governments and societies, a worldwide proliferation of Islamic organizations and societies, a diversity of ideological formulations and programs, and numerous experiments in implementing Islam. Most studies have been country specific. Comparative studies of the use of Islam through ideological interpretation and implementation by organizations and governments are sorely needed. Comparisons of the *actual* implementation, and not just the assertions or claims of governments and organizations, of Islam in Iran, the Sudan, and Pakistan could be most instructive. The reality is often far different from the ideal; in some cases the process of Islamization has been more and in others less extensive than expected. How much do we really know about the specific application of Islamic laws and punishments or about the impact of Islamization upon the nature of law, government, economics, and education in specific contexts?

Few areas of Islamic Studies have developed in recent years as fast as gender studies. Scholars from virtually all of the disciplines have chronicled and analyzed shifts in status, roles, and power. Comparative information has often been available primarily in volumes which incorporate studies of separate countries and contexts. While these studies remain important, comparative analysis of attitudes, beliefs, and practices that underscore differences in interpretation both in the past and the present and thus, the continued and changing diversity of Islamic practice over time and across different societies require our attention and support.

A key issue in the study of contemporary Islam and Muslim societies, cutting across our disciplines and areas of interest, will continue to be self-criticism of our religious and ideological presuppositions and with it a more inclusive understanding of the Muslim world – one which is more attentive to issues of religion, class and gender, more rigorous in its methodology, and more comparative in its analysis.

Response to John L. Esposito's "The Study of Modern Muslim Societies: Where Did We Go Wrong?"

Nahla A. Al-Arian
University of South Florida

Paper Summary

In his excellent presentation, Dr. Esposito makes many points that are generally missed in the current discussion of Islam's influence in Muslim societies and its study by Western scholars and social scientists. First, he indicts the Western scholarship on modern Islamic societies citing ignorance, lack of knowledge and minimal awareness not only among the general public but even in academia. He contends that the real problem in academia stems from the Western paradigm of understanding laws of modern social sciences through Western secular bias that sees religions as obstacles to change (that is, modernity). He observes that academia is part of the problem because: a) there has been no specialization in the religion or understanding of the impact of social change in Muslim societies, b) that most specialists were trained in history programs rather than religious-sociological backgrounds, and c) that the focus of their studies was mainly in the pre-modern period, or on individuals rather than on contemporary Islamic societies.

In his opinion, the Islamic revolution in Iran in 1980 proved to be a turning point for a greater interest in Islam and its impact on Muslim societies by the Western establishment: governments, academia and media. However, he questions its oversimplification and failure to understand the dynamics of social, political and religious transformation that are currently underway in the Islamic World. He observes that the contemporary Islamic resurgent movements do, in fact, challenge the liberal-secularist paradigm concerning religions and that Islam has a formidable influence in personal as well as social life. He further discusses the relationship between the West and the modern Islamic World. He contends that the modern Islamic resurgent movement was a direct consequence of colonialism and the secularization process imposed by the colonial powers on Muslim societies. The author questions the portrayal of political or popular Islam as fundamentalism; and, he dismisses the term as historically inaccurate, epistemologically inappropriate, and practically dangerous. He warns against this twisted orientalist view and understanding; he compares Islamic thought today in Muslim societies to liberation theology.

Esposito courageously calls for a new paradigm in understanding Islam and contemporary Muslim societies. This new paradigm must include: a) rich knowledge of Islamic basics of history, language, texts, law, tradition, and heritage; b) the application of a holistic social science methodology with more sensitivity towards the local experience rather than the global/secular-humanist vision (that is, the study of the social construction and dynamism of Muslim societies using sociology, anthropology, politics, literature, and arts), and most importantly, c) the serious study, understanding and analysis of contemporary Islamic movements, their leaders and thinkers. In other words, there is a need for empirical rather than theoretical orientation to the understanding of contemporary Islamic movements and their future impact in the world.

Finally, he raises many questions concerning the interpretation as well as methods of analysis facing the Western social scientist studying Islam and its impact in societies today. He cautions against finding easy answers for very complex notions, the practical manifestation of which is seen now in the tacit support of the West to the hijacking of democracy in Algeria. The Muslim world could be alienated further with this practice of double standards. In his conclusion, Esposito wisely calls for an integrated approach to scholarship with a focus on empirical research, indigenous concerns and specialization, away from newspaper reports' and the crisis management mentality's approach. He offers a challenge to the current and future Islamicists to exert their effort to understand the meaning of applying Islamic laws and the Islamization process in Muslim societies. Furthermore, he calls for a continuous and rigorous self-criticism methodology in analysis and understanding.

Commentary

Colonialism, the subsequent fragmentation of the Muslim world, the imposition of the nation-state European system in the Islamic world, the loss of Palestine and the displacement of the Palestinians, up until the destruction of Iraq and the genocide of Muslims in Bosnia are all images that have forced the Muslims to ask the question: Are the Western world's attitudes towards the second largest religion and its peoples because of ignorance or deliberate policies reflecting Western interests? Although Esposito gave some reasons for the shortcomings of Western scholarship on Islam, he did not pose these more relevant questions: Why is the position towards Islam before 1980 one of total apathy, yet after 1980 one of total absorption? Why is academia's view very similar to that of the establishment? Without a serious attempt to answer such questions, the phenomena of trivializing and de-humanizing Islam, the Islamic movements, and their impact on their societies in the West will continue to go unabated. The simple answer is that the West behaves and reacts according to its perceived interests regardless of the consequences. These interests are oil, the state of Israel, the stability of the Western oriented regimes in the area despite their dictatorial nature and human rights abuses, and the continuation of open markets to their products.

Western political establishments have no problem with Islam as a dormant religion in the secular and Western sense, but do have a problem with political Islam because it currently represents the line of defense of Muslim societies against Western dominance, hegemony, and economic control and exploitation. Another question that was also overlooked is: What would be the consequences of these hostile policies by the West, in general, and the United States, in particular, on their relationship with the Islamic world, not the governments, but the people at large?

In short, Esposito's reasons for the West's failure to respond positively or even objectively to the role of Islamic resurgent movements in transforming Islamic societies, albeit important, fall short of explaining the continuous hostile attitudes and deliberate demeaning of Islamic movements. It is not a simple failure of academic research and investigation but because of deliberate political calculations and economic interests. In fact, part of the academic establishment in the United States, for instance, has paved the road to the hostile attitude in the Western political establishment, in publications such as Bernard Lewis's "The New Map of the Middle East," Samuel Huntington's "The Clash of Civilizations," and Fokuyama's "End of History."

Several points are also worth mentioning. The fact that many activists have not been clerics is a continuation of a tradition of many Islamic scholars, imams, and leaders as attested by Islamic history since there is no clergy in Islam. In addition, while the author tries to portray modern Islamic revivalist movements positively by comparing them with the Protestant ethics and renaissance movements, it must be observed that the latter movements were revolting against the church while the Islamic movements are calling for the return of Islam to public life and are revolting against the product of secularization and Westernization.

The author falls in the same trap that he cautions others from falling into when he recognizes Qaddafi, Fahd, Saddam Hussein and Khomeini as representing different brands of Islam. All but Khomeini are not recognized by the majority of Islamists as representing a genuine Islamic authority or legitimacy. In fact, some are quite hostile towards political Islam and even persecute such movements. Therefore, the questions of "What Islam?" and "Whose Islam?", posed by the author, are not valid in the macro sense as the author seems to argue, but are valid in the micro sense. There is no debate in Islamic circles on the framework of the Islamic government or the establishment of the Islamic Shari'ah, but rather on details that are within the realm of debate and examination. In fact, there is almost a consensus among Islamic activists on many aspects of the Islamic government as can be seen in the numerous books authored about the subject in the last forty years. The question posed by the author on whether the reassertion of Islam means restoration or reformation, is practically answered by almost all Islamic movements since they call for the return to Qura'n and Sunnah (restoration) and practice many aspects of Ijtihad in their movements and with respect to their societies (reformation). So the answer is , why not both?

The impediments to progress in Islamic societies have never been the traditional ulama as stated but history attests to the fact that the ulama class was always the people's guarantee against the excesses of the state. In addition, while the author calls for a wider scholarship to non-Arab and non-Sunni Islam, the fact is that Arabic remains the dominant language of scholarship and historical texts as well as for 70 to 80 percent of modern literature in the area called the Middle East, with the remaining languages being Persian and Urdu which use Arabic alphabets and cultural linguistics. While the Shia's experience is important, and even more so after the Iranian revolution, the fact is that the Sunni experience is more representative of the vast majority of Muslim societies.

Another point the author tries to make in an attempt to quiet down Western nervousness is to classify Islamic activists as moderates and radicals or extremists. Although the notion is acceptable in general, it is nevertheless dangerous since he does not discuss the criteria that differentiate them. Violence must not be used as a criterion where the oppression and repression of the state are so pervasive that they leave the opposition no option but to defend itself as in the case of Syria in the early 1980s and now in Algeria and Egypt, or under occupation in the South of Lebanon or in the occupied territories. The author, for whatever reason, ignores this internal factor of the state's repression and dictatorship when discussing this point. What is important is that some movements that represent mainstream Islam and modern Islamic thought may find themselves fighting undemocratic and repressive regimes with violence after all options have been closed in their face. The danger here is that labeling them as "radicals", "fundamentalists", or "terrorists" becomes justified. The real point should have been: What is the position of mainstream Islam towards such actions inside Islamic societies when all other legitimate options have been closed? The author indeed correctly points out that the danger is probably more to the Muslim societies than to the outside world. The above question is being hotly debated inside the Islamic movements with many issues still being argued. Islam is an ideology that is capable of mobilizing its adherents to change corrupt and repressive societies. The Islamic revolution in Iran is a testimony to this. The more relevant question is: If it is in the West's interest to keep such societies as corrupt, repressive, undemocratic and exploited, what will the West do when organized Islamic movements try to change these societies either through peaceful means when permitted or through other means when denied?

The question of the double-talk, double-standard, and exploitative attitude of the West toward other peoples and their wealth and resources must be addressed and put on the agenda. When the West acknowledges this fact, recognizing the legitimacy of these indigenous movements, and negotiating with them its interests, only then can we hope to achieve balance in the relationship between the Islamic and Western worlds. The role of scholarship and academia is important but only if it gets to the deeper aspect of the problem, not confining itself to the peripheries.

Finally, it must be pointed out that the thrust of the author's presentation on how Islam could be better understood and analyzed in academic circles is through a genuine effort to invite Islamic intellectuals, professors, and thinkers to teach and conduct scholarly work at Western institutions (from Islamic and Arab universities,) and through an extensive program of exchange throughout the Islamic world.

V.

MIXING TYPES OF EVIDENCE:
LITERARY AND ARCHAEOLOGICAL SOURCES FOR
THE STUDY OF RELIGION AND SOCIETY

6

Babylonian Religion

Erica Reiner
University of Chicago Oriental Institute

Leo Oppenheim has a chapter in his *Ancient Mesopotamia* which has caused scandal – and I am using the word "scandal" in its religious sense. It is titled "Why a 'Mesopotamian Religion' Should Not Be Written." Amidst the furor generated thereby, he was accused to be "anti-religion," nihilistic, and the like. Ever since that time many have attempted to indeed write a "Mesopotamian Religion" – maybe using instead of "religion" some other word, say "mythology", only to prove most conclusively the point made by Oppenheim. This point is, if I try to summarize in a few words a chapter that is full of insights and rich in ideas, that first of all, our civilization is so remote from the ancient, dead civilization of Mesopotamia that we cannot grasp what lies behind the texts; that these texts reflect the life of a privileged class, not of the common man; that in the life of this so-called "common man" religion does not seem to have played an important part; that archaeological finds of temples can tell us very little of the function of these temples; and that stories about gods, the so-called mythological texts, are literary creations. What caused perhaps the greatest scandal was Oppenheim's statement that an enumeration of the gods of the pantheon can not be taken as describing, much less explaining, Mesopotamian religion.

Rather, we should try to inquire what religion represented for an individual. We can try to put ourselves in the place of a temple official, of a slave or oblate of the temple, of a scholar, of the king and his entourage. As for the private person, a lowly citizen or a member of the underclass, we cannot even hope to learn how religion affected his life, since, according to Oppenheim's opinion just cited, not only is there no evidence about his feelings and conception of the numinous, but the lack of documentation rather suggests that his life was spent without much reflection on the "ultimate things." Even for ancient Greece there is a lack of documentation on the "religious attitudes" of Greek man, as opposed to their myths and rituals, as Arthur Darby Nock stated: "...as with people of any time and place, these [personal attitudes] are more elusive, and our attempt to recapture them depends largely upon incidental remarks in literature...."[1]

Since we are not able to give answers to the social and existential questions pertaining to Mesopotamian religion, we could proceed by posing some questions, and establish some aspects by negative definitions. What was the perception of a temple official – not "priest" – of religion? We have no indication that it was based on a written text, a holy book, a revealed text. Too often are the names of various functionaries translated by "priest". Rather, they were bureaucrats, since the temple was basically an economic organization, and was one of the two "Great Organizations" as Oppenheim dubbed the palace and the temple. The functionary was kept busy with recording income and expenditure, and may not have had any part in religious activities, and was possibly only part of the larger bureaucracy, maybe having less contact with the divine service than a medieval monk who kept the accounts for his order or his monastery.

Then there were the officials engaged in ritual and cultic activities. To perform the ceremonies, written instructions for rituals and of the prayers to be recited during their performance – the "legomena" – were used. Recitations were demanded both from the priest or liturgist and from the patient. The latter, even if he was the king, recited the prayer or confession in the vernacular, while the officiating priest often had to recite in Sumerian. This bilingualism is a fascinating topic for questions of language, schooling, tradition, and the like, but it can also be viewed from the point of view of religion: Was there a transition between the religion of the Sumerians and the Semitic Akkadians who followed them in Mesopotamia? What was the influence of the nomadic tribes of the

---

[1]Arthur Darby Nock, "Religious attitudes of the ancient Greeks," in *Essays on Religion and the Ancient World*, ed. Zeph Stewart (Cambridge, Mass: Harvard University Press, 1972), pp. 534-50 (reprinted from Proceedings of the American Philosophical Society 85 [1942] p. 472-82). For general discussion about the methodological pitfalls inherent in any discussion of ancient religion, most notably the problem of dealing with texts of an educated elite as sources for traditional religion, see Momigliano "Popular Religious Beliefs and the Late Roman Historians," in G. Cummings and R. Baker (eds.), Popular *Beliefs and Practices,* 1-18 and C.R. Phillips III, "The Sociology of Religious Knowledge in the Roman Empire," Anrw 2.16.3:2681-697.

West upon the settlements in the river valleys? We are beginning to know quite a bit about these western regions and principalities from the recent rapid publications of the text from Mari on the upper Euphrates.

Secondly, we have the scholars and the scholarly professions, who were in part in the king's service and in part were set up independently in business; these latter professionals – the diviner, the physician, the exorcist – were dependent on their clients for their livelihood. As members of the class of scholars, they had the task of keeping up the tradition, by copying, commenting on, and possibly composing the texts that we regard as reflecting religious tradition: lists of gods, hymns, and various scholastic exercises. It is not well known to what extent these professions adhered to the official religion practiced by the palace and the temple, or had catered to more popular, indeed magic cults. The diviners and the astrologers, who mostly belonged to the court circles, were less prone to accept and practice what I have called "fortunetelling"; such fortunetelling, that is, divination based on the outcome of a set-up that gave a yes-or-no answer and did not require knowledge of the elaborate predictions that for example the examination of the sheep's liver provided, necessitated little book learning and could be performed by less scholarly practitioners.

The royal court again had a different role. The king's actions in appealing to the deity and satisfying his requests were meant to ensure prosperity for his land; many of the activities required from the king – offerings, sacrifices, penitential rites – have been seen, rightly or wrongly, in that perspective, for example, the famous hieros gamos or sacred marriage, the king's union with the city goddess, to ensure fertility for the land. Personal religiosity of the king cannot be divorced from his public image, except perhaps in such cases as King Esarhaddon, in the seventh century B.C.E., who resorted to penance and magic manipulations apparently because of his ill health.

When and how the "man in the street" was confronted with religion, whether the official religion of this city god or the level that is closely related to magic, is even more difficult to assess, and I will come back to it a bit later.

What are our sources and how instructive are they? To begin with, what can archaeology teach us? The ground plans of temples, usually all that remains in southern Mesopotamia where the building material was clay, do not reveal much about the attitudes and beliefs of the people who participated in the liturgy, as Oppenheim pointed out. Even where temples were built of kiln-fired brick the remains are not informative about the function of these buildings. Let me state at the outset that it is difficult to establish the difference, if any, between the two types of construction, namely brick or stone. We do not have evidence, as we do in the Old Testament, that the populace grumbled at the corvee work of building stone monuments, as they did in pharaonic Egypt. Grumbling, incidentally, is said only of the minor gods who were required to do corvee work for the supreme god, Enlil, a story which as you well know, forms the background of the myth of the Creation of Man, nowadays known under the title Atrahasis, and to which I shall return in a moment.

We recall the history of the building of cathedrals in medieval Europe, a labor of love and devotion of the stonemasons and other craftsmen. No such dedication is evident in the ancient texts. The ledgers of the temples record the disbursement of rations to workmen, but do not record any incentive that might have motivated the workers and so we assume that it was necessity alone. Still, it is not excluded that a sense of piety also drove these men to participate in the building of temples.

We do not know, again as Oppenheim has pointed out, what went on in the temples and how the sacrifices and worship were carried out, with the exception of a few, and mostly late rituals that deal with particular aspects of the cult or with particular events. At least the fact that the holiness of temples was regarded with reverence is proven by the remark of King Assurbanipal, that in constructing his palace he did not build it too high so as not to rival the temple.[2] The king's phrase was translated properly, I believe the first time, in the CAD volume A/2 under a™irtu A [mng. 1b-2']: '...did not make it too high out of respect for (the adjacent terraces of) the sanctuaries of the great gods' [p. 437b]. We have a similar, though less poetic translation under the verb *šaqû* A. Such a taboo was not, and indeed is not, unique: We read in the Talmud that "Raba b. Mehasia also said in the name of R. Hama b. Goria in Rab's name: Every city whose roofs are higher than the synagogue will ultimately be destroyed" (Shabbat 11a). A more recent example pertains to New York City:

> At the present moment, it is unfortunately the case that the New York City zoning laws contain no provisions concerning the absolute maximum height of buildings on given sites. Once upon a time, certain local traditions had the force of laws; for example, it was a tradition not to construct a building in the immediate neighborhood of St. Patrick's Cathedral which would be higher than the top of its spires.[3]

Did the "common man" worship in the temple at all? Judging from the ground plans of Sumerian and Babylonian temples, the crowd assembled in the courtyard, which was very large, but probably was not

---

[2]lapān ešrēti ilāni rabûti bēlēja aplahma tamlâ šuātu šikittašu ul ušaqqi ma'diš [Streck Asb. 86 x 78-80]
[3]Brendan Gill, "The Sky Line," *The New Yorker*, February 8, 1988, p. 91.

admitted into the inner sanctum, reserved for the priestly collegium. The god was visible probably only at his annual festival, when his statue was paraded in the streets in procession that may have resembled the processions held today at certain holy days, especially in Latin milieus. Such processions are attested for the first millennium B.C. but were held in earlier times as we can see through the terminology of administrative and economic texts, which speak of the "entrance" of certain gods, of the "greeting of the temple."

However, we must ask whether, apart from the large temples in the important cities, there were smaller buildings in less prominent and possibly smaller settlements. Or perhaps there were only street sanctuaries (Akkadian: *ibratu*) where a private person, most likely a traveler, and probably many women could stop and pray and conceivably make an offering, such as we have in the small towns and villages in Southern Europe. While the word for such sanctuaries exists, we have no record of how and when they were built and used. It is only in the West – Emar and Mari – that we find evidence of a worship – some say of, but perhaps only at – erected stones, known as *betyls* in Greek, a word that some connect with Hebrew *beyt el*.

Statues, even the so-called cult statues, do not tell much either. They rarely affect our sensibilities, and those statues that do, and that have been singled out as ancient masterpieces, are usually those that have lost their distinguishing character: the wide-open, staring eyes, inlaid with colored stone. A good example of our misplaced admiration is the often reproduced so-called I™tar-head which by the way now serves as curtain for the new production of Wagner's Ring des Nibelungen. Apart from statues made of stone, many mass-produced terra cotta figurines (that is, made in a mold) must have been available for private persons presumably for worship at home – an activity about which we know nothing.

Amulets against evil spirits that the Mesopotamian man might have worn or hung up in his house as protection are also better known from their descriptions in texts that prescribe their fabrication than from surviving examplars. There are of course the cylinder seals that may also have served as amulets, but the interpretation of their iconography has had to proceed independently from textual evidence, and thus is far from established. There are no reliable "keys" that equate a symbol or human or animal figure on the seal with belief in demons, or an afterlife, or with allusions to a myth.

Turning to literature, and to the evidence it may provide as well as the evidence it does not provide, and even obscures: Mesopotamian literature has been made available to the general public, especially lately, through the translations of ancient Near Eastern myths (Dalley, Kramer-

Bottero) and the proliferation of recent translations of the Epic of Gilgamesh. By the way, for the latter Oppenheim maintained that it was an example of court literature, composed for a king who perhaps had no male offspring and heir, and for whom the achievement of immortality was possible through valorous deeds only. The other stories, usually taken to be Meopotamian myths, are however not necessarily myths in the sense of Frazer, that is, an encoded way to come to terms with the great themes of human existence: love, death, fertility of the soil and of living beings, and the like.

Arnaldo Momigliano, the eminent scholar of ancient history and classical antiquity, once addressed a scholar of Indian literature who wished to compare Indian and Greek myths: "Maybe *you* people have myths; *we* have stories about gods." I would like to include in Momigliano's characterization the so-called myths of Mesopotamia, too. I hasten to add, however, that I claim no expertise in Sumerian, and will therefore make no pronouncements about eventual Sumerian myths. Stories, we have heard Professor Neusner quote Father Andrew Greeley, are but one dimension of religious heritages: "Religious heritages constitute storytelling communities...a group of humans who share a common repertory of symbols and a sufficiently common interpretation of these symbols so that it is relatively easy to tell them the story and relatively reasonable to expect that they will 'get it.'"

A curious fact about Mesopotamian stories that involve the exploits of gods is that, in contradistinction to what I believe Father Greeley's definition embraces, they deal with events in the gods' lives that have no connection with man, and thus, if my understanding of storytelling is correct, they can provide no lesson for behavior or reflect gods' involvement in human destiny. What are Mesopotamian stories dealing with the exploits of gods about? They are mainly about their loves, or, especially in Sumerian literature, their seductions of young goddesses, but also about fights against evil demons and monsters who threaten the supremacy or tranquillity of the divine sphere. Gods and goddesses behave like ordinary men – by ordinary we should no doubt mean men of the privileged classes who are free to engage in courtship, to marry, to enjoy good food and drink, to have servants, to wear fine clothes, and not the ordinary folk who had to labor for obtaining a livelihood, and who were subject, at least economically, to wealthy landowners, whether private landlords or the temple. Only a few stories, the story of Adapa and especially the Atrahasis epic, grapple with the problem of human misfortune and mortality.

If the divine protagonists were equated with the elite, how did our "ordinary man" express his frustration and unhappiness? In fact, there are quite a few stories, even among the so-called myths, that make fun of the gods or describe a rebellion against them. Often, of course, this moral of a story has to be veiled, and the discomfiture of a god superseded by the discomfiture of some human. We can try, nevertheless, to find the motifs underlying such stories. We have of course, the Atrahasis epic, also known as the Creation of Man. Man was created to do the labor of the gods, after the lesser gods who were assigned to this labor staged a fiery revolt. The tale goes on, as we know, with the story of the various plagues that the gods brought on mankind, culminating in the Deluge from which only Atrahasis, the Babylonian Noah, and his household were saved.

What about the story of Adapa, one of the seven sages who were god-like but still mortal? Adapa was offered immortality by the gods but was cheated of it through the malicious counsel of the god Ea. Well, Adapa was brought before the celestial tribunal after he, as the text says, broke the wing of the South Wind, that is, he rebelled against the nature of things, especially against the destructive force that frustrated his efforts of catching fish for the table of his god, again Ea, by capsizing his fishing skiff.

There are some stories, albeit a few, whose protagonists are human. These are essentially humorous, and express a veiled satire. You probably have heard the Tale of the Poor Man of Nippur. This funny story, one of the few humorous pieces we have, is significant in that it tells of the revenge of a poor devil on the mighty mayor of the city of Nippur. The story is based on a well-known motif, attested in many a folklore precisely because it deals with the frustration of the powerless and his gaining the upper hand over the rich and powerful through his greater intelligence and ruse. Yet this story takes place in a never-never land, where a poor fellow can rent a fancy carriage from the king, and has not one reference to a god or religious festival.

Other stories with human protagonists feature the physician, a comic figure in many societies, and interestingly the fuller, who is a comic figure not only in Roman literature, but must have been so known in the Rabbinic literature, as the mention of *mašalot kovēsim*, 'fables about fullers' makes clear.

The Babylonian Talmud relates[4] that among the accomplishments of Rabban Johanan b. Zakkai were "calendrical computations, gemaṭrias, the speech of the Ministering Angels, the speech of spirits, and the

---

[4]"They said of Rabban Johanan b. Zakkai that he did not leave [unstudied] Scripture, Mishnah, Gemara, Halachah, Aggada, details of the Torah, details of the Scribes, inferences *a minori ad majus*, analogies, calendrical computations, gemaṭrias, the speech of the Ministering Angels, the speech of spirits, and the speech of palm-trees, fullers' parables and fox fables, great matters or small matters."

speech of palm-trees, fullers' parables and fox fables." The phrase translated by 'fullers' parables', *mašalot kovēsim*, can of course mean not only 'parables *told* by fullers', as it has usually been taken to mean, but also 'parables, or rather stories, *about* fullers', since in Hebrew, as in other Semitic languages, the genitive construction can express a subjective or an objective relation. The phrase, then, refers to stories *about* fullers, probably similar to those that were told about their Roman colleagues.[5]

Note, by the way, that the same accomplishments are ascribed to Rabban Johanan b. Zakkai in Baba Bathra 134[a] where our phrase is translated into English as "washer's proverbs"; and, with some omissions, in Aboth d' R. Nathan, as I learned from Strack-Billerbeck [IV 535].

Among non-narrative literature, there exists poetry that is concerned with the suffering of an individual. As already the name sometimes given to this genre, "penitential psalms," indicates, they can be, and have been, compared to the Old Testament psalms. The question that needs to be posed, even though it is difficult to answer, is who the individual may have been who confesses his sins and asks for renewed divine favor, promising offerings and homage to his god or goddess. As we know from surviving exemplars of particular prayers which contain blanks into which the petitioner's name was to be inserted, whenever the blank is filled in, it contained the name of the king. Even if it was not the king alone, but possibly also members of his family and entourage for whose sakes the prayers were to be recited, we still seem to have to do not with a universal act of contrition but with one reserved for the upper echelons of society. To quote again Oppenheim, the ritual practices were devised for the king, and affected only later the lower echelons.

> A large part of what we assume to be Mesopotamian religion has meaning only in relation to royal personages – and for this reason distorts our concepts. ...the practices that originally concerned only the king influenced successively the court and even, presumably, the common man in a process of diffusion that is well known to the student of the sociology of religion. (Ancient Mesopotamial, p. 181)

---

[5]It is obvious that the Jewish scholars were puzzled by the learning of Rabban Johanan b. Zakkai. So are the modern commentators. One commentary states, with regard to R. Johanan b. Zakkai's knowledge of "the speech of palm-trees" that "Rashi professes ignorance of this. Hai Gaon writes in a responsum that on a windless day, if a man stands between two palms and observes how they incline to one another, signs can be deduced which afford information. The Gaon Abraham Kobasi d. 828. was a proficient interpreter of 'the speech of palms.'" [Footnote 16]. With regard to *mašalot kov(e)sim* the footnote [note 17] simply says,

> "The fuller is a well-known figure in Roman comedy," and to "fox fables" [note 1 (on p. 124)]" R. Meir was an adept in fox fables."

In the story often termed "the Babylonian Job," which is also known, from its first words, as (in Akkadian) *Ludlul bēl nēmeqi,* or in translation, as "I will praise the Lord of Wisdom," the suffering protagonist tries to find out the cause of his misery by seeking answers from the diviner and the dream interpreter. We cannot conclude that this was a universal recourse of a sufferer, since we learn that he has the standing of an important official. I don't think that we can extrapolate from the circumstances of a highly-placed individual to that of the man in the street.

Still, a good guide to the hopes and expectations of a private person can be found in the divinatory literature. Mesopotamian man considered the events of everyday life, especially the unusual and stranger ones, as signs given by the gods of impending events that, once forewarned, the person could evade or annul by appropriate prayers and rituals. Hepatoscopy, also known as extispicy, a process that examined the entrails of a lamb sacrificed for this purpose, and that has reached the West as one of the Etruscan divination techniques, required the not insubstantial investment of a lamb and thus was usually reserved for the highly placed of society, especially for the king. Consequently, the predictions from the appearance of the liver concerned the country as a whole, by predicting wars, plagues, and other natural catastrophes or, as the case may be, boons affecting the land. The many other forms of divination: from the smoke of an incense burner, from the shape of drops of oil on a bowl of water, from the birth of an abnormal animal, for example, a five-legged calf, or the sighting of anything unusual in or around a house or land: red ants, lichen on the wall, trees swaying without wind, etc., could affect the ordinary person. What a man saw in a dream or the various symptoms the diagnostician observed when called to a patient's bedside also predicted that individual's fate.

It is through such predictions that we learn (as was shown by Nougayrol and Oppenheim) of the everyday life of Babylonian man, of his fears and hopes, of his relations with the divine and with the society around him. We may take such typical predictions as: he will acquire a good protective spirit, or simply he will have a good personal god, which is equivalent to "he will have luck." Of course, the opposite could also be predicted: an evil spirit, or an ill-intentioned personal god will persecute him.

Apart from such non-unique illustrations, the "common man" is an elusive figure. The documentation we have of the ancient civilizations of Mesopotamia is lopsided, as it is in any civilization where literacy was not widespread. We deal with an elite, and only rarely, and by deliberate contrast, do we find the "common man."

Actually, even in those cases the emphasis is not on the man's – or woman's – status but on his or her poverty, his or her being destitute. Here I very deliberately have put the emphasis on the gender distinction since the ancient texts – be they the Old Testament or the New, or Mesopotamian texts – single out the poor *woman*, often a widow, to illustrate poverty, and to stress the fact that poverty is not an obstacle to divine favor. In fact, rather the opposite is true. Here I need only to remind you of the destitute woman who offered hospitality to Elijah, or of the New Testament parable [Luke 21; Mark 12] of the poor widow who gives all she has, and the story of the woman who lost one coin rejoicing when she found it, who serves, not surprisingly, only in Luke [Lk 15.8-10] as a pendant to the parable of the prodigal son.

In Mesopotamian texts I can point to the well-known passage in a hymn to ᵓama™, the Sun god, which speaks of the offerings brought to the god: "the rich man brings you a lamb, the widow a handful of flour." I am not so sure anymore that this often-cited line indeed speaks of offerings to the gods. Rather, it should refer to the various modes of divination: the oldest, and best known technique, the examination of the entrails of the lamb, known as hepatoscopy (the name the Romans gave to the similar divinatory technique practiced by the Etruscans), as just mentioned required the sacrifice of a lamb, that only the rich could afford; the poor woman who could offer only a "handful of flour" had recourse to libanomancy, that is, divination from the shape of the smoke on the censer, if the "flour" refers to the substance burned on the censer. Still, the divination practiced with her flour could have been aleuromancy, that is, divination from the shape assumed by poured-out flour, as Jean Nougayrol interpreted an Old Babylonian divinatory text. I do suspect, however, that the "flour" may be nothing more than a topos, the same that appears in the mentioned story of Elijah and the poor woman [1 Kings 17].

This is perhaps the occasion to say a word about the status of women. Interestingly, in this so-called "patriarchal society" women enjoyed a great deal of independence. While they most likely had no say in whom they were to marry, once married, they had power of disposition of their dowry, and could bequeath it at will. Once widowed, they could, but need not, seek the protection of their father-in-law, brother-in-law, or their own father, but they could also set up house on their own. We hear astonishingly little about religion in this connection. We know of no ceremonies in which virgins were to sacrifice before a goddess, or dedicate a symbol of their virginity to a goddess, or even women's particular devotion to a female deity. As for the custom of dedicating a daughter as votary to a goddess, attested in the Old Babylonian period, to live in a separate enclosure, called the *gagûm*, sometimes translated, albeit misleadingly, as "cloister," this may have had an economic reason, to wit, preventing the patrimony from being divided into too many parts, even though such a cloistered woman, Akkadian *nadītu*, was entitled to a dowry. The same reasons were at play, especially in nineteenth century Europe, when a family with a large number of offspring often dedicated a daughter to become a nun.

It is in the nature of records of human experience that sufferings and misfortunes are set down and insisted upon in writing, but no mention is made when things are going well. Shall we exercise our imagination to guess at how a person's satisfaction or happiness could gave been expressed? To take sickness as an example, do the crude clay models of limbs, such as feet, represent, as do the ex-votos seen in churches or at sites of pilgrimages such as Lourdes, the hopes of a sick man for recovery, or the grateful dedication after healing? Too few such objects have survived, and too few clues are extant in texts, to decide this question.

As for the clay dog figurines found in great numbers in the temples of the goddess Gula, goddess of healing and patron of physicians, as also the dog figurines found in the cemetery of Ashkalon by Stager, they have been given the most outlandish interpretations. According to one of these, the dog is associated with healing because dogs lick their wounds. The correct answer, I believe, is found through the records of a civilization that is more explicit: the Greek goddess, Hecate, has a dog as her companion, because she is simultaneously the goddess of healing and of death, and as chthonic, underground goddess she is accompanied by a dog. Only part of these characteristics are explicit in the figure of the Mesopotamian goddess Gula; we know of her only the two attributes, one, that she is the goddess of healing, the other, that her companion is a dog. The other members of the equation we have to supply on the basis of the classical counterpart. This character of Gula, as the Great Physician, but "originally – as her animal, the dog indicates – the goddess of death" was first recognized by Oppenheim (Ancient Mesopotamial, p. 197).

The gropings of us scholars to interpret the overabundant literature can be understood if not always excused by the nature of our sources. We cannot expect expository statements, philosophical discourse, on religion and its place in society. Expository writing was not a way of expression in Mesopotamia; rather, in lieu of scientific arguments and descriptions only two kinds of writings were used: the list form and the procedure texts. The list form was used to compile sign lists, Sumerian and Akkadian bilingual word lists and grammatical paradigms as well as mathematical and astronomical tables. Thus we have long lists of deities, often enumerated in groups of families and households, but these "bespeak the nature of Mesopotamian scholarship rather than the nature of Mesopotamian religiosity" (Ancient Mesopotamial, p. 180).

The other type of source, the procedure texts, deals with the particular, not the general; they describe procedures but not the justification, the underlying reasons, for the procedures; they are casuistic and not universalistic; they deal not with theory but with application. The term "procedure text" has primarily been applied to the scientific directions for making glass, dyeing wool, training horses, and, we can now add, recipes for preparing meat dishes, but it can also include directions for the physician to treat the patient and concomitant with these but also standing alone, directions for executing ritual acts, the texts that we in short call "rituals." Unfortunately, the most complete, and also the most elaborate of these rituals are late, first millennium texts, and some date to the Hellenistic period. In what measure they reflect the concerns of the individual as opposed to the routine affecting only the temple and its personnel, we cannot know. Still, speculations about these rituals have become rampant, as the interpretations based on Freudian psychology, feminist history, and other fashionable approaches show.

I will close with the analysis of one such ritual, or rather, will show how various approaches can open different perspectives. The ritual is the one called "washing of the mouth" (*mīs pî*). It deals with the all-important ceremony of breathing life into the statues of the gods, for which the Greeks had the term empsychosis, that is, providing with psyche or soul. In Babylonia, the ceremony is called the "opening of the mouth" (*pīt pî*), which is preceded by the "washing of the mouth" (*mīs pî*) of the divine statue. Divine statues, we know, were made of wood, and overlaid with precious materials, usually gold; incrustations of precious stones adorned them.[6] Their fabrication was, therefore, placed under the tutelage of the patron gods of carpenters, goldsmiths, and jewelers. Only after the inert materials were infused with breath through the mouth-opening ceremony can the statue, that is, the god, eat and drink the offerings, and smell the incense.[7]

The vivification of the divine statue comprised several stages. The first stage, the first mouth washing, was conducted in the workshop; then, the statue was carried in procession to the river bank, where a second mouth washing took place. Offerings were made to the nine great gods, among whom are the major planetary gods, that is, Sun, Moon, and Venus; then to the patron gods of the craftsmen, nine in

---

[6]Oppenheim, "The Golden Garments of the Gods," JNES.
[7]ṣalmu annû ina la pīt pî qutrinna ul iṣṣin akala ul ikkal mê ul išatti STT 200:42f. and dupl. PBS 12/1 6.

number; then to other planets and to certain fixed stars and constellations, among them Sirius, Libra, the Wagon, our Big Dipper, the Goat, our Lyra, and the Scorpion; and finally to the stars rising over the three "paths" along the eastern horizon, that is, *all* the stars.[8] The role of the astral deities in the ritual is not specified; nevertheless, that role is clear from the description of the venue, which is the river bank, and the time: at night, as indicated by the fact that the procession advances by torchlight; the stars and planets were to irradiate the statue crafted of wood, metal, and stone and thus infuse these materials with their power. The offerings are described with the words: "you set up a cultic arrangement[9] to the god"; it seems that these "cultic arrangements" or, as we might say, "altars," are the *loci* to which the astral god will descend. It is to be noted that no specific connection is made between the various materials of which the statue is made and the deity that presides over each. Only in Hellenistic times will each planet be associated with a particular metal and stone.[10]

While only the Late Babylonian version of the mouth washing ritual describes in great detail the appeal to the stellar powers, already the Assyrian kings Esarhaddon and Assurbanipal stress that the initiation of the new cult statues was taking place before not only the gods and the divine patrons of the crafts by means of which these statues were made, but also "before the stars of the sky," as the texts expressly state.[11]

This particular interpretation, one that I recently put forward in lectures, and which was naturally perceived by the first editor of the text, Sidney Smith, has left out certain elements, as it always happens when one wishes to make a case, elements that others have found to be especially significant. Just recently, at the annual meeting of the AOS, a paper discussing this ritual interpreted it as a "rite de passage", an interpretation originating in anthropological circles. According to this interpretation, the cult statue undergoes a transition ritual in order to achieve its new status, and the metaphors of this transition ritual which, as in other similar rituals, include those "of human gestation and birth," are explicated by the author of the paper.[12] In particular, the wooden

---

[8]S. Smith, JRAS 1925 37ff. = TuL 104-105:25-36; see also W. Mayer, Or. NS 47 445 W 20030/3:3-5 (copy Baghdader Mitteilungen, Beiheft 2 no. 1). The introductory instructions are partially broken; the text begins: e-nu-ma ṣip-ri DINGIR ÈBI/GA-am [x x x ina IT]I ṣal-me...'when...the work on the god,[...]in a favorable month...' lines 1f.

[9]riksu.

[10]Bouché-Leclercq, L'astrologie grecque, p. 313

[11]mahar kakkabí ṣamámi Streck Asb. 268 iii 20 (= Bauer Asb. p. 84), Borger Esarh. 91 §60 i 13, and parallels §57 r. 21, etc.

[12]Peggy J. Boden, Johns Hopkins University.

trough which holds the water is likened to the womb, the water itself to the amniotic fluid, and so forth.

Ms. Boden is not the first to suggest these analogies, even though they appear to be rooted in the feminist discourse of today. Thorkild Jacobsen, in his article "The Graven Image,"[13] had already suggested that "the waters from the river are the life-giving waters of the 'father', the river-god Ea, and represent his fructifying semen. The trough of tamarisk into which they are poured represents the womb of the 'mother', the wood, which is to conceive and to give birth to the cult statue."

These various interpretations, while I do not dispute the insights they may give us, exemplify the bias from which, unfortunately, we can only rarely divest ourselves. However, greater damage is done, a greater loss in our perception occurs, when we see Mesopotamian religion, indeed, Mesopotamian civilization, as simply reflecting universal human concerns, in whatever terms they be interpreted, from a Levi-Straussian perspective, a Freudian, a feminist, or some other current and fashionable viewpoint. Such viewpoints indeed draw attention to the common denominator in various cultures, but divert our attention from what is specific in the society we strive to understand. To describe the specific, what Benno Landsberger called, in German, *die Eigenbegrifflichkeit*, and that has been called, in English translation, 'the conceptual autonomy' of the Babylonian world, to find not only similarities but contrasts, is the way to deepen our understanding of Mesopotamian religion and Mesopotamian man. If we can describe it only in the framework of some generic model, then, indeed, as Oppenheim said, a "Mesopotamian religion" should not be written.

---

[13]*Ancient Israelite Religion,* Essays in Honor of Frank Moore Cross, edited by Patrick D. Miller, Jr., Paul D. Hanson, and S. Dean McBride (Philadelphia: Fortress Press, 1987), pp. 15-32.

Response to Erica Reiner's "Babylonian Religion"

Sarah Mandell
University of South Florida

Professor Reiner's paper on Mesopotamian religion is part of a now growing series of investigations into the practice of religion in antiquity. At one time, scholars presumed that the religions represented in or even by the myths, legends, and as depicted in various types of artifacts, were those in which people believed. So Leo Oppenheim was truly revolutionary when he entitled a chapter, "Why a 'Mesopotamian Religion' Should Not Be Written," in part three, (*Nah ist – und schweer zu fassen der Gott*) of his *Ancient Mesopotamia: Portrait of a Dead Civilization.* And this chapter did indeed cause many people to rethink their long held beliefs, to the extent that the attempt to *define a Mesopotamian religion* has become academically unfashionable. For Professor Oppenheim told us that the "emperor was not wearing any clothes." That is, he implied that our predications were not based on fact, but on hypotheses.

Professor Reiner implies that our knowledge is only partial and at times fragmentary, so we are not at liberty to draw conclusions regarding the whole enterprise. For example, even when we know the names and history of what is thought to be most characteristic of Mesopotamian religious edifices, the Temple Tower, the Ziggurat, we do not know its purpose. And what is true of our knowledge of the Temple Tower is also true regarding other archaeological finds, be they architectural, monumental, iconographic, or simply artifactual. Scholars like people in general do not want to hear such "negative" interpretations of our "data." But this type of negativity is right, proper, and incorrect (sic). Our attempt therefore to define Mesopotamian religion on the basis of what little knowledge we have about this so-called "Dead Civilization" resembles the fabled attempt of the blind men and the elephant. Each having felt a part of the animal believed that the whole beast resembled that part.

Even without the other significant contributions to scholarship made by Professor Reiner, who revised and completed Oppenheim's *Ancient Mesopotamia: Portrait of a Dead Civilization*, this book and even this chapter alone marks each as one of the foremost and *bravest* academicians of the twentieth century. It reflects wisdom, albeit not in the religio-technical sense, and rationalism alike. So it is not surprising that it is dedicated to Otto Neugebauer, whom we know to be a man of great rationalism and extensive knowledge.

Another great scholar, Professor Thorkild Jacobsen, did take the less "rationalistic," albeit more well-traveled path. As but one segment of a wealth of scholarship, he attempted to reconstruct aspects of Mesopotamian religion(s) and society. And his arguments, too, are compelling, even when they are not always based on the assumption that mankind, particularly as *homo religiosus,* is a rational being in the "scientific sense." In fact his arguments are so powerful that when new data indicate that they are incorrect and must be revised, we must still take them into account. Like the conclusions of Professors Oppenheim and Reiner alike, they are the rational deductions of an extremely sound and in fact venerable scholar. But Jacobsen's approach to scholarship is different from that of Oppenheim or Reiner.

Despite Professor Jacobsen's less "restrained" and possibly less objective attitude toward the data pertaining to Mesopotamian religious practices, he, too, did not entitle any of his works "Mesopotamian religion" without some type of qualification. Even in a major article, "Ancient Mesopotamian Religion," he qualified that title by adding the subtitle, "The Central Concerns." That is, instead of trying to define the religion itself, he looked to that with which it was concerned. Furthermore, he acknowledged the problematics of reconstructing both Mesopotamian religion and culture simply by entitling his somewhat popular, but still scholarly, book on the subject, *The Treasures of Darkness.* We must not forget, however, that it is subtitled *A History of Mesopotamian Religion.* In this case, however, the title seems to diminish the scandalous nature of the subtitle. And like Professor Reiner, I, too, use the noun scandal as well as its adjective in its various religious denotations.

But Jacobsen erred in presuming that the relationship between what is immanent and what is transcendent in ancient Mesopotamian religion is unique to and so helps to define it. So he was both right and wrong when he said:

> in asking what in ancient Mesopotamian religion seems specifically Mesopotamian, one cannot but note a tendency to experience the Numinous as immanent in some specific feature of the confrontation, rather than as all transcendent (*Treasures of Darkness* [New Haven, 1978] 5).

This is true of many religions, including many of those practiced in the Greek-speaking world; and, therefore, it does not depict or qualify Mesopotamian religion as Mesopotamian per se. Clearly Jacobsen's scholarship, like that of Oppenheim and Reiner, shows that he, too, understood many of the problems inherent in the reconstruction of a civilization that is so distant and so disparate from our own. And at the same time, Professor Jacobsen, the very scholar whose writings, like those of the members of the Cambridge and Scandinavian schools, has led many students of ancient religions to begin working on comparative bases, fell into the trap of looking into Mesopotamian religion as an entity unto itself.

In any case, Professor Jacobsen like Professor Oppenheim and Professor Reiner used what data were available. So in Jacobsen's attempts to reconstruct aspects of Mesopotamian religious rituals and practices, he did not reject the artifactual and literary data as ineffectual in speaking to us about the past. He attempted to draw what he could from them; and. using the methodology of the School of History of Religions, *Religionsgeschichtliche Schule*, he tried to tie them into universals. Professors Oppenheim and Reiner do likewise, but they come to different conclusions about the viability of the data's informing us about Mesopotamian religion(s) precisely because they only inform us about segments of those religions.

In light of Professor Jacobsen's work, I suggest that we must not be so quick to deny the possibility of writing a "Mesopotamian religion." On the other hand, considering the meticulous work of Professor Oppenheim, Professor Reiner, and of many other Sumerologists and Assyriologists who analyze what we have datum by datum without generalizing about Mesopotamian religion, I stress that we must be particular in our methodology.

It is true that we may not know anything specific about the religions, including the ritual practices, the faith, or the piety of the common man. And likewise, we may have little knowledge of the common man's way of life, be he fisherman, farmer, or what have you. But we do know something about the world in which he lived; and this itself may lead us to a generalized understanding of the religions, notice the plural, he practiced. Yet we may never know what specific prayers he prayed or what was his emotional response to any encounter with the divine. We may not even know whether he truly believed what he practiced. Nevertheless we do have some limited knowledge of occasional statements addressed by a man to his personal god as Jacobsen, S.N. Kramer, and others have shown us.

What we look for in prayers and emotional responses reflects us, not necessarily the Mesopotamian man of antiquity, be he commoner or king. An example of how people view things in light of their own *Weltanschauung* is to be found in 4QPrNab, the fragments of the "Prayer of Nabonidus," where the faith and its attendant precepts of Second Temple Judaism(s) are attributed to this last Babylonian monarch.

I would stress, however, that we cannot presume the existence of a Mesopotamian religion that was uniform and that lasted throughout the millennia. Rather there were Mesopotamian religions that were born, most likely altered normatively and sometimes became syncretized with others, and sometimes even died.

Because we look to something that we can comprehend, that is a living religion that does not alter – even when we have an academic comprehension of the fact that the only non-changing and non-changeable religion, from any time or any place, is in fact dead – we have trouble dealing with all of the religions of the Greater Mediterranean world. This includes the religions, again notice the use of the plural, of the Children of Israel. And it also includes those of their descendants, who actually stake a claim to being the "True" (Second Temple Judaisms and Rabbinic Judaism[s]) or even the "New" (Christian) Israel as it lays claims to being the "True Israel."

The interpretation of the religions of ancient Mesopotamia as unknowable because it reflects a set of predications not based on fact is itself based on the biased precept *that what we deem religious is actually religious.* But we justify our bias on an academic basis: namely, the artifacts, buildings, monuments, and literary data do not themselves offer details of the everyday practice of religion or what is believed, felt, or experienced by "Every Man." It follows then that our problems in understanding the various ancient religions, including those practiced in Mesopotamia, come not from our skepticism, but rather from our inherent Jewish or Christian faith. This is even true for those who consider themselves to be rationalists and reject that very faith.

Without understanding that our scholarship reflects our biases, even the least prejudiced of those of us who are part of the Western Tradition has wanted to limit our categorization of what we call religion. And for this reason, many scholars in Classics, Biblical Studies, and Ancient Near Eastern Studies alike have rejected or at least de- and in fact dis-valued the work of the Cambridge and Scandinavian schools. But it was precisely the scholars within these two schools that sought to find the underlying religiosity of ancient peoples, particularly by way of an analysis of their myths and rituals, insofar as we can ascertain the presence or even meaning of either, as well as by an attempt to study their societies from both a sociological and anthropological perspective.

And we rejected their findings because our personal sense of who and what we are would not allow us to accept the conclusions of those who studied the Israelites and the Greeks, whose culture we have been conditioned to interpret as the two pillars of Western, Judaeo-Christian Civilization, as *equally* representative of viable and in fact real religious beliefs and practices. And we were even more offended to find that our normatively established beliefs may have the same bases as those of the ancient Greeks; and that our "historical" narratives include myths in which the outlines of rituals are imbedded; and, additionally, that the Israelites depicted in the Hebrew Scriptures had religious and social practices that are different from ours. So Professor Oppenheim's chapter has led many of us to think about religion in a way that is certainly different from what those in *Religionsgeschicte* would have us see, insofar as and precisely because it is more in accord with what we want to see. And Professor Reiner's paper today brings us to the same end.

By acknowledging that the Mesopotamian religion(s) of which we are aware are not those of the common man, and perhaps not even those of the aristocrat, who is called a "man" (*awīlum* in Akkadian), which may something about the meaning of the word "man," a topic I shall discuss in another forum, we (re)acknowledge that there may well be a difference between a state religion and a personal religion, each of which is a workable type of religion. And unless something of the "vulgar" culture survives, we cannot determine what were the personal religion or more likely religions practiced in Mesopotamia. But we may say the same of most any ancient society of the Greater Mediterranean world, an area that both academically and at times even geopolitically was treated as including Mesopotamia.

First, we must realize that there are different types of religion in any given society. Unless there is militant opposition to more than one type of religion, these are often co-functional, existing alongside one another. And depending on the nature of the religious practices themselves, co-functional religions may be, but do not have to be, mutually exclusive.

Second, it follows from that category of co-functionality that does not demand mutual exclusivity that the same people could have practiced, and comparative data suggests they did practice, different types of religion concomitantly. So although the possibility exists that even different religions practiced by the same individual were mutually exclusive, as in the case of the twentieth-century Jew or Christian who also practices Satanism, Voodoo, or Wicca, etc., this is not probable. Moreover this exclusivity may itself be unilateral: for example, Judaism and Christianity may forbid the practice of Satanism, Voodoo, or Wicca, but any or all of the latter group may not preclude the practice of Judaism or Christianity.

The fact that traditional practices "die a hard death" clearly affects co-functionality. More often the traditional practices, representative of what has transformed into a subculture, are assimilated and incorporated into the more powerful or main-cultural practice. So for example, the Medieval European Christian peasant went to Mass and practiced other, often non-church-sanctioned rituals and conventions. But he or she envisioned them in light of rather than in opposition to the dominant, that is "Catholic", religion he or she practiced. The same thing is true of the native rituals and conventions that have been incorporated into Roman Catholicism, as attested to by the type of worship represented by that of the "Virgin of Guadeloupe." She is a syncretization of an Indian and a Catholic deity, who was worshiped by the local Indians who were "Christianized" after the Conquistadors took their land. And she has continued to be worshiped by the Hispanics, who come to her shrine as their "native" forebears had done long before the syncretization. The syncretization of types of worship, although not necessarily of objects of worship, is to be seen in various Jewish ritual practices within the self-enclosed, and thereby religiously sheltered, Eastern European world before World War II. Some of these conventions, moreover, are still a part of Hassidic Judaism.

But what is more important concerning Ancient Mesopotamian religions, these syncretisms are found in at least several ancient Greater Mediterranean cultures about which we are knowledgeable, including those of Israel, Judah, Greece, and Rome. In the various Greek civilizations – it would be a mistake to think of one, uniform Greek civilization predicated on a nineteenth-century Germanic sense of what is classical – diverse non-Olympian religious practices are subsumed under the names of Olympian gods. But what little we know of the mystery cults or of everyday piety suggests that the worship of the Olympian gods within their traditional pantheon represents a vastly different type of worship and even of religion. And we cannot say what the common man, if we can even define such a person, practiced, and how that differed from what the aristocrat practiced.

Although we acknowledge our relative ignorance about the non-Olympian religions that nevertheless centered on the Olympian gods, we presume to know something about the worship of the Olympian gods as predicated by their myths, the religiosity of which we deny. But we must not be so sure that we know how the Greeks interpreted the so-called Greek myths *vis-à-vis* the worship of the Olympians within what we consider the established tradition.

The same may well be true of the Romans although their allegedly "sub-cultural," but actually para-cultural, practices are less well known or understood than what little we do know of those of the Greeks. And in Israelite and Judaean writings, Prophetic literature shows how practices pertinent to non-Yahwistic worship were still being syncretized with the Yahwistic as late as the sixth century B.C.E.

In any case, exclusivity of worship insofar as it precludes more than one type of worship is not characteristic of religions that are not monotheistic. Exclusivity generally pertains to who may worship which gods. And in many societies, certain types of worship are exclusively for "natives" or "citizens."

The universal god, who is worshiped by all men, is not a characteristic "type." And we must note here that the precept on which the Judaeo-Christian tradition is based – whereby Yahweh, syncretized with Elohim, is the god of all people – is itself both late and revolutionary. It was brought in with the eighth-century prophets, and was not accepted by the "official" religion of either Israel or Judah at any time in its history, including Josiah's reform. And P and Dtr[1 & 2] do not presume that deity to be god of all even where they, or for that matter, J or E attribute the worship of him to outsiders.

So acceptance of the syncretized monotheistic deity is either something some sectarian groups, but not that represented by P or Dtr[2], first took up during the Babylonian Exile or it is something that developed during the Restoration Era. Hence it is more than likely that there was no conflict between the different types of religions practiced respectively by the same individuals.

Third, we cannot presume that lack of knowledge about personal religion means there was no such thing or that the common man was not concerned with what is ultimate. Rather what we do know about *Religionsgeschichte* in general and about the Greater Mediterranean cultures is that state cults or religions and personal religions, be they cultic or not, co-existed and were co-functional. And where we can ascertain this co-functionality without mutual exclusivity, it is clear that each served a different end, but for the same individual.

So we may hypothesize that even in Mesopotamia, it is likely that all free "citizens," that is those of native stock, took part in the state cult(s), be it actively or passively. We cannot say the same of those who were freed-men since we do not know whether they were considered citizens or even whether there was any consistency in their classification throughout the millennia. And we can say even less about slaves, particularly those who were not from the city or even country in which they lived. Were they required to worship the gods of the state even while retaining their own forms of personal worship? Or were they totally excluded from each type of state worship for fear of pollution, etc.? Mary Douglas's observations about pollution and danger may well be applicable here.

Mesopotamian religion in particular has to be problematic regarding the inclusion of non-native slaves in the worshiping body. It is characteristic of Mesopotamian society throughout the millennia preceding the beginning of the Common Era for men to be thought of as servants or slaves of the gods. This includes kings and common men. In fact it includes all whom we define as human beings. (Do not take it for granted that every society holds to the same, biologically defined categorization of the species.)

Moreover, there existed some sort of pyramidal structure in which the king was the slave of the gods, and then the aristocrats, that is the "men," (the *awīlū*), were the slaves of the king, etc. But they were not categorized as *wardū*, or "slaves" per se. And there are some problems about how the Temple and its "people" fit into this pyramid. Insofar as we can tell, this varied according to the prevailing precepts in different eras. So we have problems distinguishing between the Ensi, the Lugal, or simply the En.

This, however, does not mean that there was no "transition between the religion of the Sumerians and the Semitic Akkadians who followed them in Mesopotamia". But the problem is complicated. Semitic Akkadians may have lived in Mesopotamia as early as the middle fifth millennium B.C.E. And we do not know whether they or the Sumerians, or both or neither, were indigenous to the region. But we cannot say what their religious practices were before their brief hegemony over Mesopotamia toward the end of the third millennium, and their lengthy one that began shortly after the beginning of the second millennium.

The extant, albeit sometimes fragmentary and sometimes relatively complete legal codices do tell us something about the constraints on the actions of various classes of individuals, and more particularly about the punishment for abridgment of those constraints. But when we find a stela in which there is a depiction of a god, as in Hammurapi's codex, then we can see that even the civil law is religious, not secular, and it is tied into the state religion *whether or not the code defines itself as religious*. But despite any pictographic representations on a stela in which it is reproduced, or any statement in the text of the codex, we learn but little about the actual practice of the religion(s) of the greater Mediterranean area in any time in antiquity from the legal codices.

Before beginning to attempt to distinguish between the types of religion and/or religious practices, that is *religio* and *superstitio* respectively, it would be helpful to define the terms being used. "Religion", derived from Latin *religio*, has as its base meaning "scruple" or "a binding back" or "a binding down." On the other hand, "superstition", derived from Latin *superstitio*, has as its base meaning, "what remains" or "what is left over" or "what stands over and above." And it would help if we realized that some of the types of worship that we would call superstition may have been included in the ancient *religiones*, and some that we call religion may have been included in the ancient *superstitiones*. I suggest that these distinctions are more meaningful than that between the king, the temple bureaucrats, the priests, all as one group, and the lesser classes as another group.

Much of what we term religion today would have been classified as *superstitiones* by the Romans and, using the equivalent term in their own language, by most people in antiquity. And what the Romans called *religiones*, we would call cold, hard, unfeeling, and impersonal: hardly religious and far from what we call religion. And *religiones* would have included the work of the diviner, the physician, and even the exorcist, each of whom was, as Reiner notes, dependent on his client for his living. We, however, would be hard put to equate the latter with religion *qua* religion.

Perhaps we may define the ancient interpretation of *religiones* as an external and imposed type of faith, requiring orthopraxy although not necessarily orthodoxy, and *superstitiones* as the practice of a faith that comes from within, requiring neither orthopraxy nor orthodoxy for the entire body of practices. But each category of *superstitiones* would itself demand some type of orthopraxy and orthodoxy.

This however is hard for us to grasp because the private communion with the deity we have come to expect today does not seem to be characteristic of ancient religious practice. And even the communality of the state religion may be seen in the private household, clan, or tribal practices. In fact there are times when it is hard to say when a religion is private, when it is characteristic of clan or tribe, and when it is characteristic of city-state or nation. The boundaries are fine indeed, and they often reflect our modern precept of what a religion must be to be so categorized.

So it is important to realize that the Roman categorization is characteristic of religion and its practice for much of the greater Mediterranean world, including Mesopotamia. And it is representative of religious practice in that area from as far back as we can trace up to the period of the early Roman Empire. Moreover, it is characteristic of the state religion as represented by the Roman Church up to Vatican Two, after which the formal Mass became a personal type of communion between worshiper and worshiped, and the deity became more immanent than transcendent, and so less imminent.

It is also characteristic of many segments of Rabbinic Judaism that excluded a personal encounter. This is not to say that there was not a personal communion between deity and individual, but it was not part of the formal practice of either Judaism or Christianity. In fact, unless some miraculous event can be tied into it, it is what the Romans of classical antiquity would have categorized as *superstitiones*. So the personal communion is relegated to the realm of the individual, be he common man, saint, or martyr, precisely because it is not a formal part of even the modern religious worldview of those whose practices fall into the category of Jewish or Christian orthodoxy.

On the other hand, those of the Protestant sects that are based on the personal encounter between worshiper and worshiped, like those Jewish sects that do likewise, practice a more developed form of religion – developed in the sense of altered and advanced, but temporally, not necessarily for the better. So academicians do not like to acknowledge that much of what we think of as epitomizing "religion" today would have been called *superstitiones* by the Romans. And other people in antiquity would have used an equivalent term had they thought to differentiate at all.

It is ironic then that it is this personal type of interaction with the divine, be he or she defined as wholly other or as merely one who is supra-human, that defines what we think of when we seek to define religion. So from this perspective, but only this one, Otto was correct in his definition of religion; and likewise those who view religion as a dialogue or even a contract between individual men and "god" are also correct.

But when religion is treated as a social contract, or even part of one, as it had been throughout the Greater Mediterranean world, then we are dealing with an official, state type or category of religion. And it does not matter if the state is constituted by a city-state, a nation, or merely a church as defined by Durkheim. (And this includes the so-called "mystery cults" of antiquity, but with the stipulation that these cults also represented personal types of religion as well.) It is the worship by a collective body on behalf of that collectivity rather than by an individual member of that body on his own behalf alone. And it is the collective body that seeks to live forever, with the individual living through it. I'm sorry to startle you by reverting to Animism and Totemism. I do not treat either as a type of "buzz word" for some archaic precept that we have outgrown. Rather, I treat them together as a basic component and possibly unifying component to all religions. But I deal with this very component as a part of, but not a defining factor in, the architectonics of non-primal religions.

Which brings me to the crux of the problem. Our real difficulty is threefold. First, it is a matter of definition: What do we mean by religion? Second, it is a matter of arrogance. We all want *our* version of religion to be defined as the archetypal form of religion even if we do acknowledge that it is not the only real and valid religion. We are looking for what we know, what is meaningful to us. But our society is an "open," not a "closed", one. We do not put the state before the individual, and so our world is taken up with prayer for the individual save in moments of pomp and circumstance or of grave national emergency. But third, and from an academic perspective, it is a matter of academic integrity: we are not willing to use our knowledge of some parts of what is clearly a composite entity to hypothesize the structure of the entirety. That is, we are unwilling to define Mesopotamian religions using the limited data we have about temple buildings, Ziggurats, icons, be they monumental or merely miniature representations on cylinder seals, ritual practices, literary representation of religious stories or the embedding of those stories in literature – which is not one and the same thing, etc. Rather, we analyze each entity as it stands.

And that brings me back to the particular works of Professors Oppenheim (and Reiner) *Ancient Mesopotamia,* and of Professor Jacobsen *The Treasures of Darkness,* and most importantly to Professor Reiner's presentation today. Jacobsen was right in trying to write a chapter treating Mesopotamian religion(s), both from the perspective of the *Religionsgeschichtliche Schule* as well as from a cultural historic standpoint. It does not matter whether we yet have all the data we need. We must make do with what we have, and alter our conclusions as newly uncovered evidence directs. And it does not matter how many times scholars in the future will have to alter our or successors' conclusions. We must dare to generalize. Else we will never have even a limited perception of what the real "shape of the elephant" might be.

Professor Reiner's and Professor Oppenheim's shared belief, one that is accepted by a great many but not all Sumerologists and Assyriologists today, that we cannot write a Mesopotamian religion, is therefore by definition incorrect, both from a *Religionsgeschichte* perspective and a cultural historic standpoint. The state religion really is a religion, and whether we like it or not it is a real religion even when it goes so far as to revert to a denial of deities, and fall back on the primal self-worship inherent in both Animism and Totemism. Notably, it even offers a form of eternal life as I have just suggested, but one that is embodied in the state and its ruler. That is, the state has become what clan or tribe had once been; and Animism together with Totemism must be treated as inherent in its practices until additional data is obtained that demand that we revise this opinion.

Because of the social and presumed geopolitical implications, whereby the well-being of the state and its ruler depends on the correct practices and proper worship on the part of the citizens, it is most likely that the common man, that is the man who was not an *awilum*, was part of the state religion. But in addition, he practiced other co-functional religions, some of which included aspects of personal piety. And since we do not expect the syncretization to reflect both upward and downward religious mobility, the non-state may possible have been totally different from what we predicate as the state practices; but we cannot discount the possibility that the co-functional religious practices were also syncretized to one another. This is at present an unresolvable problem.

What we know from Graeco-Roman religions is that the various gods who seem to have been the "great gods," those of the state, were also those of individuals. But they were worshiped differently by the individuals, frequently having specific roles in the mystery cults that were not characteristic of their "Olympian" character. So they are related to both, as I have just suggested, and therefore that may have served as some type of bridge between the state religion(s) and the personal ones.

And there are indications in various categories of Mesopotamian literature, in which cultic or otherwise religious data are embedded in a literary text, that some sort of mystery cults did exist in Mesopotamia and/or that man did consider the way(s) in which he related to his deities. Likewise we know of specifically religious material such as the Namburbi texts that consist of rituals and of prayers; that may tell us something of personal as well as state piety; the Omen literature to which the Namburbi texts may well be responsive; and Balag Lamentation liturgies, that also tell us something of the state religion and its practices; etc.

We must be wary of drawing conclusions from literature that is literary-based rather than theologically based, when archetypal models are subsumed and can be seen to be part of the literary architectonics. Nevertheless we may presume that at some time, albeit not that of the literature itself, these models were valid for rituals currently in practice. So we may not be able to ascertain the "religious attitudes" of the people we study, precisely because that is subjective. Witness Reiner's citation of Momigliano's statement "Maybe *you* people have myths; we have stories about gods."

Unless its context suggests that he is being facetious, Momigliano should have known better. Myth, from Greek *mythos*, simply means "story." And all people consider their sacred history historical. So these stories about gods are not myths in the early Greek sense, and they are not myths, that is stories in which gods act. Rather what Momigliano calls myths here are myths in the latter Greek sense of being false stories.

Keeping in reserve the usage of the *Religionsgeschichteliche Schule*, I would like to suggest that today, for Western man in general, the belief that our stories about gods are history, but yours are myth, prevails. And we excuse away your worship by suggesting that there is only one true god, namely ours, whom you worship unknowingly under different names and different functions. So unlike the Greeks who paid tribute to the unknown god so as not to slight him, we, following Paul even if we are not Christian, presume that unknown god, whose name or even existence, is unknown to the worshiper who gives him accord, to be our own.

Rather I agree with Father Greeley as quoted by Professor Neusner and Professor Reiner: "Stories", as Reiner notes, "are but one dimension of religious heritages". And Greeley, via Neusner and Reiner, states "Religious heritages constitute storytelling communities...a group of humans who share a common repertory of symbols and a sufficiently common interpretation for these symbols so that it is relatively easy to tell them the story and relatively reasonable to expect that they will 'get it.'" As is well known, these stories alter as the society(ies) for which they are or become pertinent alter. And even written texts are changed, whether because of the alterations accounted for by the concomitant oral traditions, and their presentation by remembrancers, or by design of a redactor.

So we do not find the "truth" about ancient religions depicted in literary or nonliterary texts or on the art, be it glyptic or otherwise. But we can learn something about the religious practices of antiquity: and from Mesopotamia we can study, for example, the Omens, which tell us a great deal about the state religion; the art, which is of major importance in ascertaining how the gods were envisioned and which also helps to support some of the religious interpretations of the texts that in their received form are purely literary; and, we can study the nonliterary writings including the penitential psalms as well as the Wisdom literature.

What do these data tell us about the religions of Mesopotamia? I think that such information can ultimately help us to write a study of Mesopotamian religion, but not of Mesopotamian personal piety. I iterate that these are two different subjects. And so at last, I do agree with Professors Oppenheim, Reiner, and Jacobsen despite the latter's different and sometimes contradictory approach. The "'common man' is an elusive figure. The documentation we have of the ancient civilizations of Mesopotamia is lopsided, as it is in any civilization where literacy was not widespread."

I do not however believe that we can only "deal with an elite". Rather we must deal primarily with the state religion, which seems to pertain to an elite, but most likely was practiced by all whether or not it was believed. And it does not matter whether the common man could enter the temple or had to remain in the courtyard. If he gave no more than lip service to the state religion, which was most likely more concerned with orthopraxy than faith and piety, he participated in it. And finally, we must deal with the paradigms embedded in literature, which did reflect cultic matters although they may not always have been concurrent with the literary presentation itself.

7

Archaeology and the Social Order

James F. Strange
University of South Florida

Archaeology is a systematic retrieval and examination of material remains. It is also a construction of explanations of social change and development; at least it aspires to do so. Archaeology is also the interpretation of material remains with a view to reconstructing societies, their histories, and their relations with other societies. We are concerned here with a narrower aspect of archaeology, and that is how archaeologists deduce social order so that then archaeologists can impart their new found knowledge to practitioners of other disciplines, such as historians.

What kinds of questions typically occupy archaeologists when dealing with religion and the social order in ancient Near Eastern remains? Typically it is *not* the question of social order, rather typically it has been merely the simple identification of cultic remains as cultic. The truth is that religious systems are quite difficult to tease out of the material culture, but that activity cannot even begin until we have identified cultic activity. This is not to say that artifacts or architecture in service to worship or ritual cannot be identified, for indeed they can be.

In fact, here are some indicators of ritual that have been used by archaeologists to interpret the remains of material culture. These are expanded from a list in Renfrew and Bahn 1991 (359f).

Focusing of Attention:

1. Ritual may take place in a spot with special, natural associations (for example, a cave, a grove of trees, a spring, or a mountaintop).

The places appropriate for ritual are defined as so by the society in question; therefore an inspection of the ancient literary record gives a valuable clue where to look first. It is no accident that Israel's temple and the Samaritan place of worship are on mountain tops.

2.   Alternatively, ritual often takes place in a special building set apart for sacred functions (for example, a temple, synagogue, or church). The "setting apart" is often accomplished by building a walled, open space (a sacred enclosure or temenos) around the special building. The setting part may also be in the sense of deliberately using building methods or building decoration that do not appear elsewhere in the society in question.

3.   The structure and equipment used for the ritual may employ attention-focusing devices, reflected in the architecture, special fixtures (for example, altars, benches, hearths), and in the movable equipment (for example, lamps, gongs and bells, ritual vessels, censers, altar cloths, and all the paraphernalia of ritual).

4.   The sacred area is likely to be rich in repeated symbols, sometimes called "redundancy". It is interesting to read the biblical descriptions of the decoration within the first temple and realize how much of that was repeated.

5.   The sacred area may be much larger than expected. That is, the scale does not depend on human measure, but suggests that beings larger than humans inhabit the structure. Doors and ceilings are too high, doors are too wide, columns are oversized, paving slabs are too large, etc.

6.   There may be special provision architecturally for pomp and circumstance as part of worship.

The Boundary Zone Between This World and the Next:

7.   Ritual often involved conspicuous public display and expenditure. This is not only in terms of the raw materials for the ritual building, but also in terms of the skill of the artisans employed to build and finish the structure.

8.   Concepts of purity/impurity may be reflected in the facilities and in the maintenance of the sacred area. For example, one may find pools or basins of water within the sacred precinct or ritual baths beneath the approach steps on the south side of Second Temple Mount.

The Presence of the Deity:

9.   The association with a deity may be reflected in the use of a cult image, or a representation of the deity in abstract form. Since ancient Judaism is understood to be aniconic, archaeologists search for substitute forms, such as a standing stone or stones. These were found in the putative Israelite temple found at ancient Arad in the Negev. In other words, standing stones may be abstract ways to represent God to worshipers.

10.   The ritualistic symbols will often use animal symbolism (of real or mythical animals) with particular animals relating to specific deities or powers. One wonders in this connection what was the function in Solomon's temple of the twelve bronze calves upon which the great bronze sea was set or the cherubim on the ark of the covenant.

11.   The ritualistic symbols may relate to those seen also in funerary ritual. Here we must admit a great dearth of symbolic material in ancient Israel until the fourth century C.E., when we have a veritable explosion of art and symbol.

Participation and Offering:

12.   Worship will involve prayer and special movements – gestures of adoration – and these may be reflected in the art or iconography of decorations. Typically we use ancient art to deduce gesture in worship.

13.   The ritual may employ various devices for inducing religious experience, for example, dance, music, sensory deprivation or over-stimulation, or the infliction of pain or exhaustion.

14.   The sacrifice of animals may be practiced.

15.   Food and drink may be brought and consumed as offerings or burned/poured away.

16.   Other material objects may be brought and offered, so-called votive offerings. The act of offering may entail breakage and hiding or discarding.

17.   Great investment of wealth may be reflected in the equipment used, in the offerings made, or in the effort expended. The wealth may be reflected in the resources used for the equipment, such as silver, gold, or lapis lazuli or in the craftsmanship lavished on the equipment or both.

18.   Great investment of wealth and resources may be reflected in the structure itself and the facilities. The wealth may be reflected in

the building resources (beautiful, rare stones) or in the building workmanship or craftsmanship (beautifully cut, rare stones).

I would like to use these indicators to show how one might interpret a find as an indicator of ritual. In the present instance I refer to the claims of Adam Zertal that he has found the Israelite altar mentioned in Joshua (Zertal 1990).

The structure in question is nearly three meters in height, roughly rectangular, with exterior dimensions of 7.3 x 9.9 m. Its walls are about 1.4 m. thick, which is surprising for a structure this small, unless it once held an upper story. Zertal and his staff first thought that this was a field tower or perhaps even a farmhouse. However, it has no entrance on any of the four sides, which rules out interpretation as a house. On the other hand, it did not serve well as a watchtower, as there are no communication routes in the vicinity. Furthermore, the building exhibited a curious method of construction, one which neither Zertal nor anyone else has explained satisfactorily. Namely, two cross walls divide the structure. The two walls emerge from the two narrow sides and were built in a straight line toward the center, but they do not meet in the center. Furthermore the *corners* of the structure are oriented on true north-south, true east-west. This is most sophisticated, as it takes some careful astronomical observations over time to establish true north.

The fill inside the structure was alternating layers of field stones, earth and ashes. The ash was from burned oaks, which occur naturally in the region. Each layer contained a great deal of Iron IA pottery, or pottery from the very beginning of the Iron Age. A large quantity of animal bones also was found in the layers of soil and ash.

According to the laboratories of the Hebrew University, the bones came from young male bulls, sheep, goats, and fallow deer. Many of the animals had been butchered before burning, and most of the animal bones had been burned in open fires at low temperature (200-600°C).

Further excavation beneath the structure revealed a circle of stones in the exact geometric center of the rectangle of the structure. The circle was 1.95 m. in diameter. The circle was full of a thin, yellowish material, perhaps the remains of something organic, and on top this yellowish layer lay a thin layer of ash and animal bones.

On the southwest side of the structure were two courtyards with a total of seven chalk-lined pits. Each pit was filled *either* with ashes and animal bones *or* pottery vessels in the forms of jars, jugs, juglets, and pyxides. A ramp erected at an angle of 22 degrees leads upward to the structure from between the two courtyards. If the ramp originally gave onto the top of the structure, then its original height was about 3 meters.

The whole of the structure is surrounded by a low wall nearly 0.5 m. high forming a roughly elliptical space enclosing about 3,500 square meters. A gateway through this wall consists of two parallel walls perpendicular to the enclosure wall about 7 m. apart. The gateway leads upward along a carefully paved walkway, also about seven meters wide, equipped with three steps. Within the enclosure Zertal and his workers found caches of pottery vessels, but with no traces of fire or ashes.

What are we to make of this whole installation? Does it conform to the markers of cult mentioned above? The answer is yes. First, it is on a mountain top. Second, the structure is set apart by means of the low wall. Third, an attention-focusing device is used in terms of the ramp. Fourth, there is no repeated symbolism, but the very lack of any symbolism at all is as striking as its presence. Fifth, the structure is built on a grand scale, including the path leading up to the structure. Sixth, the low wall that surrounds the enclosure is not for defense, as it is too flimsy and too low. It seems to have no other function than to mark the space, a prerequisite for marking limits for purposes of distinguishing pure and impure. Seventh, although there is no cult image, there are animal bones in abundance, and always of the same species. It is typical that sacrifice is only of specific animals. (The fallow deer, by the way, are a surprise.) Eighth, the deposits of pottery vessels, always of the same vessels, resemble votive offerings more than anything else. Ninth, although great wealth is not reflected in the workmanship nor in the materials of the structure and its associated enclosure, it does represent a major earth and stone-moving undertaking. Ordinarily such massive expenditures of energy, time, and manpower reflect either religious motives or royal patronage or both.

I am aware that there is controversy in interpreting this structure (Shanks and Cole 1990: 94-122). An Israeli archaeologist has insisted in print that the whole is for grain threshing. Another interprets the structure as a watchtower. But the clincher for me is actually simply the find of alternating layers of soil, ash mixed with animal bones, and field stone inside the structure. Zertal points out that the bronze altar of Exodus 27:8 was hollow, and we also know that often Greek altars were filled with alternating layers of stone and earth. I think we have a much better than even chance that this is indeed the altar of Joshua 8:31ff.

I leave this controversy aside to call your attention to a simple fact of the matter, and that is that many of the characteristics of cult also can be found in royal architecture. Of course this is no accident, for the language of kingship is used for God over and over in the Hebrew Scriptures, and this language is adopted in the New Testament.

My second example is also taken from archaeology in Israel. In this case I am speaking of the identification of the Hellenistic Jewish temple

at Beer Sheba: In the course of the third century B.C.E. a temple was built
at Beer Sheba, presumably for worship of a mixed population of minor
deities. Images of the Egyptian deities Bes, Horus, Neith, and Serapis
were found within the sanctuary with the Hellenistic deities Demeter
and Persephone along with the Semitic deity Astarte. A dolphin figurine
may have represented the Nabatean deity Delphinios (thirteen Nabatean
coins were also found in the temple). The building measured about 13 by
25.5 m., with an open courtyard taking up most of the interior space,
about 10 by 18 meters. The building was oriented on the summer
solstice, or about north 50 degrees east. This sanctuary was destroyed no
later than 126 B.C.E. according to its excavators, probably by John
Hyrcanus I. The temple was then re-established, presumably for
Yahwistic worship. What is the evidence for this radical re-use of the
temple? In the interests of the new worship a new floor was laid down
in the central courtyard covering over all evidences of the earlier
worship. A stone altar was established in the courtyard measuring the
traditional 5 by 5 cubits or 2.25 by 2.25 m. (Exodus 27:1ff.). With the
renovation of the courtyard came renovation of the combined sanctuary
and holy of holies, which may have resembled that of the earlier temple
at nearby Arad. This temple continued in use until the intervention of
Rome in the Negev about 63 or 62 B.C.E. (Derfler 1993).

Please note that in this instance only the barest inferences about
religion have appeared. Certainly nothing about religion and society or
the interface of the religious systems that belong to the temple with the
social systems of the city of Beer Sheba in the period of the building and
use of the temple. I would call this an archaeology in a classical mode, or
archaeology as cataloguing of material remains, not archaeology as I
have been discussing it.

That is, what is absent here is an understanding of religion as that
system that forms society by generating and preserving values, ethics,
and morality. On the other hand what is also missing is an explicit
understanding that society forms religion as a social system by
sanctioning religious values, enforcing the claims of religion, and
providing the societal structures for these two functions.

What are some of the conditions that archaeologists expect to pertain
before formulating their theories of society of Ancient Israel? First, in
order to reconstruct the social order with any degree of accuracy in the
ancient Near East, it is necessary to have at hand great quantities of
interpreted archaeological data of the most diverse kind. We must see
complete reports from dozens of tombs, many villages, towns, and cities,
farmsteads, and much detail from public space and even private spaces
in homes and farms. The greater the amount of archaeological detail

from a given society, the greater the possibility of reconstructing the social order.

Second, it is necessary to understand that archaeology is a search for ordered or organized distributions of archaeological observations. The choice of such abstract language is deliberate. It is simply not the case that archaeology is the science or art of digging up interesting things. Such an approach may be antiquarianism at best, but it is no longer archaeology. Instead, archaeologists hunger and thirst for distribution patterns and for strong correlations of one distribution pattern with another, for these are the clues to the system of social organization that belongs to each society. It is never enough to dig up and display a few beautiful and proud items, as attractive as they might be. Without the detection of order, of pattern, of repetition in the organization of the material record, there will be no reconstruction of the social order.

Third, I am mainly speaking of times and periods when writing systems were fully developed. From the adoption of a form of the ancient Phoenician alphabet on the part of the Canaanites and of ancient Israel to the period when Greek became triumphant, an enormous Israelite literature developed in Hebrew, Aramaic, and Greek, only part of which has survived. Archaeologists and other scholars of the ancient Near East therefore use written documents as a major source for developing hypotheses about the types of social systems in ancient Israel, about the structures of the society, and about other issues, such as the role of religion and values in Israelite society. As literacy spread in ancient Israel other written sources become available to the archaeologist such as inscriptions on various media and on coins after the striking of coins began in Persian Yehud in the fourth century B.C.E.

But these reconstructions from documents will remain untested hypotheses without endless checking against the archaeological record. It is simply not enough to examine documents and inscriptions, even in appropriate, scholarly detail, with a view to deducing the social system in which they were produced. Rather, it is equally important to check the alleged facts read in the documents against our accumulated observations of archaeological data. It is also necessary to reason about the documents in their ancient societal, that is, material contexts. In other words, the documents are read with one eye on the archaeology, and the archaeology is studied with one eye on ancient documents. In practice this means that neither documents nor archaeological data stand in isolation. Each provides important insights to interpret the other, and both form the whole of the evidence at hand for reconstructions of society.

Furthermore, we freely borrow theories of society from the social historians, the sociologists, and from the anthropologists. Therefore there are many kinds of archaeologists, just as there are many kinds of historians, anthropologists, sociologists, and the like. Archaeology is not all one thing, as much as someone may like to believe so. Furthermore the various archaeologists practice differing hermeneutics of material culture, so that unanimity is an elusive goal.

Yet there are a few invariants in terms of ancient societies in general and ancient Israel in particular that we know we will find. This pattern was first articulated for us by Lewis Binford, but it has been followed in many texts since then based on Old World archaeology (Binford 1972).

1) Someone exploits the natural environment directly. In other words, we expect to find farmers, miners, fishermen, hunters, artisans, and others who pursue natural resources. Art may also appear at this level of society if it is understood as use of the natural environment. At this level of exploitation of the natural environment we find traces of social organization appropriate to that level. In other words, human beings peruse exploitation of the environment in an organized fashion, when viewed as a society. Some interpreters have insisted that such organization is more like hunter-gatherer bands than it is like bureaucracy. In any case, farmers, miners, and fishermen are often responsible to the next level of society.

2) Someone keeps track of the social order and spends more time interacting with other human beings than with the natural environment. These are bureaucrats in service of the state, clerks of the court, judges, bailiffs, tax collectors, bookkeepers, bankers, business people, architects, and the like. But this category also includes kings and queens, members of the court, generals and career military personnel. Strangely enough it also includes bandits, robbers, and rebels, who earn their keep robbing from the other two groups and from one another.

Their elaborately organized niche in society at this level consists primarily in dealing with one another and with those who exploit the environment. Such bureaucrats and representatives of government are often concentrated in cities or towns, and often they contribute to the power structure as well as to the bureaucracy that government always develops. Bureaucrats are often beholden to the next level of society.

3) Someone keeps track of the divine order inhabited by God and his angels, gods and goddesses, Satan or the satan, demons, principalities and powers, and so forth. We understand these to be pre-eminently priests, but they may also be prophets, cult personnel, diviners, seers, or even sorcerers and witches. In view of the latter, may I remind you that those who see to the divine order are not necessarily socially acceptable. Into this category we might put all the practitioners of alternative religious systems from the point of view of ancient Israel. Often chiefs, kings, and queens are expected to do their part in maintaining order in

the spiritual domain, that is, they double as priests and either prosper for it or suffer for it.

Archaeology reveals the social order in the following domains:

Priests interact with the divine order: gods and goddesses, values, religion, and ethics;

bureaucrats interact with citizens: societal structures;

farmers, miners, hunters, artisans exploit the natural environment.

So what does archaeology tell us about society? Let us begin with some assumptions that will lead us to examine some archaeological data in a specific way.

I. The Power Landscape

In our analysis of archaeological data I have insisted that we seek patterns in the data above all. I did not make explicit that these are spatial patterns first and foremost, and then these are patterns in time second. I think most scholars understand the concept of time as a variable, but may not be so conversant with space as a variable.

We know that societies do not distribute themselves evenly over the natural landscape. All things being equal, it is possible to analyze the spatial distribution of isolated farmsteads, villages, towns, and cities to deduce how the net has developed. Inequities in spatial distribution imply that some force or forces are at work to introduce inequities into the net. The most common such variable is political power, and imbalance is of the essence of power relationships. Furthermore power is normally concentrated into the hands of a few in the ancient world, and these few ordinarily live in cities and towns of some size. Therefore for the past twenty years archaeologists in many parts of the globe have understood spatial distributions of human settlements on the natural landscape to be an expression of political power, or, to use the term of the social archaeologists, polity (Renfrew 1984: 30-77).

We note that human beings organize themselves typically in modular units, and the larger the unit the greater the power it exerts over the landscape (Renfrew 1984: 94-101). This has given rise to a whole analysis of political space called central place theory, though it has many forms. In concrete terms, we expect villages to be within less than one-half day's walk of the central market town. This allows villagers time to get up early, travel to market, sell and buy, then return home that night before dark. There has been no formal application of central place theory to ancient Israel, to my knowledge, except to the place of Jerusalem as a presumed central place. The scholar in question could not figure how topography skewed the presentation of the data. Suffice to say that it is possible to develop a simple algebraic equation that predicts the distance of a village from its central market, if one knows the difference in elevation and therefore knows how effort increases with travel to the central market and return. It is also possible to arrange sites from a specific region in a histogram by their size. Then one examines the histogram to look for "breaks" in the curve, or sudden changes in size. The assumption is that smaller sites are dependencies on the larger sites, which will be laid out naturally in a more or less hexagonal net.

We must modify this exercise with what we know from ancient literature. We know from Josephus that Acco, Sepphoris, and Tiberias were important central places, no matter what their size within their walls. We also have enough information in ancient written sources that we can deduce a testable model of polity distribution on the landscape and use our archaeological data to test the model.

To our dismay we find that almost no artifacts serve as markers of human administrative units. That is, it may be quite reasonable to use the data of Pliny, Josephus, Strabo, and others to deduce the administrative system of ancient Judea. Furthermore, the administrative units so deduced may cohere with the system deduced from estimating site size and placing in a hierarchy. But the postulated boundaries between units are permeable. Artifacts, people, and ideas flow through them with regional and long distance trade.

So far the most helpful artifact to use to deduce polity or administrative units, at least in the Roman period, has been the Roman milestone. When these have been found in place we have an excellent means of demarcating the lines of power over the landscape. Interestingly enough, such milestones provide a map of the power landscape that coheres rather well with that drawn more theoretically from the clues in ancient written sources.

II. Agriculture

It is probably safe to say that agriculture formed the fundamental fact of life in antiquity, as one may wish to argue today (Borowski 1987). Whatever one might contend about the role of agriculture in contemporary society, it is clear that we are bound to infer agricultural systems which ancient Israel relied upon for the foundation of its life. Whatever historical period we may examine in whichever part of the world we choose, agriculture is the base of the society. Without manipulation of the environment to produce food, raw materials for family and village consumption, finished materials or agricultural products for trade, and subsistence itself, there will be no society.

But societies do not manage their agricultural resources at random. Rather, a complex set of trade and distribution patterns evolve early in the history of Israel to ensure that not only do most of the inhabitants of a region get enough to eat, but that they are also clothed and housed. This is not necessarily a conscious decision on the part of a monarch, it is simply the system that human beings hit upon in order to meet basic needs.

Furthermore, the tax and trade systems that Israel developed also functioned in such a way that there will always be an imbalance in availability of goods, particularly in terms of elite hoarding so as to accumulate wealth. Other factors that also created an imbalance in the availability of agricultural produce were the vagaries of market economies and natural disasters such as calamities of weather, tremors in the earth's crust, or swarms of insects. Therefore the task of the archaeologist is to deduce the patterns of production and management of agricultural produce where possible. Even if the whole pattern is not amenable to reconstruction, enough of its outline must be sketched from the available literary and archaeological data so as to fill out at least partially our knowledge of the social structures of ancient Israel from period to period.

But what are the social structures we can infer related to agriculture? Let us pick the period of the kingship of Herod the Great, 37 B.C.E. to about 4 B.C.E. (Fiensy 1991). Archaeological excavation and survey of the areas of Galilee, Samaria, and Judea during this period reveal a simple pattern. The land appears to have been organized into large estates, farming villages, and isolated farms. The literary evidence for large estates is detailed, persuasive, and well known, and includes allusions to royal estates in the gospels, specifically in the stories that include absentee landlords (Herz 1928; Hengel 1968). I will only mention here the edict of the Roman Senate of 44 B.C.E. preserved in *Antiquities* 14.207:

> It is also the pleasure of the senate, that as to the villages which are in the great plain, which Hyrcanus and his forefathers formerly possessed, Hyrcanus and the Jews have them, with the same privileges with which they formerly had them also....

Albrecht Alt is the one who traced the history of the Jezreel Valley or Jezreel Plain as it is sometimes called as a royal estate probably formed in the Seleucid period (Alt 1959: 384-395). The famous Greek inscription from Kibbutz Hefzibah near Beth Shean, which contains six letters from Antiochus III to Ptolemy, Strategos of the district of Beth Shean and of Jericho and two letters from Ptolemy, tends to confirm this picture (Landau 1966). This correspondence must date between 201-195 B.C.E. and demonstrates that certain villages of the Jezreel Plain belong to

Ptolemy the Strategos as his property. These had been ceded to him from the royal estates of Antiochus III. These in turn were part of the royal estates of the Seleucids and Ptolemies, which estates may in fact have been royal lands as early as the kings of Israel. Archaeological survey in the region has identified seven Hellenistic villages scattered throughout the eastern end of the valley which apparently formed at least part of this governor's estate (Isaac and Roll 1982).

Thus we can find evidence for large estates, and some of them are likely royal estates. Since these estates are large enough to contain whole villages, it is reasonable to infer that the residents of the villages worked the estates. Either these were day laborers paid by the absentee landlord, or they were roughly the equivalent of serfs, paid from the land to work on the land.

Other large estates in the Herodian period are to be found in the Bet Netopha valley and the Beth Ha-Kerem valley in Lower Galilee, around the oasis of Jericho in its great plain, around Azotus (that is, Roman Ashdod) and Askelon near Gaza, and in Gaza itself. Dar's survey of Samaria and Judea revealed nearly 1,000 field towers built so similarly that they imply central administration. Dar interprets these as evidence for large estates (Dar 1986). Of course large estates can be inferred from literary references elsewhere. Excavation and survey in these territories confirm that farming villages are to be found within the estates, but no market city in the sense of a market patronized by independent farmers and freeholders. This allows is to deduce what we probably have already hypothesized from the ancient literature, namely, that the estates supported an elite, and that the estates included a system of villages in private ownership to support the elite population.

Excavation and survey within the confines of ancient Galilee, Samaria, Peraea, and Judea encounter, besides estates, small farms ranging in size from one to fifteen acres (Golomb and Kedar 1971) with an average of about seven acres. For example, Dar's survey of Khirbet Buraq, a farming village in Samaria, showed that about 70 households worked 445 acres, which averages about six acres per household (Dar 1986). According to some calculations, this amount of land could only feed a family of six for four months (Fiensy 1991: 95). Thus the freeholders or landed peasants, who were themselves responsible for their harvest, had to supplement their subsistence by hunting and gathering (Freyne 1980). But it was also necessary to increase their income by working as artisans, by hiring out as a day-laborers, or by turning to banditry. All three of these alternatives are well attested in the ancient literature (Horsley and Hanson 1985; Wolf 1966).

It is scarcely appreciated by modern city dwellers how precarious life on the land can be. Small freeholders, who in some cases, at least on the average, cannot feed their families for the entire year, always stand in danger of losing their crops or their land or both. A small freeholder who loses his land to increasing debt, successive drought, or to other natural disaster is most likely to turn into a day-laborer, according to recent scholarship, though he also has other choices as I mentioned earlier (Fiensy 1991: 85-90).

So far, however, we encounter a limitation in current archaeological methods and theories. We are at a loss how to detect day-laborers – or slaves – in the archaeological record. Of course it is possible that we have been seeing their evidences for years, but not recognizing them. I am thinking of the traces of "squatters" in and among ruins after earthquakes as reported here and there by expedition staffs. The first interpretation one might think of is that the "squatters" were the owners of the devastated buildings, but it is also possible that they are the sought-for day-laborers. We will leave this door open for further discussion.

Therefore, from our survey of Herodian period agriculture, it is possible to deduce that a large population of farmers bound to large estates supported a much smaller population of aristocrats and royalty. It is also possible to infer that a large population of isolated farmers and farming villages worked the land either as small freeholders or as something approaching the medieval serf. That is, the population distribution was skewed in the direction of what collectively today we might call "peasants", though that term has social implications that may not pertain.

What was said above about agricultural products is also true of water, one of the most basic needs in any society, except that water is not traded at a distance until the invention of aqueducts in the Hellenistic period. But people in the societies we study do not merely drink water or use it to grow their crops. Our ancient forebears also gathered water in complex schemes, stored it above ground and under the ground in elaborate systems, and then handed the commodity around, as it were, in equally complex systems. The archaeologist, then, spends sufficient field time and energy to detect Israel's sources of water, methods of storage, and if possible, methods of allocating water to the population at large.

May I register an aside that we notice that ancient aqueducts generally do not cross administrative borders. In other words an aqueduct is wholly the product of a specific administrative unit, and as such it remains within the territory of that unit. This is true even for Jerusalem, which brought its water overland in two aqueducts which originate at Bethlehem, hardly five Roman miles to the south. Bethlehem lies within the administrative territory of Jerusalem.

It has been noted before that plaster-lined cisterns appear to proliferate in the Iron Age, or about the time of the early history of Israel (Aharoni 1978, 1982: 161f.). Such plaster-lined cisterns cut into the bedrock near fields and orchards allow for an intensive agriculture in the dry season, which is sometimes nine months of the year. Although most of these appear to be family cisterns, that is, there is not a standardization of form that would imply a centrally managed resource, there is a record in the Bible of royal patronage at a time of higher rainfall in which Uzziah had cisterns cut in the wilderness (2 Chronicles 26:10). Sure enough, isolated farmsteads of this period are also well known in the wilderness of Judea and in the Negev that rely upon field cisterns for agriculture in areas that had not hitherto supported such exploitation of the natural environment. That is, a government decision, in this case by a monarch, resulted in extension of existing cistern systems so as to extend agriculture and presumably multiply wealth.

Other natural resources Israel exploited in a more or less organized fashion included animal and plant life, clays for pottery, natural earths and ochres for paint, and stone for architecture. One gathered plant life (such as reeds for mats or lumber for furniture), hunted game for food, mined the earth for clays for the potter, and quarried stone for the mason. The exploitation of these resources was surely managed by ancient Israel with complex societal structures which leave their imprint in the archaeological record.

For example, it is possible to deduce in one region of ancient Palestine in the Persian and Hellenistic periods, that is, from 537 to 200 B.C.E., that the city called today by the name of its mound, Tell el-Hesi, exploited the region as a wheat growing area (Blakely and Bennet 1992). The evidence for this are the many grain pits found always at about the same level in the tell or city mound. These pits are sophisticated, as they are clay-lined, they can be sealed, and a small fire was built in them before they were used (a small deposit of ash and charcoal was always found in the bottom). Such careful preparation of storage pits allowed for long-term storage of the major crop, namely, wheat. (The wheat is detectable in the form of charred whole grains.)

Storage is a means society uses to tide the community over when drought occurs. (We forget in a mechanized society that three years of unbroken drought in the ancient world could depopulate an entire region.) However storage is another way to deal with a relatively efficient agriculture which produces a surplus, that is, wealth. Social systems develop to manage the wealth, and the artifacts follow (storage pits). Therefore, in a real sense, the Persian storage pits of Tell el-Hesi are the imprint of the social structures of the ancient town in which someone agreed to store grain in more or less standard pits. Since standardization is a pattern, we are in a position to deduce that the pits are most likely an artifact of social organization, not of simple happenstance or of merely copying a successful innovation.

Another example of archaeological detection of exploitation of the natural environment which has consequences for deducing the polity of the village in question is in the Bet Netopha Valley north of Nazareth. There in 1988 the University of South Florida Excavations at Sepphoris carried out preliminary surveys in sufficient detail to identify a rather extensive Roman and Byzantine period ruin as ancient Shikhin, mentioned in ancient Jewish sources many times as a pottery-making village. The find of ancient pottery wasters in a modern olive orchard seemed to clinch the definition. Then it became possible to explain a huge pit which was still to be seen in the maps of the area that dated as late as 1924. This was surely the clay pit from mining the clay directly from which the famous pots of Shikhin were fired. Here an entire village was devoted to pottery manufacture, which meant that some sub-set of the villagers were engaged in clay mining.

2. Trade Systems

One of the prime tasks of archaeology is to deduce trade routes and trade systems, sometimes called "action at a distance." From where did Israel get certain commodities at certain times? Earlier in this century one deduced trade routes by simply assigning a given artifact that appeared to be out of place, such as a Mycenaean vessel, to its original find spot by seeking parallels. That is, pots made in the same way as the pot tentatively identified as "Mycenaean" were comparative data for deducing the beginning of a trade route, whether by land or by sea. Now we are more sophisticated, using neutron activation analysis to deduce the origins of the clay in the vessel in question. To our surprise as archaeologists, some of the vessels historically identified as Mycenaean IIIb turned out to be of local manufacture in Israel. Now we have changed the data, for it is still the case that we recognize that this pot is made according to the conventions of an alien culture, namely, the Mycenaeans, but the pot itself is not alien. Is therefore the *potter* alien? This surprising turn of events has overturned some earlier interpretations and disclosed some new patterns of society wherein artisans appear to move, or their craft moves, and not necessarily the pot.

Long-range trade is one of the easiest systems to deduce from the archaeological record. As you may know, we have one well publicized Late Bronze shipwreck that contained a cargo from various port cities in the Eastern Mediterranean (Bass, Pulak, Collon & Weinstein 1989). That is, Israel emerged into a world already well traced with international trade routes. This fact is also reflected in ancient economic documents from a variety of cultures ranging from Ebla in Syria to Mari in Mesopotamia and to Egypt in the Amarna period.

What is not always so easy to do is to distinguish the movement of peoples with their material culture from the movement of material culture by trade. I have already alluded to one such surprise above. A further complicating factor is the movement of ideas in the form of artifact manufacture. That is, as innovations in artifact manufacture spread, it is often the case that the first imitators of the innovation in manufacture also imitate the form in which it comes. This principal has been invoked to explain carved ivories with Egyptian motifs found in Israelite contexts.

Regional trade is in some ways more interesting and more complicated than long-range trade. We can deduce the movement of goods and materials over regions, given enough archaeological data. We can also deduce a rough regionalism in pottery manufacture north and south, which should not be a surprise, as we know from Israel's own court history in the Bible that two kingdoms developed where once there was one. Any isolation at all, so the cultural historians tell us, results in regional vocabularies and usages in language and regional forms and even habits of manufacture in daily goods.

For most of this century we have relied upon the services of the natural scientists to help us identify the provenance of manufacture for many items of metal and clay. The movement of an item, such as a specific kind of cooking pot or a specific type of glass vessel, can be tracked by identifying trace elements that provide a signature for its place of manufacture. Thus David Adan-Bayewitz has identified the signature of the pottery manufactured at Kefar Hanania in the Galilee and used that signature to trace the movement of this commodity throughout the Galilee and into the Golan (Adan-Bayewitz 1993). But this movement of the commodity through two and one-half centuries of the Roman period amounts to tracing a local trade network, a social system used in the movement of goods and services, as well as ideas and news, throughout this region. Such a pattern is more characteristic of the movement of peddlers than it is of family movement of the commodity on market days (Adan Bayewitz 1985).

Many other issues in the social order come under the aegis of archaeology and the interpretation of archaeological remains. These include city-town-village relationships, issues in cityscape planning, architectural choices and the public use of space. Archaeology is also called in to aid in interpretation of villages as economic centers or of village specialization in industry, agriculture, and trade (Strange, Groh, and Longstaff, 1994).

Regionalism is also an electric issue in archaeological interpretation today. "Regionalism" means that we can identify consistent use and exploitation of the environment in some distinguishable part of the land, or a similar consistency in landscape, or planning the environment. Some would insist that political choices and ethnic settlement are reflected in the archaeological record and regional communication systems.

Other social issues that stand to gain from archaeological analysis are intra-city relations, ethnic distributions within cities, family structure, endogamous vs. exogamous marriage, age distributions, recreation, gender roles, the specialization of artisans in quarters of a city, and the development of public space.

However, all of this is still in a very undeveloped stage in ancient Near Eastern archaeology at any period. It will be some time before we see the kind of detail which I have proposed here actually appear in the analysis of ancient Israel.

172   Religion and the Social Order

Bibliography

Adan-Bayewitz, D.

1985 The Itinerant Peddler in Roman Palestine. *Jews in Economic Life*, N. Gross, editor. Jerusalem.

1993 *Common Pottery in Roman Galilee: A Study of Local Trade.* Bar-Ilan Studies in Near Eastern languages and Culture. Ramat-Gan: Bar-Ilan University Press.

Aharoni, Y.

1978 *The Archaeology of the Land of Israel.* Philadelphia: Westminster. Translated by A.F. Rainey 1982.

Alt, A.

1959 *Kleine Schriften zur Geschichte des Volkes Israel.* Vol. 3. Munich: C.H. Beck Verlag.

Bass, G.F., Pulak, C., Collon, D., and Weinstein, J.

1989 The Bronze Age Shipwreck at Ulu Burun: 1986 Campaign. *American Journal of Archaeology* 93: 1-29.

Binford, L.R.

1972 *An Archaeological Perspective.* Studies in Archaeology. New York: Seminar Press.

Blakely, J.A. and Bennett, W.J.

1992 Tell el-Hesi: The Persian Period. The Tell el-Hesi Publications, vol. 3. Winona Lake: Eisenbrauns.

Borowski, O.

1987 *Agriculture in Iron Age Israel.* Winona Lake: Eisenbrauns.

Dar, S.

1986 *Landscape and Pattern: An archaeological survey of Samaria 800 B.C.E. - 636 C.E.* Oxford: BAR.

Derfler, S.

1993 *The Hellenistic Temple at Tel Beersheva.* Lewiston: Edwen Mellen Press.

Fiensy, D.A.

1991 *Social History of Palestine in the Herodian Period: The Land is Mine.* Studies in the Bible and Early Christianity 20. Lewiston: Edwin Mellen Press.

Freyne, S.

1980 *Galilee from Alexander to Hadrian.* Wilmington: Michael Glazier.

Hengel, M.

1968 Das Gleichnis von den Weingärtnern Mc 12:1-12 im Licht der Zenonpapyri and der rabbinischen Gleichnisse, *ZNW* 59: 1-39.

Herz, J.

1928 Großgrundbesitz in Palästina im Zeitalter Jesu, *Palästina Jahrbuch* 24: 98-113.

Horsley, R.A. and Hanson, J.S.

1985 *Bandits, Prophets, and Messiahs: Popular Movements in the Time of Jesus.* Minneapolis: Winston.

Isaac, B. and Roll, I.

1982 *Roman Roads in Judea: The Legio-Scythopolis Road.* Oxford: BAR.

Golomb, B. and Kedar, Y.

1971 Ancient Agriculture in the Galilee Mountains, *Israel Exploration Journal* 21: 136-140.

Landau, Y.H.

1966 A Greek Inscription Found Near Hefzibah, *Israel Exploration Journal* 16: 54-70.

Renfrew, C.

1984 *Approaches to Social Archaeology.* Cambridge: Harvard University Press.

Renfrew, C. and Bahn, P.

1991 *Archaeology: Theories, Methods, and Practice.* New York: Thames & Hudson.

Shanks, H. and Cole, D.

1990 *Archaeology and the Bible: The Best of BAR.* Washington, D.C.: Biblical Archaeology Society.

Strange, J.F., Groh, D.E., and Longstaff, T.R.W.

1994 University of South Florida Excavations at Sepphoris: The Location and Identification of Shikhin, Part 1. *Israel Exploration Journal* 43.

Wolf, E.R.

    1966   *Peasants.* Foundations of Modern Anthropoloogy. Englewood
           Cliffs: Prentice Hall.

Zertal, A.

    1990   Has Joshua's Altar been found on Mt. Ebal?, pp. 76-93 in
           Shanks and Cole.

VI.

SOCIAL SCIENCE'S PERSPECTIVE ON THE STUDY OF RELIGION AND SOCIETY BY HISTORIANS OF RELIGION

8

A View from the Fringe:
A Survey Researcher's Perspective
on the Study of Religion

Andrew Greeley
University of Chicago
University of Arizona

Introduction

My purpose in this paper is to discuss some of the lessons I have learned about the study of religion from my work as a collector of data and a builder of mathematical models which may be useful in fashioning a response to the question of whether religious comparisons may be made between the past and the present.

- All generalizations are false.
- All models are deceptive.
- All theories are wrong.
- Evolutionary change in human behavior doesn't happen. Or if it does we are yet incapable of understanding it.
- What most people know to be true, often isn't.
- The good old days never happened.
- When trying to account for changes, do not overlook technological development (the birth control pill), disease, weather, and shifts in commerce.
- There are no trends.
- Human nature hasn't changed all that much.

I began to think on this subject when two colleagues made observations about the study of religion. The Rabbi (as Jack Neusner is called in my office, as if there were no other!) suggested that I might cast this paper in the form of a survey research questionnaire that I might be able to administer with the help of a time machine at some previous point in human history. We could ask them, I said, remembering his work on the decorations in the synagogues from the Second Temple era about whether they believed there should be no sculpture in a synagogue. Indeed we could choose maybe a dozen talmudic regulations and ask the Jews of the Second Temple era whether they obeyed them. My guess based on my premise that human nature hasn't changed much is that some would be very observant, some very unobservant, and a large number in between, sometimes observant and sometimes not. In this respect they would not be much different from contemporary Jews – or Catholics or Protestants either for that matter.

The second conversation was with by birthday mate, Martin Marty. He mentioned that his *projet* had brought him up to the nineteen thirties and he was learning to use the SPSS data analysis system where he could look at the survey data which was available from that and all subsequent years.

I pondered the serious constraints under which those who work from texts and ruins must work – and of course the brilliance of their reconstructions. Suppose at some time in the future historians should try to study Catholicism in the second half of this century from published material in the Catholic press and from the ruins of Catholic churches built in the last thirty years. I think they would be forced to conclude that Catholics had enthusiastically accepted the Pope's teaching on birth control and at the same time were drifting close to Protestantism because they were breaking from the architectural traditions of their past and building houses of worship which would delight low-church Protestants.

Both conclusions would be erroneous. Most Catholics in fact see nothing wrong with birth control and, while many Catholic churches are being built without saints and angels, without a corpus on the crucifix, without holy water fonts and votive candles, it does not follow that the average Catholic likes such churches. Quite the contrary, they dislike them intensely; but they didn't get to vote.

Reifying the Model

The most serious temptation I see in the study of religion – indeed in all social science – is to reify models. Like Middle Ages-Renaissance-Modern. Or Rural-Urban. Or Ego-Id-Superego. Or Working Class-Capitalist. Or Secularization. Or Baby Boomers. Or my friend Hans

Küng's Paradigm Change. Or Analogical and Dialectical Imaginations. I submit that in the real world such realities simply do not exist. They are of the same order of fiction as Jung's collective unconscious. We all must use models to arrange our data so we can make sense out of them. But we must also understand that a model is heuristic, designed for exploration of reality and indeed to provide a temporary, provisional, tentative and inadequate description of reality. When we slip into the temptation of believing that the model represents the way things really are and begin to force the data to fit the model, we are using reality (fact, if you will) to prove assumptions (fiction, if you will).

When the survey researcher hears a generalization – say, Robert Bellah's fiction that Americans are more individualistic and less concerned about civic problems than they were in the time of Alexis deTocquiville – the survey person immediately want to know (after they have laughed if they realize what a monumentally chaotic and selfish era the time of the Second Great Awakening really was) how many Americans now compared to how many Americans then are concerned with the problems of the *civis* and how do you define individualism and civic concern and how do you measure such variables. Surely the assertion can't be that all Americans were oriented towards the community then and that all Americans are individualistic now. Obviously some Americans in both eras were individualists and some were not. What changes have there been in the distributions of Americans on the axis of civic concern in the last century and a half?

We demand this information not merely because our evidence shows major increases in civic concern and responsibility in the last twenty years (arguably the nation has too much of such concern instead of not enough), but because we know that the nature of human nature is such that some people will be responsible and some less than totally responsible and some irresponsible and want to know how, in Bellah's alleged change, these proportions have rearranged themselves. But one looks in vain at the explication of such models for the word "some." Rather they are presented as describing a total change in American culture and behavior.

I am not persuaded that Bellah's model is of much use even for heuristic purposes. But if it was presented as something that has been subject to verification and falsification, has been refined by nuance and qualification, and is offered only as a tentative description of reality which is subject to latter refinement, change and even abandonment, then I might be inclined to say that it could be a useful model for further investigation. In fact, Bellah presents it to us as the Truth. No model is ever Truth, in great part because there always will be some in any population who don't fit the model. For a serious scholar it is the deviant cases, those who don't fit the model, who are interesting and a challenge to the model itself.

Most Poles did not protect Jews from Nazis. But some did. Who were they? The research literature, as I understand it, suggests that they were disproportionately devout Catholics who were intellectually independent from the Church institution. Not everyone in this category actually protected Jews, but people in the category were more likely to do so – another imperfect model – than other Poles. Now that, I submit, is a very interesting finding, and one that knocks most theories of the sociology of religion into a cocked hat.

It is often said, to cite another example, that the Aztecs believed in human sacrifice. Certainly there is ample reason to conclude that this belief was widespread in the priestly caste and the nobility. The rest of the people? They appeared to have come to the ceremonies in large numbers (as the Romans came to the Coliseum). But did they believe that the gods demanded such rituals? Did any of them feel sympathy for the victims? I would not be prepared to bet against it.

Or again we know that the peasants in the Middle Ages were heavily involved in magic and superstition, from the beginning, as documented by Irene Flint, to the end, as reported by David Gentilecore in his study of the documents of the Roman Inquisition (which was relatively fair and benign with such matters and let most offenders off lightly). But how many actually practiced magic or engaged in superstitious practices? We simply don't know. Some, including clergy, surely did. Others apparently did not. And among those who didn't engage in it, how many nonetheless believed in it and how many did not? If one constructs a continuum from no-belief and no-practice of magic to both belief and practice, how would the peasants in the heel of the Italian boot distribute themselves? One would be ill advised to bet against a fairly even distribution.

Nor has magic disappeared from the world, even the North Atlantic world. In a recent study of the International Social Survey Program it was found that more than thirty-five percent of the people in Great Britain and Germany believed in some form or the other of magic. Is it as important to "moderns" as to "medieval?" Perhaps not and then again perhaps. Religion exists because humans need reassurance. Magic exists because sometimes they need (or feel they need) absolute reassurance. Medicine and improved public health has diminished quantitatively the number of things about which we seriously have to worry (no more bubonic plague, it would seem) but there remain plenty of uncertainties in life for which some kinds of humans will need absolute reassurance.

Lenin said that religion was cheap vodka. But there seem to be times when many people need a drink of vodka, cheap or not.

Evolutionary Models

The most dangerous models are those which purport to measure evolutionary social change, an inevitable and irresistible social process which the researcher has discovered. Thus many European Catholic sociologists (not including the Irish by the way) believe that a trend towards "secularization" – a decline of religion – is at work, for which there can be no effective responses by the Churches. This is the result, they tell us, of other developments such as "rationalization, modernization, urbanization, individualization, and industrialization." In each of these alleged social change models one detects the ghosts of Joachim of Flora, Auguste Compte, and Charles Darwin – to say nothing of Georg Whilhelm Freiderich Hegel. When I am presented by this argument and the scraps of data which are supposed to support it, I am struck by four facts:

1. Generally the scholars have taken a small correlation and converted it into a powerful social reality whose importance and meaning far exceeds the correlation and whose predictive power for the future is dubious indeed. (I will turn later to "trend" analysis.)

2. Those scholars who have carefully applied the model of "Modernization" in Asian and African countries are extremely dubious about its predictive power. When western industrial culture encounters indigenous cultures, some phenomena change in one direction, some in another direction, and yet others do not change at all. Industry can function moderately well in India and Iran, for example (to say nothing of Japan) without the collapse of the indigenous culture or the indigenous religion.

3. There is no evidence at all that biological evolution provides a useful model for social change and surely no mechanism which explains how social evolution works (like natural selection in Darwin's theory).

4. Human behavior and human culture is obviously too complex and too intricate to be explained by any one-directional, one-dimensional model.

I often wonder why intelligent and able men succumb to this "Hegelian" temptation. I suppose that they are trapped by the lure of the single all-powerful explanation, our version of the "unified field" theory for which cosmologists search as they try to reduce electromagnetism and gravity to a single common force. I am unable to say whether this latter search admits of success. Perhaps it does. But human behavior is far more complicated and far more unpredictable than the results of the "Big Bang" which involve only matter and energy and which can be predicted precisely when we know the elements of the equation. Humans are different.

Humans are Different

At a conference in Washington, a participant expressed the usual liberal lament that it was a disgrace that we could put a man on the moon and yet not educate a child. Jack Feldman, a sometime colleague at NORC, replied that it was an easy matter to put someone on the moon. All that was needed was lifting power and logistics, both of which we were capable of providing. To educate a human child required knowledge of how children learn and of how the schools can overcome the influence of family and neighborhood. Despite our all research, we were relatively ignorant on both subjects.

A unified field model of human behavior, especially of human religious behavior, seems improbable in the near future. Or ever. A paradigm from the physical sciences (of the sort we imagine, often wrongly, that the physicists possess) is inappropriate for studying humankind. Perhaps the most diligent attempt to produce a single field model in history was that of the late Arnold Toynbee. As I understand the common opinion on Toynbee today, the model is not accepted, in great part because it omits much of the relevant data – and is far too simple to fit the complexities of the changes which historians have studied. Those of us who do survey research are painfully aware of the problem. Our models, if we are very fortunate, may explain as much as twenty percent of the variance in the dependent variable. It's difficult to deceive yourself that this makes the model a powerful social evolutionary mechanism. Nonetheless, some of us, I admit, still deceive themselves.

We can predict the outcome of an election with reasonable accuracy if we do the right kind of survey the day before an election. We are even more successful with our exit polls, again if we do them right. However, it is much more difficult to explain the voting. The commentaries you hear on election night or read the next morning in the *New York Times* are merely descriptions of correlations. As in "white Catholics returned to their Democratic voting patterns because they were concerned about the economy." Some white Catholics did indeed return, but by no means all of them. And some of the returnees did indeed have worries about the economy, but not all of them. Using all the correlates they can tease out of the data, election analysts must leave much of the variance in voting patterns unexplained. This is not to say that they have failed. Indeed because of their work we understand much more about the dynamics of American voting behavior than we used to comprehend. The models of the election analysts are ingenious and sophisticated and extremely useful. But they present at best an incomplete approximation of reality.

I contend that in what one might broadly call the Social Sciences those are the best models we are going to have, even for present behavior, to say nothing of past behavior. They are useful heuristic tools, which is about all any model of human behavior can be. Some are more useful than others. To speak of models developed by two friends: I would not find Küng's "modern/post-modern" very useful even if he had not reified it. I don't believe in "post-modernism" save as a rarified fashion in obscure literary analysis and philosophical and theological happy talk. On the other hand, I find Tracy's model of "analogical/dialectical" imaginations (which he has not reified) extremely useful. I disagree completely, however, with Tracy's apparent assumption that "post-modernism" exists in the real world – though it may have a limited existence in the culture that theologians inhabit and may even be a useful, though limited, model for discussion in that culture.

Models, to repeat my theme, are useful, sometimes very useful; moreover they are absolutely necessary for human knowledge. They are stories about reality and we humans basically understand reality through stories (as Roger Shenk has argued) but they are not True in any sense of that word. They are at best provisional pictures in which some truth might be contained with perhaps hints of further truth which we might be able to explore.

It might seem unnecessary to say these things. They seem to me to be self-evident. Nevertheless many scholars slip into the error of reifying models, so it is indeed necessary to repeat that models are at best useful and are never True.

There are no Trends

Perhaps the most common abuse of the social evolutionary model is in the study of "trends," which absorbs many scholars and fascinates to the point of obsession the media. As a general rule of thumb never believe any story in the media about trends. Thus there is the Doonesbury strip in which Michael wants to engage in sex with Joanie. That latter worthy replies that research has shown that young married people make love after a couple of years of marriage only because they want children. She and Michael don't want children yet, so why make love? Michael objects and she dismisses him with the decisive comment,

"It's a *proven* trend." Whereupon, Michael goes of to the refrigerator to find some meat so he can resist the "ecological" trend.

The most fundamental weakness of this kind of "trend" analysis is that it assumes that the dynamics built into the trend are permanent and irresistible. The divorce rate increased sharply in America in the late 1970s and the early 1980s. Robert Michael, then the director of NORC, asked what were the reasons for the change. He thought that greater occupational opportunities for women and control over their fertility with the Pill might account for the change. (It is much easier to account for change in behavior than it is for the behavior itself.) Perhaps the increase was the result of women getting out of marriages in which formerly they were trapped. He constructed a big econometric model with these assumptions built in and predicted a leveling of the divorce curve in the in the middle 1980s. Unfortunately the article was rejected by several journals (perhaps because it offended then fashionable feminist ideologies) and when it finally appeared the curves had already fit his projections.

You will hear repeatedly from educators and clergypersons and media commentators that one out of two marriages will end in divorce – some hysterical clergypersons have recently upped the projection to two out of three. In fact two-thirds of Americans have never divorced their first spouse (though they may have been separated by death). In the case of cohorts in their thirties and forties the proportion of those never divorced slips into the middle fifties. Demographers make their projection that half of marriages will end in divorce, to oversimplify the matter somewhat, by assuming that the increase in the present level of divorces for these two cohorts will continue at the same rate as did that of the earlier cohorts and when they moved into their fifties. There is nothing wrong with this assumption as such. One could make another assumption, however: the younger cohorts got their divorces out of the way earlier and their rates after fifty will be less than their predecessors in the life cycle. Whether this will actually happen remains to be seen. However, if there is one thing we know from past demographic projections (such as the confident projection of the late 1930s of permanent population decline) that people often change their attitudes and behaviors and thus make hash out of projections.

The difficulty with the projection in the hands of those who are not demographers is that it becomes deterministic. "Your marriage has a one out two chance of ending in divorce" is said as though there is an inexorable law dooming the young couple to that fate. A trend is no more reality than any other model, especially because behavior and values can change.

Much less is the increase in divorce proof of a "decline in the family." Those who leave a marriage now often do so for the same reasons that their predecessors would have had in earlier years if they had the economic freedom to so. The departure of couples from marriage says nothing about the condition of the family life of those who remain – though this self-evident fact does not seemed to be perceived by many who propose to comment on the contemporary American family. (My own research on this subject shows that those who remain in a marriage when they are free to leave are quite happy indeed). I know of one couple who, incredibly, decided to end their marriage because, while they were quite happy in it, they believed, because of the trends, they would have to end it eventually and they wanted to end it while they were still in love and hence have a pleasant divorce. Joanie and Michael in the real world!

A similar trend analysis which obsesses the media and some sociologists is their picture of religion in the United States since 1945. In this paradigm there was a major religious revival after the war as part of the increased domestication of the 1950s. Then there was a falling off in religion during the troublesome 1960s and selfish 1970s and another revival in the late 1980s perhaps because of economic hard times. This is all rubbish.

Research that I have done on the polls about religion since the late 1930s shows that American religious behavior has changed hardly at all in the last half century with two exceptions:

1. Catholic Church attendance declined from 1968 to 1975 as a result of the birth control encyclical, but has since stabilized, though Catholic financial contributions have not.

2. The proportion of the population with no religious affiliation increased from 3 percent to 7 percent in the late 1970s and early 1980s because of the postponement of the age of marriage and the increased proportion of those who do not marry. Both phenomena have leveled off.

Some sociologists (mostly those who had never been faced with data) reacted to my analysis by creating the "resacralization" phenomena. Americans had been secularized but now they were resacralizing themselves. There is no evidence for this assumption, but that doesn't bother these folk. One of them even wrote that in fact what was happening was that "secularization" and "sacralization" were canceling each other out exactly so there was only the illusion of continuity. Think about that one for awhile.

Once a month or so, a media person, digging deeply for a story, calls me to ask if I have any evidence for a "return to religion of baby-boomers." Each time I have say, as carefully and as clearly as I can, that religious behavior in America (as in most countries) follows a life-cycle curve, beginning in the middle teens, bottoming out in the middle twenties and then increasing at the time of marriage so that by the time a person is in the forties, he/she is likely to be as devout as his/her parents were. The illusion of the "great return" is caused by the fact that those who are currently returning (a little later because the age of marriage is a little later) are members of the largest cohorts in American history. So, is there a "return?" Yes, there is. Is it a " revival?" No, it is not. Rather it is merely the working out of the life-cycle curve on a very large cohort. They rarely understand what I'm talking about.

The baby boomer model is especially stupid because it combines those who matured during the Vietnam war and those who matured after it – two very different generational experiences. It is not as stupid, however, as the superstition that eras in human history nicely fit into decades, something so absurd that you'd think even a journalist would have perceived that it is wrong. There were surely a depression between 1929 and 1945 and a surge of prosperity and confidence between 1945 and 1963. Whether historians of the future will consider these to be two different periods in twentieth-century American history remains to be seen. We are too close to the years after the Kennedy death to make any judgment about them. The instant history of the media is dangerously shallow.

The "trend" and "evolutionary" models are deeply imbedded in the perceptive mechanisms of many half-educated Americans (like Joanie and Michael). While the media are partially responsible for this phenomena, some scholars are also responsible because they have contributed to it, largely because they have succumbed to the Hegelian temptation of reifying the model.

Humans Are Human

Finally, I suggest that in our research on religion we try to avoid the assumption that we are all that different from our human predecessors. We live longer; are better educated; have more leisure time, more physical comfort, and better health; and understand more about how the world works than they did. It does not follow, once you take those variables into account, that we are either wiser or more moral than they were. Rudolph Bultmann, the German theologian, once argued that when humans can control electricity with a light switch, lightening is no longer a source of awe for us as it was for them. Yet most people still find thunder storms impressive and scary, despite their light switches. Barbara Tuchman in her book about the thirteenth century *A Distant Drum* treats the men and women of that era with absolute contempt as though they were so utterly different from and inferior to us that they were scarcely human. This comes with singularly ill grace from a product of the present century which murdered countless numbers of people in wars and massacres – each death being a terrible tragedy for the person and those relatives who remained alive.

As I read Emmanuel Leroy Ladurie's book on Montaillou I had the exact opposite impression. Despite the author's intrusion of his (very French) theory of *"Mentalitè,"* I was struck about how very like us those men and women were. I have the same impression when I read the love poetry, the letters, the wills and burial memorials from previous eras. I am skeptical that human nature has changed very much since Neolithic times. We can do more than our Neolithic ancestors and have more power than they did but it remains uncertain that we are in any important ways fundamentally different from them. We live, we worry, we love, we die. Some people in both eras are more moral (by the moral standards of the time) and some less moral. In both eras where was generosity and selfishness, brutality and gentleness, honesty and corruption.

Levi-Bruhl's "primitive mind" has been sent to the ash can in which it belongs, but there is still a powerful temptation to assume, perhaps implicitly or even unconsciously, that we are somehow superior to them. I think that such an assumption needs to be proven in every case when we are studying an "ancient people." Otherwise we are guilty of temporal ethnocentrism, an offense which has yet to become politically incorrect.

Conclusions

Models then are essential but dangerous. We must use them in our scholarship. But in our use of them we must be modest, humble, cautious, careful, and restrained. We must resist the Hegelian temptation to see disembodied forces or energies or "trends." We must also resist the Toynbee temptation to find the Grand Explanation for everything. Such things are not real. Models are only tools, useful but fallible for exploring that which is real – that which will always be more complicated than our explanations, but also more challenging.

Is it possible then to make comparisons between the religious past and the religious present? I think the answer is that of course it is so long as:

1.   We assume at the beginning that except for health, longevity, literacy and leisure time, they are more like us than different from us.

2.   We realize that the ordinary and the common people are not perfectly reflected in the elites about whom we have more data.

3.   We are cautious in the application of our theories and models

All of which may merely be a way of urging that we all use the indispensable qualifying word: Maybe!

Interpreting Religion Sociologically: A Response to Andrew Greeley's "A View from the Fringe"

Danny L. Jorgensen, Ph.D.
University of South Florida

Little that Professor Greeley says about religion, viewed from the perspective of the methodology of survey research and efforts to form sociological generalizations, troubles me. Unlike the mass media and other lay consumers, some public opinion pollsters, and many sociologists who employ survey research technology, he appreciates the limits of this social scientific methodology. He understands what can and cannot be said based on survey research data.

Throughout his career Greeley has used survey research carefully and skillfully to inform sociological generalizations about religion, particularly religion in America and especially Catholicism. His 1972 work, *The Denominational Society: A Sociological Approach to Religion in America*, although seldom recognized as such, is one of the most important and insightful statements on the subject published over the last thirty years.[1] Although it mostly has been neglected, I have found

---

[1]Andrew M. Greeley, *The Denominational Society: A Sociological Approach to Religion in America* (Glenview, IL, 1972: Scott, Foresman).

189

Greeley's *The Sociology of the Paranormal* immensely useful in my research on esoteric religions and occultism in America.[2]

These and many of his other scholarly works serve as shining examples of how survey research may be used to illuminate our understanding of religion. His critique of this technology provides a healthy reminder of its limitations for scholars of religion who too often forget them, and it performs an invaluable service for the uninitiated, especially the media and other concerned consumers of this information. In spite of his modesty, Dr. Greeley's scholarly work also is illustrative of the sociological imagination and it represents an impressive body of theorizing about religion. I am troubled, however, by some of what is hinted at and implied without being developed explicitly in Professor Greeley's essay. Several fundamental theoretical and methodological concerns need clarification. I focus on and unpack two perplexing issues. First, what is the nature of human nature, and why is it permitted to do so much explanatory work? Second, what is the "truth," and how is it to be determined? In selecting out these two areas of concern, I am not being arbitrary. Understanding Professor Greeley's essay hinges on unraveling where he stands on these crucial questions.

Human nature does a lot of explanatory work in Professor Greeley's essay. Although he does not tell us what it entails, he repeatedly notes that it has not changed. He is certain that, because human nature has not changed, particular contentions about religious trends are false. His heavy reliance on the nature of human nature to account for the social phenomenon of religion is very problematic. If I understand him, Dr. Greeley thinks that by their very nature, human beings somehow need religious meanings. What exactly, I wonder, is this need? Is it an intellectual or cognitive need for some explanation of the unknown? Is it an emotional need for reassurance, a shield against fear, particularly of death? Is it a product of some combination of both cognitive and emotional needs? Or, is it the result of some other image of the composition of the human animal?

Professor Greeley's dependence on the nature of human nature as a central theoretical assumption or premise is similar to the basic point of departure of many nineteenth-century scholars of religion, particularly the early sociologists and anthropologists of religion.[3] These thinkers, almost without exception, were social evolutionists, and many of them

---

[2]Andrew M. Greeley, *The Sociology of the Paranormal* (Beverly Hills, CA, 1975: Sage). See, for example, Danny L. Jorgensen, *The Esoteric Scene, Cultic Milieu, and Occult Tarot* (New York, 1992: Garland).
[3]See, for example, E.E. Evans-Pritchard, *Theories of Primitive Religion* (New York, 1990: Oxford University Press).

also were biological determinists. Greeley, however, does not subscribe to determinism, biological or sociological, and he is highly critical of evolutionary accounts of religion. He – like Emile Durkheim and Max Weber, the two most influential founders of a modern sociology of religion – seems to think that the distinguishing characteristic of the religious life is an ideational component, especially the ways in which religious symbols define what is humanly meaningful about the world around us and, thereby, how they inform what we do and how we interact with the world of everyday life.[4] Like Weber, but unlike Durkheim, Greeley also envisions religious conduct and interaction in a non-deterministic way as involving some degree of human freedom and choice. Consistent with the predominant tendency of American sociological theory, his view of social reality (social ontology) is characterized by a certain voluntaristic nominalism.[5]

In all of these ways Professor Greeley's image of religion is similar to the sociological theory of religion proposed by Peter Berger.[6] Unlike Greeley, however, Berger does not permit the nature of human nature to remain an unexamined premise. He takes great pains to show – in what I think is a rather convincing fashion – how the biologically *indeterminate* nature of human nature, our lack of a biologically encoded program and our biological openness and flexibility, require the social construction of reality. The social construction of religious meanings consequently is necessary because of what the nature of human nature *does not* provide, not because religion is a need that derives from human nature.

Greeley and Berger both advance sociological theories of religion; that is, interpretations of some socially fashioned religious reality. Yet, all interpretations are not equal – contrary to the radical epistemological relativism currently fashionable among some post-modernists – even if they all ultimately fail to grasp truthfully social reality in all of its complexity. What makes one theory preferable to another? In this instance it is the difference between accounting for a central premise versus leaving it hanging, unexamined, in the air. If the nature of human nature is to carry such a heavy load, how it relates to the social construction of religious meanings and their consequences for human

---

[4]See Max Weber (translated by Ephraim Fischoff and introduced by Talcott Parsons), *The Sociology of Religion* (Boston, 1964: Beacon, first published in 1922); and Emile Durkheim (translated by Joseph Ward Swain), *The Elementary Forms of the Religious Life* (New York, 1965: The Free Press, copyright 1915).
[5]See, for example, Roscoe C. Hinkle, *Founding Theory of American Sociology 1881-1915* (Boston: Routledge and Kegan Paul, 1980), and *Developments in American Sociological Theory, 1915-1950* (Albany, 1994: SUNY Press).
[6]Peter L. Berger, *The Sacred Canopy: Elements of a Sociological Theory of Religion* (New York, 1967: Doubleday).

action needs clarification. Human nature, whatever it may be, probably is constant. What is important about religion, that its meanings are socially fashioned and highly consequential for human action, is highly variable temporally and cross-culturally.

Professor Greeley's stance on the matter of truth (epistemology or sociological epistemology) and its connections to sociological methodology and theorizing is even more confusing. He begins, in the very first sentence of the essay, with the observation that the lessons to be discussed derive from his "work as a collector of data and builder of mathematical models." Within sociology, collecting facts by way of survey research and constructing mathematical models are regarded generally as distinguishing features of some form of methodological positivism or neo-positivism. Greeley, however, clearly rejects many of the key features of sociological positivism. He observes, for instance, that: "All generalizations are false" and "all theories are wrong." Even more explicitly, he says that "a paradigm from the physical sciences...is inappropriate for studying humankind."

Is Greeley, therefore, taking an anti-positivistic stance? Perhaps he is advocating some form of methodological humanism? Maybe he has converted to one of the newer, stylish versions of post-modernism and a radically relativistic epistemology? Certain of his comments – the idea that models or theories simply are stories about reality, provisional pictures, but not otherwise true – might suggest this conclusion. Yet I do not think that Andrew Greeley is a humanist, methodological or otherwise. Nor do I think that he has joined the ranks of the post-modernists. His repeated references to matters of truth and reality, and especially their opposition to falsehood and fiction, indicate very powerfully that he thinks there are ways of determining the difference. That he practices survey research and regards its products as data (facts) leads to the conclusion that Greeley is some sort of empiricist. He thinks, in other words, that claims to truth, at least those deriving from interviews with representative, probability samples of the American population, can be adjudicated by sensory observation. This view, furthermore, presumes a correspondent theory of truth. There is some reality out there, Greeley repeatedly implies, that may be captured, even if imperfectly, by social scientific concepts.

This, then, I submit, is how we are to hear and understand Professor Greeley's essay. As a practitioner of survey research, he thinks that questionnaires and interviews, a form of sensory observation or empiricism, produce social facts (data). He thinks that it is possible to form generalizations based on these facts. Presumably, when they are collected in conjunction with some scientifically defensible sampling procedure (such as probability theory, for instance), these facts may be generalized cautiously to the population they are thought to represent, such as the American people. The resulting generalizations, furthermore, then may be arranged into larger patterns forming propositions or equations of mathematical models.

Although Greeley does not claim that theories of social and religious behavior are anything more than approximations of certain facets of social reality, they do have some truth value. They, in other words, provide interpretations (or explanations?) of religion, even though "all generalizations are false," "all models are deceptive," and "all theories are wrong." Based on what Professor Greeley says and does, I feel safe in noting that he thinks that this form of methodology and theorizing is *more adequate* than some of the other options. Perhaps it is less false, less deceptive, and less wrong? I think he overstates the case against sociological theorizing; but, all kidding aside, I, too, share his concerns and reservations about the reification of theoretical constructs and models.

Evidence supporting this reading is abundant throughout Professor Greeley's essay. Robert Bellah's "fiction" is rebuked with facts derived from survey research supported by a parenthetical statement about American history. Similarly, contentions about the Nazis and ethnic Christians, the Aztecs, magic, secularization, Catholic voting patterns, as well as social and demographic trends, all are disputed from the standpoint of survey research data or logic. I find no difficulty with any of these arguments, so far as they go: The counter evidence he presents seriously challenges certain popular contentions. I am perplexed, however, by what is left unsaid and where all of this leaves us in terms of our efforts to make scholarly sense out of religion.

I am much less certain than Professor Greeley about what we take to be social facts and how we arrive at them. All of our "facts," it seems to me, depend on human judgments and evaluations. Like generalizations, models, and theories, they ultimately are based on human *interpretations* that rest on certain assumptions; they are no better or worse than what we presume about social reality; and, like all symbols, they are constructs or fictions that we employ to make sense of reality. Unfortunately, perhaps, whatever reality is, *we know it only through socially constructed symbols and their meanings.* I, therefore, find no reason to grant the "facts" of survey research an ontological status superior to other social scientific or scholarly methods and procedures for fact finding.

Gathering facts through survey research requires us, for example, to assume that we know what questions are relevant to respondents and the responses or range of responses that meaningfully reflect what they think, feel, and do. We must assume that they all hear the same thing in our questions and mean the same thing by their responses. We assume that they respond to us truthfully or as truthfully as is humanly possible. Since we rarely have an opportunity to verify the relationship between their attitudes (what they feel and say) and what they actually do in particular situations, we also assume that they do what they say. Perhaps obviously, some of these assumptions hold all of the time, some of them hold true some of the time, and some hold true none of the time. In short, then, the procedures whereby survey researchers construe what is and is not a social fact depends on these assumptions.

The assumptions and results are different when I collect them by participating while I observe religionists, or when I base them on bits and pieces of historical evidence.[7] The procedures also differ when scholars of religion construe the facts based on the systematic examination of texts or other artifacts. Although they differ, I find no reason to presume that the facts collected in these ways are inferior to those gathered by survey research. Depending on the intellectual problem or question at hand, the facts produced by one method or another may be more or less suited to addressing and resolving the matter.

The facts of survey research suffer from all of the usual problems of any scholarly effort to ascertain the truth. Just as experimental research designs are superior to other methods for definitively identifying casual relationships among social variables, survey research methods are invaluable for ascertaining the public's opinion at a particular moment or moments in time. There is no better way of getting a snapshot of where particular categories and collectivities of people stand on matters of relevance to religion.

Professor Greeley's essay serves us well by pointing out many of the pitfalls of efforts to interpret these and other facts and arrange them in terms of some sort of coherent picture that tells us about religion in the world today. While the facts of survey research are extremely useful for the purposes indicated, like all facts they, too, have serious limitations. The most interesting sociological questions about religion, those involving what it means to people and how it influences their actions, are just beginning to emerge once we have sketched out the basic parameters of public opinion with survey research.

Why Professor Greeley thinks it is fruitful to arrange the facts of survey research in the form of mathematical models is not obvious. By his own admission, these types of models explain very little. I detect a certain contradiction: Mathematical models typically presuppose that human interaction is causally determined, but Greeley assumes that it is guided by human intentions and choices among alternatives. The

---

[7]See, for example, Danny L. Jorgensen, *Participant Observation: A Methodology for Human Studies* (Newbury Park, CA, 1989: Sage).

problems I note are cumulative. Professor Greeley thinks that human nature is constant and that it somehow explains religion. What is significant about religion, however, is that people act intentionally on the basis of socially constructed meanings. He thinks that all theories are fictions but reality exists out there, it may be captured and measured by strict sensory observation, facts collected by survey research are somehow superior to those gathered by other means, and they can be arranged coherently in mathematical models in spite of human intentionality. Is this what Professor Greeley means to indicate by the essay's title, "A View from the Fringe?"

In spite of these apparent contradictions as well as his modesty and caution, Professor Greeley's hard-headed use of public opinion information contributes significantly to our thinking about religion. Even more importantly, his willingness to generalize from the data and theorize about religion challenges all of us to think more deeply and rigorously. In all of these ways, Professor Greeley's scholarship represents a far-reaching and lasting contribution to an understanding of religion and society.

VII.

UNCONVENTIONAL EVIDENCE PERTAINING TO TIMES PAST AND ITS LESSONS FOR CONTEMPORARY SENSIBILITY

9

Why Are Mythologists Political Reactionaries? An Investigation of C.G. Jung, Mircea Eliade, and Joseph Campbell

Robert S. Ellwood
University of Southern California

The question, "What kinds of lessons does history teach?" can be nearly equated with the question, "What kinds of lessons do historians teach?" For history is pre-eminently a human science. Its subject matter is human beings, not the natural world save as it impacts the lives of humans. Its investigators are human beings, and as such inevitably inhabitors of a matrix of time, place, and culture. Its audience is also human beings who inevitably hear and read the historians within their own topical, temporal, and cultural matrices, often more or less the same as those of their favorite historians.

To say this is not to adopt an extreme historicism about history. It is well known, of course, that all history entails interpretation, if only in the matter of the selection of data as significant, and that the interpretation may be unconscious and unintentional as well as otherwise. Yet it is, perhaps paradoxically, also the case that history, perhaps even more than other social sciences, sees itself as transcendent over the particularities of its own cultural matrix, able to relativize *it* and interpret *it* by telling where it came from, how it compares with other times and places, and to suggest that it, like all other moments in the stream of human time, is ephemeral. In this way many historians – and even more, one is tempted to say, many earnest but naive lay consumers of history – would like to imply that "history" as an objective reality teaches lessons independent of the historian, and which stand over against the society, and in judgment of it.

Even those lessons, however, may be taught in a way which is not, in fact, independent of the society. The historian's well-meaning judgments on his or her time and place may reflect less the view of eternity than a perspective from within the tensions and cleavages of one's specific society. It may offer only judgments and "lessons" that, though put in the grammar of transcendent history, really use only the vocabulary of options and opinions readily available in that society.

This paper will endeavor to show that this was, in fact, the case with three historians – if one may use the term broadly enough to include mythologists – who set the world of ancient myth over against the troubled world of the mid-twentieth century to critique its spiritual emptiness. Their judgments were often acute, yet the language and reactionary terms in which they were expressed undoubtedly reflected less archaic realities than an intricate interplay between that material and the historians' own times and places – with which they were profoundly engaged. The modern world within which they lived, and which dominated the academy and the psychotherapeutic professions with which they were intimate, had effectively pre-empted the future. It was expected to be only more science, more therapy, more democracy, in a word, more "progress" as they understood it. Radical dissent from modernism's values, critiques of what was perceived to be its destructive influence on the lives of millions, disdain even of the therapeutic language of modernism in favor of other tongues like those of myth or religion, could then only be expressed in a vocabulary that sounded reactionary though it was meant to be radical, and individualistic when it was meant to point toward the healing of society. Unfortunately other meanings and moods were in fact latent in that language, like those of mid-century fascism, another nostrum for the ills of modernity. This brought the mythologists much criticism, some probably deserved and some not. In any event, their case is an interesting study of the advantages and perils awaiting the historian as transcendent social critic.

The three men named in the title of this paper, C.G. Jung, Mircea Eliade, and Joseph Campbell, undoubtedly are the persons most responsible for the fresh mid-twentieth century blossoming of interest in myth. This interest was moreover often associated with profound belief that somehow a recovery of the meaning enigmatically embedded in ancient mythologies could do much to alleviate the deep wounds and dysfunctionings of the times in both individual and collective psyches. Through their mythological prescriptions for the ills of their times these three did much to foster belief in the meaning of myth. Largely because of that conviction and its powerful resonance in mid-century, they acquired large and devoted followings.

At the same time Jung, Eliade, and Campbell, at least at times in their careers, embraced political positions or the sort commonly categorized as conservative or reactionary, and all three have been accused of anti-semitism and sympathy for fascism. This paper will briefly examine these perceptions, and will then endeavor to interpret the stances on myth and politics of the three scholars in light of their intellectual and cultural worlds and the tensions between it and their archaic subject matter.

First, however, a discussion of terms may be in order. All the major terms in the title question are, I am aware, loaded and provocative. Some will no doubt protest that these writers were not really mythologists (or folklorists) in a strict academic sense. They did little field work, it will be said, or serious textual and philological work on myth; rather, depending largely the labors of others, they employed myth – sometimes selectively and cavalierly – in the service of other agenda: promoting a school of analytic psychology, establishing a history of religion academic discipline, addressing the spiritual problems of the day. It will be pointed out that there are other "working" mythologists, including some now active in the scholarly world, who undoubtedly do not share the politics of Jung, Eliade, or Campbell. I take the point, but will have to ask you for the moment to accept the term mythologist on the grounds of their intense interest in myth and their avid concern for promoting awareness of myth.

Then there is the term "reactionary." I debated in my mind for a long time over the correct word to use here. None, in fact, seemed exactly right. Despite the charges, and a few incriminating passages in their voluminous writings, I do not think the terms "fascist" or "antisemitic" are fair or accurate as primary categorizations in light of the total corpus of these individuals. I thought of "conservative," but like its antonym "liberal" its meaning is often slippery, more rhetorical than precise, and moreover has somewhat different connotations in Europe and America. Furthermore, the surface meaning of just keeping things as they are hardly does justice to the radical overtones, as over against their contemporary world, of some of the visions involved. Adriana Berger, in calling Eliade a "radical traditionalist," caught something of that flavor.

"Reactionary" is also not quite right, if it implies merely a Colonel Blimp sort of yearning for days that are no more, or a Bourbon-like passion to recover lost aristocratic privileges, but it was better than any other label I could think of. For all three men did in fact want to return to pasts they deemed preferable to their present. The difference is that for them reaction was an urgently felt ideological and even spiritual cause, which would bring them no economic or social gain, and indeed much obloquy in some quarters, but which they felt entailed a message the world desperately had to hear. The past they evoked was no subject of mere nostalgia, much less of material benefit, but a time when values and spirituality now almost forgotten reigned. The loss of that kind of a past, well fused by mythology, was memorably outlined by Campbell:

> The rise and fall of civilization in the long, broad course of history can be seen to have been largely a function of the integrity and cogency of the supporting canons of myth. For not authority but aspiration is the motivater, builder, and transformer of civilization. A mythological canon is an organization of symbols, ineffable in import, by which the energies of aspiration are evoked and gathered toward a focus. The message leaps from heart to heart by way of the brain, and where the brain is unpersuaded the message cannot pass. The life is untouched. For those in whom a local mythology still works, there is an experience both of accord with the social order and of harmony with the universe. For those, however, in whom the authorized signs no longer work – or, if working, produce deviant effects – there follows inevitably a sense both of dissociation from the local social nexus and of quest, within and without, for life which the brain will take to be for 'meaning.' Coerced to the social pattern, the individual can only harden to some figure of living death; and if any considerable number of the members of a civilization are in this predicament, a point of no return will have been passed.[1]

Those (for the mythologist) still living and workable pasts were in fact twofold in each case. On the one hand, there was the undated primordial golden age when myths were strong and human life meaningful under its aegis; on the other hand, there was a more immediate secondary silver age within the last few hundred years, more fallen but also perhaps more accessible, for which they pined: Jung for a medieval harmony of symbol and life before it was fractured by the triple evils of the Reformation, the Enlightenment, and the Industrial Revolution; Eliade for the silver years of Romania's nineteenth-century cultural renaissance; Campbell for an idealized early America of moral virtue and sturdy individualism. To put it another way, all admired the primitive, believing that, largely through the power of myth and ritual, primal humanity was better integrated spiritually and cosmically than moderns, and they also held that enough recent examples obtain to

---

[1]Joseph Campbell, *Creative Mythology: The Masks of God* (New York, 1968: Viking), pp. 5-6.

suggest that primal integration can be recovered at least in part, though perhaps only on an individual basis.

Now let us look at the political views of the three mythologists, beginning with Carl Jung. I realize that this is hotly disputed terrain. Nonetheless a few observations must be made. In the case of Jung, key terms are "collective unconscious" and "psychic epidemic." By collective unconscious Jung means mental contents shared with others, either the entire human race or a subdivision of it, such as a culture or nationality. Being unconscious, this collectivity obviously does not include a people's articulated beliefs, ideas, or vocabularies, but rather points to the preconscious mental energies which activate them. Being preconscious, they can express themselves only in camouflage, usually through emotions bearing symbolic archetypal forms: a culture's particular versions of the Father, the Mother, the Hero, the Shadow.

In a traditional society, these images are best found in its religious or folkloric myths and symbols. In a well-integrated culture, like those of primal humanity, or indeed (in Europe) of humanity up through the Middle Ages, the archetypes – including the Shadow, representing evil – are well balanced-off in its mythic scenarios and its symbolic symmetries, creating what Jung called a mandala. These symbols then provided for the orderly release of the irrational energies that welled up from the unconscious's fountains of the deep, and so kept society on an even keel. For Jung was quite convinced that rationality is a precious but precarious epiphenomenon on the surface of human life, that our real drives are irrational and far more powerful than reason.

Jung therefore had little faith in the modern notions of development and progress, for he did not think that such superficial changes in the conditions of human life could really change the equation between the rational and irrational, so heavily skewed toward the latter. Indeed, he perceived the situation as really getting worse, for what modern developments from the Reformation on have done is break up harmonious symbolic outlets for psychic energy, therefore separating people from their unconscious and instinctual natures. The Reformation shattered the symbolic unities of medieval Catholicism (though Jung was not a Roman Catholic, he appreciated that faith's archetypal richness); the Enlightenment, by creating the illusion that life could be rational and its worse illusion that the psyche is a tabula rasa, further alienated moderns from life's powerful and rich but irrational sources; the Industrial Revolution augmented the damage as it alienated humanity's conscious and psychic natures from each other through its one-dimensional values and robot-like occupations, and by herding people into the sterile life of urban centers where they are torn from nature, and from traditional communities in which healthy instincts and symbolic harmonies can be nourished. The result has been what Jung called "mass man," humans isolated socially from others, while also separated from their unconsciousness and their instincts. They are therefore susceptible to "psychic epidemics," the virulent expression of this extreme inner imbalance. These epidemics are most likely to take political form, because Enlightenment rationalism inculcated that the sources of good and evil are to be found in the objective social environment rather than in the psyche, and so require political rather than religious solution; and because mass man's urban social isolation urges him to deal with his inner demons through some kind of compensating collective expression.

For what mass man's alienation had done was to leave a vast cloud of unreleased and irrational psychic energy floating in the air, so to speak, not tied down to benign symbols or understood through living myths, but just there, capable of working tremendous destruction and waiting to be employed at the whim of any demagogic personality – most likely political – who knew how to harness it. This figure would be what Jung called a "mana personality," like Napoleon, whose excess of psychic energy magnetically draws others into its pattern, and then is able to organize and direct its flow in one direction. This process will produce a collective psychic "inflation" as rough new channels are cut, the modern alienation is short-circuited, and a group again identifies with the archtypes of its collective unconscious – or rather, because of the sudden and violent nature of this preemptory operation, with only one or two of them in an unbalanced way; the group is also likely to project the "shadow" archetype on its perceived enemies and demonize them.

In the Europe of his time Jung had no lack of opportunity to observe this process and to see his views apparently confirmed. The most egregious case was across the border from his native Switzerland in National Socialist Germany. In his powerful essay "Wotan" Jung described the volcano-like upsurge of raw long-repressed irrational psychic energy that produced the Hitler state.[2] Yet Jung's own attitude toward the "New Germany," especially as reflected in his acts when the presidency of the International Society for Psychotherapy fell to him in 1933 upon the resignation of the anti-Nazi German president, Prof. Ernst Kretschmer, has been much debated. The strong German section, under intense pressure to attain *Gleichschaltung* with the ideology of the new regime, was being forced to purge itself of Jews. It contained some Nazis (including the meddlesome Prof. M.H. Göring, the Reichsmarschal's brother) and Nazi sympathizers; and some, Jews and others, unsympathetic but whose position was most precarious. The Society

---

[2]"Wotan," *Civilization in Transition: The Collected Works of C.G. Jung* (hereafter C.W.), vol. 10, pp. 179-93. First pub. 1936.

was made international in order to contain the German maelstrom within a larger context. Yet Jung's presidential role in it has left questions in the minds of some.

I cannot undertake to sort out all the factors of this situation now. Aniela Jaffé, herself a German-Jewish refugee and Jung's secretary, has made a reasonably convincing case that, at least on his own conscious level, Jung had no sympathy for National Socialism as such, though at first like others he was perhaps naive about its full potential for evil; in any case, in his presidential role he was, she thinks, trying to do the best he could as mediator in an extremely difficult situation. He also helped countless individual Jews in those terrible years.[3]

Yet questions remain, perhaps having more to do with the full political implications of Jung's system than with any specific actions of the well-meaning Swiss. These center around a 1934 article of his translated as "The State of Psychotherapy Today," in which he expressed some hope for fruitful development in Germany out of National Socialism. The doctor of the soul opined that the "Aryan" unconscious contained creative tensions and, though now still possessed of a "youthfulness not yet fully weaned from barbarism," may hold the "seeds of a future yet to be born."[4] In the same essay, Jung expressed views of the Jewish psychological character which have given much offense, stating that "the Jew, who is something of a nomad, has never yet created a cultural form of his own...since all his instincts and talents require a more or less civilized nation to act as a host for their development," and that Jews "have in common with women being physically weaker, they have to aim at chinks in the armor of their opponents...having a civilization twice as old, they are vastly more conscious than we of human weaknesses....But the Jew like the Chinese has a wider area of psychological consciousness than we....In general [it is] less dangerous for the Jew to put a negative value on the unconscious...the Aryan unconscious on the other hand, contains explosive fires...."[5]

Such gross stereotyping was perhaps slightly more acceptable in Jung's time than today, and one does not need to be a Nazi to at least raise the issue of the distinctive psychological qualities of different peoples, including Jews.[6] Many Jews have themselves. But two points

---

[3]Aniela Jaffé, "C.G. Jung and National Socialism," in her *Jung's Last Years and Other Essays* (Dallas, TX, 1984: Spring Publications).
[4]C.W. 10, p. 165.
[5]Ibid.
[6]In a 1933 editorial in the *Zentralblatt* of the Society of which he was editor, published in Leipzig, Jung went on to say at this incendiary moment, "the differences which actually do exist between Germanic and Jewish psychologies

stick in one's mind, even apart from the crudity and plain erroneousness of this particular example of comparative psychology. First, the appalling lack of moral judgment on Jung's part in choosing to write on racial psychology, including that of Jews, precisely at a time when such rhetoric could only fan the flames of racial fanaticism, and when the relative heat of such fanaticism could well be a matter of life or death for Jews. Second, the sweeping, unqualified manner in which he applied various attributes to Aryans and Jews as such suggests the truly breathtaking extent to which Jung was prepared to think only in terms of the collective unconscious when dealing with social and political matters, and not with individual differences.

Richard Stein, in fact, contends that despite his protestations Jung became identified with the image of the "mana personality," a condition that led to an inflation of the power and vitality of the Third Reich. Stein sees Jung's attitude toward Jews as a manifestation of his father complex, acted out both toward Freud and toward the God image of the Hebrew Bible. Ambivalent both toward the feminine and his own father, Jung allegedly identified through the "mana personality" with the "Great Father."[7] This would explain, in terms of the recondite language of his own system, why Jung could write, from somewhere within himself, what he did about Aryans and Jews, while maintaining outward independence. These observations are now chiefly of value insofar as they show how the system itself can support racist and (in a certain sense) reactionary mentalities while at the same time offering a powerful and valuable critique both of the anomie of modernity and the destructiveness of the National Socialist upsurge of irrationalism. After the fact, needless to say, Jung offered trenchant diagnoses of Germany's "epidemic insanity."[8]

Yet, paradoxically and significantly, in light of the immense German failure, the only solution Jung had to offer for the ills of "mass man" was individual – individuation, the harmonious rearrangement of the archetypes on an individual basis and within a modern individual. As Hans Schaer has pointed out, if "modern man" cannot avail himself of a

---

and which have long been known to every intelligent person are no longer to be glossed over, and this can be only beneficial to science....At the same time I should like to state expressly that this implies no depreciation of Semitic psychology, any more than it is a depreciation of the Chinese to speak of the peculiar psychology of the Oriental." "Editorial (1933)," *Zentralblatt für Psychotherapie und ihre Grenzgebiete* VI:3, Dec. 1933. C.W. 10, pp. 533-34.
[7]Richard Stein, "Jung's 'Mana Personality' and the Nazi Era," in Aryeh Maidenbaum and Stephen A. Martin, *Lingering Shadows: Jungians, Freudians, and Anti-Semitism* (Boston, 1991: Shambhala), pp. 89-116.
[8]See, for example, "After the Catastrophe," C.W. 10, pp. 194-217, First pub. 1945.

universal symbol, the process which Jung calls individuation must now set in.[9]

Jung seemed to be able to hold out no hope that modern humanity could produce any satisfactory political solution to its dilemma. Regarding his views of democracy, Volodymyr Walter Odajnyk wrote, in *Jung and Politics,*

> Jung does not espouse liberal democracy as a generally applicable, ideal form of government. Rather, he holds an organic view of the relationship between the individual, the society, and the state, so that, where there is no historical, social, and political basis for a democratic order, it is unwise to graft it on by decree. Moreover, given his opinion of the pernicious influence of sheer numbers, Jung would certainly argue that democracy is possible only on a small scale.[10]

Perhaps the small scale is reflected in Switzerland, for in 1928 he wrote of his democratic homeland as a "European center of gravity," despite its stolid and conservative citizens.[11] Among humans as among animals, he viewed progressives and conservatives as both having a place in the order of things.[12] The basic impression one gains from writings in this vein is that Jung was conservative in a democratic, Burkean sense; it is better for a society to be, like Switzerland, open, democratic, stupid, frustrating, and changing only slowly, than to be carried away by psychic epidemics. For what such a small, isolated society could really mean is a society of individuals rather than of "mass man," and again the only salvation is through the full individuation of the individual. In "The Undiscovered Self" Jung spoke of "modern man" in terms of "mass-mindedness," "mass role," "the blind movement of the masses," "the infantile dream state of mass man," and the like.[13] "Mass man" is always less real than the individual, seeing himself only as a statistical average, and easily becomes the victim of modern authoritarianism. (The "mass man" analysis, incidentally, is not an

---

[9]Hans Schaer, *Religion and the Cure of Souls* (New York, 1950: Pantheon), p. 121.
[10]Volodymyr Walter Odajnyk, *Jung and Politics: The Political and Social Ideas of C.G. Jung* (New York, 1976: Harper & Row), p. 182.
[11]"The Swiss Line in the European Spectrum," C.W. 10, pp. 579-88. First pub. 1928. Jung wrote: "Does neutral Switzerland, with its backward, earthy nature, fulfill any meaningful function in the European system? I think we must answer this question affirmatively. The answer to political and cultural questions need not be only: Progress and Change, but also: Stand still! Hold fast! These days one can doubt in good faith whether the condition of Europe shows any change for the good since the war..." p. 487.
[12]C.W. 7, p. 116. In "General Remarks on the Therapeutic Approach to the Unconscious." First pub. 1917.
[13]Cited in Peter Homans, *Jung in Context* (Chicago, 1979: University of Chicago Press), p. 180.

original observation on the part of Jung, having been common coin of alarmed social critics of the day, such as Ortega y Gasset and Max Scheler, who heavily influenced Jung.)

Obviously all that can be done is to awaken mass men from their dreams by individuation, and that is achieved by opening channels to the unconscious, including the archetypes and the collective unconscious. Myth and ritual can have a very important role in this awakening process, for they are able to penetrate mass man's amnesia and recall to some level of consciousness the archetypes and finally the mandala of full human/divine glory they embody when realized and in balanced harmony. Jungian works like *Archetypes and the Collective Unconscious* are full of studies of the Trickster, Kore, Fairy Tales, the Mother and Child archetypes, the last (as the marvelous child, the *puer aeternas*, the Christ Child) being the emblem of rebirth and new transformed selfhood.

So awakened, the archetypes can then fairly contend for the soul of the persona and forge it as with hammer and anvil; "Between them," Jung said, "the patient iron is forged into an indestructible whole, an 'individual.'"[14] Iron must be heated to a burning red to be forged, and one can perhaps see why the upsurge of Wotan "like an extinct volcano" roaring back to fiery life in National Socialism could have given Jung a glimmer of hope, since at least connections were once more being made between conscious and unconscious. But it was quickly evident this effort had very badly misfired; it prematurely released nothing but raw and therefore destructive energies of the unconscious, with no truly conscious control at all, naught but that of the infantile dream state of mass man with a hysterical mana personality as psychopomp. It was no breakthrough, but the worst of both sides: semi-conscious mass mind energized by the fires from below.

Jung was undoubtedly confirmed by this realization in his belief that the way out can only be individual; there is little hope in mass movements or political action, for they are generally part of the problem instead, annealing mass man more than healing him. This is not to say that Jung did not affirm the need for a background of minimal democracy in the Swiss or Anglo-American style, for certainly a pioneering doctor of the soul needs adequate freedom to publish ideas and analyze patients without totalitarian interference. But if the modern world, with its bizarre mix of freedom and depersonalization, had not happened, perhaps he would have been a monk or mystic instead.

Mircea Eliade's name is often linked with that of Jung, but Eliade always insisted he was not a Jungian, and in a strict sense that is

---

[14]"Conscious, Unconscious, and Individuation," in *The Archetypes of the Collective Unconscious* C.W. 9, p. 288. First pub. 1939.

probably true. More important, the two Europeans had rather different personalities and careers. Jung was a doctor, and though a doctor of the spirit rather than of the flesh took his professional role quite seriously. Eliade was a professor and as a young man a lively, sometimes scandalous, novelist, journalist, traveler, and public personality in his native Romania. Jung came from one of the best governed countries of Europe, Eliade from one of its most notoriously corrupt.

Mircea Eliade's life (1907-1986) divides neatly into two parts. The years until 1945 were lived in, or in relation to, his native Romania, where he emerged in the years between the wars as probably the best known and most controversial of the passionate young Romanian intellectuals of his generation: a prolific and provocative newspaper columnist whose political and cultural views kindled fiery debate, a novelist whose works were praised extravagantly and denounced as pornographic; a dynamic lecturer at the University of Bucharest who virtually established history of religions and Indology as disciplines there; a political activist who was to be accused of fascism, but who suffered imprisonment for his loyalties under the rightist dictatorship of King Carol II.

Then there was the second "life," when, in exile from his homeland after it fell behind the Iron Curtain, Eliade – now apparently nonpolitical[15] and noncontroversial unless on arcane scholarly levels – became the pre-eminent historian of religion of his time, widely known through such classics of that field as *The Sacred and the Profane, The Myth of the Eternal Return, Shamanism: Archaic Techniques of Ecstasy,* and *Yoga: Immortality and Freedom,* among many others. After 1945 he taught first at the Sorbonne in Paris, and then from 1956 at the University of Chicago. I myself had the privilege of studying the history of religion under Professor Eliade in the 1960s, and was first drawn to that field through his luminous books.

Until recently little was widely known in the West about Eliade's prewar and wartime life. When I was a graduate student at Chicago, only a few rumors – some of them wildly inaccurate, it turned out – floated about among his docents. The professor himself talked about his past very little, and though kindness and graciousness itself in his relationship to students, he was not the sort of person into whose life one pried freely. But now it has been reconstructed, first through Eliade's

---

[15]Apart from some articles directed against the Communist regime in his homeland which appeared up to 1954 in Romanian émigré periodicals.

own two-volume *Autobiography*.[16] Second, Mac Linscott Ricketts, the splendid translator of the autobiographies and other Romanian works of Eliade, has compiled a massive and definitive documentary portrait of the years up to 1945, based on countless hours of digging in Romanian archives and libraries, and with the help of Professor Eliade himself up until his death.[17]

One can here trace the problematic story of Eliade's relationship to the Legion of the Archangel Michael, a political/spiritual movement with fascist and antisemitic leanings powerful in Romania during the 1930s; out of a wing of the Legion emerged the pro-Nazi and virulently anti-semitic Iron Guard influential in Romania's tilt toward the Axis powers in 1940-41. Although Eliade had always been a cultural nationalist who liked to speak of Romanian "messianism," meaning that the country had a cultural heritage to redeem and a special destiny to fulfill, these views usually were relatively non-political. As for anti-semitism, on several notable occasions he befriended Jewish colleagues and acquaintances in his notoriously anti-semitic land.

But in late 1936 the brilliant young commentator began publishing articles clearly showing disillusionment with democracy and the leaning of his favor toward the Legion. What appealed to him most about that militant movement was its "spirituality," the dedication of its young cadres who went into the villages to help peasants and the movement's own ostensible dedication to social rebirth and the creation of a "new man." Though perhaps with distaste, he seemed willing to accept the Legion's occasional violence and anti-semitism as a price that had to be paid for national resurrection; he wrote columns of a "Romania for the Romanians" sort, suggesting that the influence of the country's numerous minorities – Jews, Hungarians, and others – was excessive and needed to be curbed.[18]

Though nothing can excuse such sentiments today, two factors may at least help us to understand: first, the abysmal corruption and incompetence of the nominally democratic monarchy that ruled Romania in those days; and second, the natural attraction of the Legion's romantic,

---

[16]*Vol. I: 1907-1937, Journey East, Journey West,* (San Francisco, 1981: Harper & Row); *Vol. II: 1937-1960, Exile's Odyssey,* (Chicago, 1988: University of Chicago Press).

[17]Mac Linscott Ricketts, *Mircea Eliade: The Romanian Roots, 1907-1945* (Boulder, CO, 1988: East European Monographs). Distributed by Columbia University Press, New York. 2 vols., p. 1453.

[18]See, for example, Ricketts, *Mircea Eliade,* II, pp. 909-12, 915-17. It should be pointed out that in some places Eliade urged merely that the minorities be assimilated, and unlike other Rightists even at his harshest did not urge any particular action against them, such as the use of force or punitive legislation.

spiritual and mythic rhetoric for one of Eliade's susceptibilities. The way in which all fascist movements appealed to deep instinctual yearnings for communal solidarity, spiritual rebirth, and enacting deeds of mythic dimension, feelings not far removed from the religious, is not to be underestimated.

During most of the 1930s the King had tacitly encouraged the Legion and its nationalism. But in 1938 Carol II squelched the squabbling parties to establish a royal dictatorship, and turned against the Legion as a rival source of power. Eliade, with many others, was imprisoned after refusing to sign a document dissociating himself from the Legion. (He said, first, that he had never joined so could not leave it; and, second, that he did associate himself with many of its aims.) Eliade was released after four months and, in 1940, enabled to depart his increasingly desperate country to become its cultural attaché in London, where he endured the Blitz, and then, when Britain declared war on Romania in 1941, in neutral Lisbon, Portugal, until 1945.

During the latter years Eliade (who had never completely endorsed the Mussolini or Hitler regimes) found time to compose a book in praise of Portugal's "benevolent" dictator António Salazar, a fellow professor raised to a position of power whose administration he recommended as an example to his countrymen. (The book, he earnestly says in the introduction, was written to answer a question: "Is a [national] spiritual revolution possible?" The answer, he now found, is Yes! Salazar has "achieved a miracle"; "a totalitarian and Christian state, built not on abstractions, but on the living realities of the nation and its tradition."[19])

The most important question, however, is not whether Eliade made serious political misjudgments at particular times, but – as in the case of Jung – what relation those judgments may have to his lifework as mythologist and historian of religion. In this regard we may note that Eliade was fundamentally a structuralist who began with an ideal type, *homo religiosus*, religious man, and then analyzed the structures of the world as seen by this person. His religious cosmos is first of all not "homogeneous" but divided into the sacred and the profane, sacred space and time, the space of temples and the like, the time of rite and festival, over against their "ordinary," nonsacred counterparts. The sacred ultimately cannot be contrived but only discovered through "hierophany," communicated by means of myth and preserved in rites whose "gestures" symbolically repeat those of the mythical time, *illud tempus*.

All this was best realized by archaic peoples who still lived in the world of "cosmic religion," in the "paradise of archetypes" before time

---

[19]Ricketts, *Mircea Eliade*, II, p. 1108-09.

has been "allowed to become 'history'" through discovery of the "irreversibility of events"; in those days of innocence its corrosive effects could be periodically reversed and evil expelled through rites of renewal.[20] Post-archaic man has fallen into historical time and hence into the dolorous "terror of history," a place of nightmares and *ignes fatui* in which "modern man's boasted freedom to make history is illusory for nearly the whole of the human race."[21] But shadowy relics of the old cosmic sacred still abide on the fringes of consciousness, and can be evoked. Why should one call them up? In a word, to be free. In contrast to the false freedom of which moderns boast, which is really slavery to history, and to "leaders" who promise freedom only to take it away,

> ...the man of the archaic civilizations can be proud of his mode of existence, which allows him to be free and to create. He is free to be no longer what he was, free to annul his own history through periodic abolition of time and collective regeneration....[T]he archaic and traditional societies granted freedom each year to begin a new, a 'pure' existence, with virgin possibilities.[22]

Something of that vision can be recovered, though perhaps only individually and vicariously, through the history of religions. Nonetheless Eliade was excited about the contemporary cultural importance of his discipline as "a new humanism," ultimately I believe because he saw it as offering the prospect of transcending the tyranny of history. He wrote that "the history of religions is destined to play an important role in contemporary cultural life...especially because, by attempting to understand the existential situations expressed by the documents he is studying, the historian of religions will inevitably attain to a deeper knowledge of man...[because] by studying the religious expressions of a culture, the scholar approaches it from within...."[23]

But let us return to the observation that Eliade began with an ideal type, the concept of *homo religiosus*. What this ought to mean, of course, is not that all persons, or all conventionally religious persons, always think and act like *homo religiosus*. But when they are acting religiously they "become" *homo religiosus*, and the *homo religiosus* way of viewing and being in the world is what their ritual or other religious behavior says through its own language the world is like, regardless of the extent to which conscious belief is attuned to it. Like Jung speaking of mass man and collective unconsciousnesses, however, Eliade's

[20]Mircea Eliade, *Cosmos and History: The Myth of the Eternal Return* (New York, 1959: Harper and Row), pp. 74-75.
[21]Ibid., p. 156.
[22]Ibid., p. 157.
[23]Mircea Eliade, "A New Humanism," in *The Quest* (Chicago, 1975: University of Chicago Press), p. 3.

phenomenology tends to slide over that last qualification, and to assume that subjectivity follows ritual action.

Being Eliade-trained, I am adamant myself that religion should not be reduced to inward belief – the Protestant temptation – and that it is very important to listen to the languages of the ritual, art, and other nonverbal signs of any religious community. But it is equally important not to presuppose that the subjectivity behind such "gestures" is necessarily holistic and homogeneous throughout the community. To return to the political case and, for examples, to the National Socialist era, in a published interview Eliade responded to a question by Claude-Henri Rocquet about religious murder, such as that of the Aztec sacrifices. Rocquet had inquired, "What criterion enables us to decide that the Aztecs lived out a justified illusion whereas the Nazi Storm Troopers didn't? What is the difference between ordinary murder and sacred murder?" In reply, Eliade said, "For the SS, the annihilation of millions of people in the concentration camps also had a meaning, and even an eschatological one. They believed that they represented Good versus Evil....We know what Good was for Nazism: fair-haired, Nordic man, what they called the pure Aryan. And the rest were incarnations of Evil, of the devil. It was almost a form of Manicheanism: the struggle of Good against Evil."[24]

The point is not that Eliade was justifying the Nazis. He was not. Later in the same discourse he spoke of them as "those sick men, or zealots, or fanatics – those modern Manicheans" who "saw Evil as being embodied in certain races: the Jews, the Gypsies," and so for them, "Sacrificing them by the millions was thus not a crime." It is rather that, first, he never really answered Rocquet's question as to how one can tell the difference between Aztec ritual murder (if one makes the questionable assumption that it was a "justified" religious "illusion") and the Nazi crimes; and second that, in a peculiar reflection of the Nazis' own mentality, he saw the Nazis themselves collectively rather than singly, an ideal type like the Aztecs performing roles (or rather one role) in their own myth.

In fact not all Storm Troopers liquidating their millions saw themselves consistently and homogeneously as acting out a "Manichean" Aryan myth of Good versus Evil. Some were sickened but fearful of resisting orders, some were numbed, some were just ordinary sadists, a few did resist in various covert ways, some probably were True Believers. While Eliade's mythology may help us to understand the

---

[24]Mircea Eliade, *Ordeal by Labyrinth: Conversations with Claude-Henri Rocquet.* Translated by Derek Coltman (Chicago, 1982: University of Chicago Press), p. 127. Originally published in French, 1978.

message of the grim overall pattern, it is these individual nuances that one misses: for him the individual becomes his/her role in myths and rituals that are essentially social. For Eliade the phenomenologist, unlike Jung the physician, there is not even talk of individuation out of those roles – unless through a still-mythologized transformative process like that of the shaman or the yogi, or unless that is attained in the privileged position of the "new humanist," the modern scholarly observer like Eliade himself!

Eliade went on to talk similarly of the "myth" then afflicting his homeland: "Exactly the same can be said about the Gulags and the apocalyptic eschatology of the great Communist 'liberation': it sees itself as confronted by enemies that represent Evil, that constitute an obstacle to the triumph of Good, the triumph of liberty, of man, and so on. All this can be compared with the Aztecs...."

Although after 1945 Eliade – doubtless chastened by the almost apocalyptic-scale events of that year – no longer much committed himself publicly to any political or other myths, there is a deep level continuity to his work. He saw the world as the arena of, in his term, the "dialectic of the sacred," or, to put it another way, as an arena of myth against myth and ritual against ritual, for in such a world even the profane is still part of the myth. This is a view that is reactionary, if the word may now be used in a neutral descriptive sense, because it implies that the archaic world is needed to interpret the modern. The modern world really acts out myths as much as ever, including those sodden with blood sacrifice, but knows not what it does. By returning to the archaic world which lived much more consciously by myth and ritual we can understand how we, too, are *homo religiosus* behind the secular masks. In doing so we may find the rather rarefied salvation offered by Eliade's New Humanism, and spice it with the humane excitement he found in scholarly exploration.

Joseph Campbell (1904-1987) was undoubtedly the best known of all interpreters of myth to late twentieth-century Americans, thanks to a series of learned but highly readable books, assiduous lecture hall performances, and above all his posthumous PBS appearances with Bill Moyers. The response to that series of six interviews was remarkable. As Mary R. Lefkowitz put it, "On television Joseph Campbell was the embodiment of the ideal academic: gentle, fatherly, informative, reassuring, unworldly, spiritual, and articulate without being incomprehensible. He was knowledgeable about what we didn't have time (or inclination) to discover for ourselves, pleasantly remote, and (unlike most of nontelevision professors) entertaining. Campbell could tell a good story...."[25]

But there was more to it than simply the personality. Something in Campbell's message clearly resonated strongly with the yearnings of those late Reagan-era years. Certainly the appeal was rooted in Campbell's conviction that myths are not past but present, embodying the eternal essence of life. When Moyers asked if myths "are stories of our search through the ages for truth, for meaning, for significance," Campbell replied,

> People say that what we're all seeking is a meaning for life. I don't think that's what we're really seeking. I think that what we're seeking is an experience of being alive, so that our life experiences on the purely physical plane will have resonances within our own innermost being and reality, so that we actually feel the rapture of being alive. That 's what it's all finally about, and that's what these clues help us to find within ourselves.[26]

Campbell could make others believe with him that myths are important because they are vivid and timeless vehicles of human life. People respond to people who care, and Campbell manifestly cared about people and about myth – perhaps in that order.

For despite his academic credentials as a Professor at Sarah Lawrence College, and though remarkably widely read in mythology, Campbell exhibited scant interest of the usual academic sort in his subject matter. He evinced little concern about mythic variants or philological issues, or even about the cultural or ritual context of his material. For him a myth seemed to be a rather disembodied, timeless story of eternal human significance. It might happen to come from here or there, but in the final analysis all myths are equal and interchangeable – with the possible exception of those of "the Yahweh cult" upon which the Judaic-Christian-Islamic tradition is based, and which Campbell clearly disliked.[27] Otherwise, what myths all say, finally, is that behind all forms there is a Brahman-like Oneness, and that in moving toward its realization one should "follow one's own bliss" – a saying no doubt capable of interpretation on several levels.

---

[25]Mary R. Lefkowitz, "The Myth of Joseph Campbell," *The American Scholar*, 59:3, Summer 1990, p. 429.
[26]Joseph Campbell, with Bill Moyers, *The Power of Myth* (New York, 1985: Doubleday), p. 5.
[27]In *The Power of Myth* Campbell says, "The Yahweh cult was a specific movement in the Hebrew community, which finally won. This was a pushing through of a certain temple-bound god against the nature cult, which was celebrated all over the place. And this imperialistic thrust of a certain in-group culture is continued in the West." p. 21. The text is taken from the PBS series.

Robert A. Segal, probably Campbell's most measured and perceptive critic, asserted that Campbell's draw lay in the "unashamed romanticism" of his theory of myth. Myths have been regarded in various ways by modern interpreters. For Victorian rationalists of the stamp of Tylor and Frazer, they were primitive science, quaint but of no deep interest now that their views of natural phenomena have been surpassed. For psychoanalysts in the Freudian style, myths also represented metaphorical accounts of natural, though intrapsychic, processes which now can also be put in more universal scientific language. All this was quintessential modernism.

But for Campbell, a myth is an eternal, not merely a primitive, narrative. Nothing can supersede it, because it is not about proto-scientific explanation, but about the human condition, which in the last analysis is always expressed metaphorically, and always has to be spoken. Thus for Campbell, according to Segal, myth is indispensable, and the primitives who first bespoke it were really wiser than moderns because they knew implicitly that the metaphors of story tell human things better than the false abstractions of science, and they constructed a worldview centered on their stories.[28]

Elsewhere the same commentator remarked that actually Campbell "is oddly not much interested in myth – as myth. He is much more interested in human nature, which he simply finds revealed in myths. He sees myths as a respository of the experiences and beliefs of mankind. He is far more concerned with the information myths contain than with myths themselves."[29] But while it is easy for academics to disparage such an attitude, this is in fact no more than the approach most predicants, more concerned with saving the world than with footnotes, take toward their scriptural and other sources, and no doubt represents one legitimate level of hermeneutics.

Of more interest in the present context is Campbell's own social and political views. Although, unlike Jung and Eliade, he never expressed himself fully and explicitly in print on such matters, they were known to acquaintances, and posthumously created something of a furor. The ruckus was essentially started in a 1989 article in the *New York Review of Books* by Brendan Gill, who claimed to have known Campbell well. Gill complains that, though one might have expected a person given to a lifelong study of diversity of cultures and points of view to accept a variety of points of view in his own culture, this Campbell was never

---

[28]Robert A. Segal, "The Romantic Appeal of Joseph Campbell," *Christian Century*, April 4, 1990, pop. 332-35.
[29]Robert A. Segal, *Joseph Campbell: An Introduction* (New York, 1987: Garland Publishing), p. 137.

able to do – toward minorities, toward feminists, or toward liberal social programs. The mythologist was reportedly anti-semitic, anti-black, and in 1941 unable to grasp the threat represented by Hitler. Needless to say, the sixties did not meet with his approval at all, despite his frequent lectures at one of its most celebrated shrines, the Esalen Institute.[30] Brendan Gill commented, "So far was Campbell from applying the wisdom of the ages to the social, political, and sexual turbulence that he found himself increasingly surrounded by that he might have been a member of the Republican party somewhere to the right of William F. Buckley. He embodied a paradox that I was never able to resolve in his lifetime and that I have been striving to resolve ever since: the savant as reactionary."[31] He advanced several scraps of evidence, largely anecdotal and hearsay, to support Campbell's reactionism.

As to why Campbell's Moyers interviews were so well received, Gill opined that most viewers assumed his was a liberal message – religiously liberal, at least, with its relativistic openness toward the myths and faiths of many cultures. But, Gill claims, the covert message of the tagline, "Follow your bliss" – whatever makes you happy – is none other than the philosophy of "Wall Street yuppies, junk-bond dealers" – or an Ayn Rand type of elitist individualist with no discernible social conscience.

This article was followed by an orgy of letters-to-the-editor activity. Further anecdotal support was given the legend of Campbell's rightest biases. He was called a "romantic fascist"[32] and virulent anti-communist, was said to have objected to admitting blacks to Sarah Lawrence, and at the time of the Moon landing in 1969 to have remarked that the earth's

---

[30]It might also be added that Campbell enjoyed friendship with, and influenced, a number of prominent figures of the sixties and seventies who did not necessarily share his political views but appreciated his creative intellect and who applied his mythic vision to their art or social role. These included Bob Dylan, The Grateful Dead, the psychologist Joan Halifax, California governor Jerry Brown, and the filmmaker George Lucas.

[31]Brendan Gill, "The Faces of Joseph Campbell," *New York Review of Books*, Sept. 28, 1989, pp. 16-19.

[32]However, in the Introduction to his *The Masks of God: Primitive Mythology* (New York, 1959: Viking), p. 12, Campbell had referred to the destructive power of mythological racism and Aryanism in such writers of the nineteenth and twentieth century as Gobineau and Chamberlain, and drawn from them the moral that "mythology is no toy for children," but can have explosive power in our own as well as any other age. On the same page he wrote, "And the world is now far too small, and men's stake in sanity too great, for any more of those old games of Chosen Folk (whether of Jehovah, Allah, Wotan, Manu, or the Devil) by which tribesmen were sustained against their enemies in the days when the serpent could still talk."

satellite would be a good place to send all the Jews.[33]   One woman recounted that she had been in a class of his at the height of the sixties campus upheavals; Campbell had said he would flunk any student who took part in political activism – and when she did, he made good on his threat.[34]

---

[33]This may well be apocryphal; the major biography of Campbell to date, Stephen and Robin Larsen, *A Fire in the Mind: The Life of Joseph Campbell* (New York, 1991: Doubleday), states that Campbell was anti-Zionist but not anti-semitic (pp. 510-11). Gill claimed that Campbell liked Jung but disliked Freud, and thought this had to do with anti-Jewish prejudice; but it seems to me that even the original premise here can be questioned.   One of Campbell's most powerful pieces of writing is a long section on "The Psychology of Myth" in *The Masks of God: Primitive Mythology*, a real *tour de force* interpretation of myth in highly Freudian terms, from birth trauma to breast to discovery of genital sexuality.   The most direct influence there was that very orthodox Freudian anthropologist Géza Róheim, to whose *festschrift* Campbell also made a significant contribution ("Bios and Mythos: Prolegomena to a Science of Mythology," in *Psychoanalysis and Culture: Essays in Honor of Géza Róheim*, eds. George B. Wilbur and Warner Muensterberger, New York: International Universities Press, 1951).   Róheim, and behind him Freud, is also prominent in the Prologue of his early *magnum opus*, *The Hero With a Thousand Faces*.   But Campbell always seemed to accept the common wisdom that Freud is the best guide to the first half of life, Jung for the second.   While Campbell appears to have become more Jungian and less Freudian as the years advanced, there is certainly no evidence of nonacademic bias.   At the same time, his bias against the Hebrew God, and that deity's manifestations in three religions, is evident repeatedly.   In the last year of his life, when he finally got a computer for writing, he named it Jahweh.   "A lot of rules and no mercy," he explained (Larsen and Larsen, p. 539).

[34]The Larsens state that Campbell did not actually flunk students for political activism as such, but did hold them responsible for material presented in class even during strikes and demonstrations.   They describe the late sixties atmosphere at Sarah Lawrence, with its highly visible posters of Mao and Vietcong flags, and its student strikes, which so inflamed the conservative mythologist, though he himself had been infatuated with Communism in the early thirties.   On other points, Campbell's 1941 belief that artists should remain above the war is reflected in a notable series of letters Campbell exchanged then with the great German novelist and anti-Nazi exile Thomas Mann.   They are alluded to unfavorably in the Gill article and reproduced in the Larsens' book. (In later writing, such as *The Masks of God*, Campbell refers to Mann frequently and very positively.)   It might be noted also that in 1941 Campbell wrestled earnestly with the issue of pacifism, seriously considering becoming a conscientious objector before finally registering for the draft in February 1942, rather in contrast with his much later strong support of the Vietnam War.   The Larsens were friends of Campbell and their biography is generally sympathetic, though they acknowledge that in the Vietnam era they "leaned to the left" and often disputed Campbell's pro-war Republicanism with him, trying to get him to see such sixties dramas as the march on the Pentagon sympathetically as contemporary events of mythic dimension.   They attribute his then unpopular (at least in the circles in which he and they generally moved) stance to his visceral

Other correspondents rose as vehemently to the mythologist's defense. One contended that his position at Sarah Lawrence had to be understood in light of the fact that he had fallen foul of a faculty "Marxist clique" – the same academic politics satirized in Mary McCarthy's *Groves of Academe*. Others argued that "Follow your bliss" has nothing to do with Ayn Rand individualism, much less materialistic selfishness, but the opposite – follow your own way to spiritual liberation.

Admittedly, it is hard to connect the Campbell of the bigot stereotype with a man who for nearly forty years was an immensely popular teacher at Sarah Lawrence, until recently a women's college and one which has long had a reputation as a liberal bastion with a large Jewish enrollment. Yet, if even some of the anecdotes are true, there does appear to be a paradox, the paradox which Gill called "the savant as reactionary" – in this case, not so much a sophisticated intellectual reactionary, a de Maistre or even a Jung or Eliade, as a smooth articulate nonpolitical mythologist who, off the record, dropped remarks that seem to be from an entirely different sort of person. One almost senses a double life.[35] That perception would not, however, be entirely correct; there were relationships between the mythologist and the political reactionary, and Campbell's political views, though strongly held and on occasion forcefully expressed, were more subtle than might appear on the surface. Harold Taylor, president of Sarah Lawrence in the McCarthyist era when Campbell's passionate anti-Communism alienated some colleagues, recalled that Campbell also believed a college should reflect a diversity of opinions, that "each person who came in should be given leg room to move in whatever direction his legs took him," and remarked that "Campbell's view was always more complex than could be easily grasped by most people."[36] How is Campbell to be resolved?

---

anti-Communism, his idealization of American individualism, and his stubborn independence. They point out that later he also had problems with the Republicanism of the eighties on three important points: its alliance with Christian fundamentalism (he believed strongly in separation of church and state and did not care for either Catholic or Protestant authoritarianism), its opposition to abortion (perhaps because of his radical individualism, he believed in a woman's right to choice), and the GOP's inadequate stand on ecology (a great lover of nature, Campbell supported strong measures for its protection). As the decade advanced, he claimed he was so disillusioned with all parties that he might not vote at all.

[35]Even the Larsens, though clearly endeavoring to present a generally favorable image of Campbell (and successfully so), suggest in several places that, perhaps especially as he grew older, in certain moods he could be very persistent, blunt, and opinionated in his "reactionary" social and political views.

[36]Larsen and Larsen, *A Fire in the Mind*, p. 357.

The best effort I know of is in Toby Johnson's *The Myth of the Great Secret,* an interesting account of the author's personal movement away from conventional Roman Catholicism under the aegis of Campbell's perception of myth. Johnson, who did not and does not share Campbell's politics, reports he was quite taken aback when, unaware of Campbell's views, he first met him in 1971, during the years of turmoil over Vietnam, and found that his mentor identified himself as a Republican and a supporter of Nixon and the war. (Johnson had, in fact, steeled himself to oppose the war through the power of certain lines about the hero's resolve in Campbell's 1949 classic, *The Hero With a Thousand Faces.*[37]) He found also Campbell opposed to sixties-style sexual and psychedelic drug experimentation, and "sounded like he'd been listening to too much Art Linkletter."[38]

In further conversations, Johnson came to understand Campbell better. The mythologist called himself a "classical conservative," citing the story of the Grail Quest as an example of the staunch individualism on which that position is allegedly based: the knights agree among themselves that they will not follow in another's footsteps, but that each should pursue his own path to the holy object, beginning at that place in the forest which was darkest and most alone. Campbell, in fact, according to Johnson prided himself on not really being part of the modern world. He never watched television and had no interest in popular culture. (Eliade, too, incidentally, during the Chicago years when I knew him, never read newspapers or watched TV and had virtually no awareness of what was happening in the outer world.)

Extreme and obviously idealized individualism – the assumption that the knights of capitalism would voluntarily all start equally distant from the prize – combined perhaps with something of the puritanical Jansenism of his Irish Catholic background, were the dominant constituents of Campbell's social views. He explained to Toby Johnson that the real danger in modern society was the threat of swamping personal freedom with concern for collective needs, which would lead the government to meddle in people's lives and cater to nonindividualized pressure groups.[39]

---

[37]Joseph Campbell, *The Hero with a Thousand Faces.* Bollingen series XVII (New York, 1949: Pantheon. 2nd ed., Princeton Univ. Press, 1968). This often brilliant and magical study of the hero myth was Campbell's first single-authored book, and also is his most sustained piece of scholarly writing. It had a definite influence on a generation of literary critics and historians of religion.
[38]Toby Johnson, *The Myth of the Great Secret* (Berkeley, CA, 1992: Celestial Arts), pp. 48-49.
[39]In the Moyers interviews, reproduced in *The Power of Myth,* Campbell did talk at some length about the American "myth," or rather myths, for he held that

The mythic model is clearly the free enterprise "rugged individualist" of a romanticized American past, not the type of heroic individualism represented in his own day by, say, a Rosa Parks or a draft resister.[40] How Campbell's political worldview was reconciled with such further seeming contradictions as, for example, the mythologist's love at a distance for such an extremely nonindividualistic society as the Hindu (though he did visit India in 1954-1955, and remarked on the lack in contemporary India of the "forcefully heroic attitude" it had had in "the periods of the great dynasties" now past[41]), or at least for its myths; or his disdain for the Judeo-Christian tradition out of which at least some of Western individualism derives, is not explained. But it seems to me that Joseph Campbell's thought can only be considered a collection of unassimilated fragments, many brilliant, some not thoroughly thought through, some frankly based on prejudices. Toward the end of his life he seemed to realize that he was out of step with both left and right, and – like, eventually, Jung and Eliade as well – ready to give up on the whole political world. In a late interview he said,

> I don't know what politics can do. I think it's fair to say that I'm a little bit discouraged by the people who are involved in the political life of this country. I begin to feel it has been betrayed. Its potentialities have been sold for values that are inscrutable to me.[42]

Why were these three mythologists reactionaries? Our view will be that their rightist sympathies stemmed from a semi-conscious and unresolved tension between the nature of their material based on an

---

America in its pluralism has never had a single, unified mythology. The classic American goals of life, liberty, and the pursuit of happiness, he said, are *for the individual* -- but are buttressed by the cosmic orientation of the Great Seal, reproduced on the dollar bill, with its four-sided pyramid representing the earth, and the descending eagle, the bird of Zeus, indicating the "downcoming of the god into the field of time" (p. 27). See Dabney Gray, "Campbell, America, and the Individual as New Hero," in Kenneth L. Golden, ed., *Uses of Comparative Mythology: Essays on the Work of Joseph Campbell* (New York, 1992: Garland), pp. 235-48.

[40]Karen L. King, in "Social Factors in Mythic Knowledge: Joseph Campbell and Christian Gnosis," in Daniel C. Noel, *Paths to the Power of Myth: Joseph Campbell and the Study of Religion* (New York, 1990: Crossroad), p. 69, speaks of Campbell's "American Romanticism," which held that truth lay in authentic experience of the inner self; a view which, she holds, was shared by the ancient Gnostics and helps explain Campbell's interest in both the Gnostic and Romantic traditions.

[41]Larsen and Larsen, *A Fire in the Mind*, p. 382.

[42]John M. Maher and Dennis Briggs, ed., *An Open Life: Joseph Campbell in Conversation with Michael Toms* (New York, 1989: Harper and Row), p. 101. The interviews in this book are undated but took place over a ten-year period beginning in 1975.

unretrievable archaic worldview, and the modernist milieu within which they worked and whose concepts of knowledge they largely accepted.

Jean-François Lyotard, the noted exponent of post-modernism, has identified the two great "metanarratives" of modernism as, first, the emancipation of humanity by progress, both political and scientific; and, second, the unity of knowledge in a way amenable to rational, "scientific" abstraction and technological implementation.[43] The second metanarrative means, more explicitly, that there are universal languages – that is, those of science and social science – by which particular cultures and their particular knowledges can be interpreted universally, and so to which the particulars are subordinated, for it is the universal language which gives power. Needless to say, the modern university was above all the custodian and power dispenser of these two modern metanarratives. Our mythologists were university people or closely related to university ways of thinking.

Archaic myth was undeniably an outsider in the university world of nineteenth and early and middle twentieth-century modernity. On the surface at least, myth is that which scientific progress has progressed beyond. From the scientific point of view, it does not unify knowledge but fragments it into a thousand faces. Myth might be studied, but only as "mythology," that is, in a way which subordinated it to the metanarratives, treating it as prescientific and bringing to it the tools of the unified knowledge of modern science, social science, and philology. Our three mythologists were enough persons of modernity to profess to do this. As scholars, they took the panoptic privileged position of the modern observer, surveying the world past and present to bring all its myths into their purview, and subordinating them to various kinds of hermeneutics. But Jung, Eliade, and Campbell were not able to subject myth simply to the rationalist reductionism of the Victorians. They lived a little too late for that, in a world which seemed far more dangerous and nonrational than theirs. Over against this, the mythical world, the world of a cosmos that is alive and harmonizes soul and matter, in which processes of individual transformation obtain, and where heroes go on adventures of ultimate significance, seemed an appealing "otherness" to set beside the drab world of "mass man."

For by the mid-twentieth century when the mythologists were in their prime, talk was rising to high decibels of how science and reason, far from unifying knowledge or humanity, had produced deep levels of alienation: humanity from nature, humanity from its own soul. The

---

[43]Jean-François Lyotard, *The Postmodern Condition: A Report on Knowledge*, trans. Geoff Bennington and Brian Massumi (Minneapolis, 1984: University of Minnesota Press), p. ix.

problems were becoming visible, but no antidote was at hand. It may be, first Jung and then Eliade and Campbell thought, that the archaic peoples whose language was myth had done it better.

But to make myth accessible to modernity as a remedy it also had to become sufficiently modern to be heard: it had to be made compatible with what was left of the idea of progress, and speak some species of universal tongue. The mythologists sensed the vast saving potential of their archaic material, yet they were also people of their time. They could not simply become archaic. Rather, the mythical empowerment had to be advanced through the means of modernity, which meant in effect through the metanarratives of progress toward emancipation, and of the unity of knowledge. Whatever the case in archaic times, myth now had to bespeak some kind of progress, individual or social, and become a universal language.

These mythologists lived before the frank fragmentation of postmodernism; they lived in a time when it was still possible to think in terms of a grand theory or an overarching symbol system that would unify everything. But they did live at a late stage of modernism when scientific rationalism had sufficiently broken down that the proffered symbol system could, in fact, be mythical and nonrational, unifying history and experience in terms of the worlds of myth rather than of science or reason. It would be scientific in the sense that it was based on modern comparativist and psychological studies, but its appeal would be to levels of human nature deeper and more powerful than the rational.

The two major apertures available to generic myth in the modern world were in individual psychological procedures and in nationalism. Other possibilities were pre-empted. Liberal or radical reform was taken over by secular myths such as Marxism or by the myths of specific relevant religions, as in the Christian social gospel. Social roles had their indigenous mythic models: Victorian reconstructions of chivalry for the English gentleman, Daniel Boone for the American frontiersman.

But the very individualism on which mass man quixotically prided himself, together with the notion of progress, made him want to progress inwardly, to inwardly simulate growth and evolution, in moving from one psychic state to a better one. In the hands of Jung and Campbell, mythic scenarios were ready-made models for individuals in the process of inner transformation. Nations also could move on to what they trusted were higher stages of their own development through attaining the inner cohesion and unity of purpose afforded by a mythic model, with reference back to the "organic" society supposedly realized in mythic times and touted by mythological and other reactionaries.

But because these two processes, the individual psychological and the nationalistic, were ostensibly at odds with the fundamental character of modern society – its scientific, "statistical" homogenization, its supposedly democratic institutions – and since the modern mind cannot really countenance the possibility of any sort of large-scale change except through the political process, the mythology movement had to be in some way (maybe only a mythic one) political. It could not be liberal or progressive in the ordinary sense, since that implied only more of the same, scientizing and bureaucratizing human life rather than mythologizing it. It could not be conservative in the usual sense either, since that also implied more of the same science and bureaucracy, save perhaps now in the hands of business corporations more than of government. A radical change, such as the mythologists required, could only be reactionary, returning in significant ways – maybe only individually, maybe nationalistically – to the idealized archaic world.

In conclusion, I believe we can affirm there is much that is appealing and profoundly true in the sermons of the mythologists to the modern world. Undoubtedly that world is often alienating and dehumanizing, denying people easy access to the depths of their own souls. Myth, like all great literature, can become universal, transcending its particular cultural setting to provide general models of the human predicament and ways out of it. This is true even though the mythologists, in their generalized reverence for their subject, did not always take into account that myth, like everything human, can be of quite varied moral worth: the Aztec myth by which the sun must be fed daily the blood of sacrificial victims, or the Babylonian myth, criticized by feminist scholars, in which Marduk created the world by carving up the body of the female entity Tiamat, are not necessarily to be received on the same level as love-suffused stories of Krishna or Jesus.

Moreover myth, unlike much later "civilized" literature, has one peculiar characteristic: it deals almost entirely in generic, "archetypal" categories, reducing individuals (and races or peoples) to types and roles, stereotyping them as Hero or Trickster, as Good or Evil.

Here lies the great danger in applying mythic categories to contemporary affairs, above all political. The mythologists under discussion were aware of the danger, but not always sufficiently. The problem was not only their occasionally succumbing to dubious political myths, or in thinking of collectives of people from Jews to Storm Troopers in generic "bloc" terms, but also in a more general tendency to think of the modern world in a stereotyping, homogeneous, and pessimistic way – as "mass man." They thereby pre-emptorily dismissed it as hopeless for any kind of salvation but individual, or through some (equally hopeless) corporate reversion to the mythic world in a healthy sense. It was too late for that, and the pseudo-mythic worlds were far more dangerous than the ailment. But both alternatives left the mythologists political reactionaries in effect: the individual salvation option being politically reactionary by default, the reversionary endeavor reactionary in concrete political terms. What was lacking, perhaps, was a rational, humane myth of the future.

Response to Robert S. Ellwood's "Why Are Mythologists Political Reactionaries? An Investigation of C.G. Jung, Mircea Eliade, and Joseph Campbell"

Dell deChant
University of South Florida

Robert S. Ellwood has presented and offered support for a new and exciting theory. It is his claim that three of the twentieth-century's better known and more publicly popular "mythologists" are political reactionaries. Ellwood's concern is not that the "mythologists" may have had an uncritical appreciation for the object of their inquiries or that they may have held decidedly conservative political views at a time when much of the scholarly community was politically liberal. Both of these claims are fairly well known and Ellwood supplies adequate support for them – especially the latter claim.

Rather than reporting the presence of these two elements (each notable and together worthy of special comment), Ellwood utilizes their presence to construct the novel, and potentially controversial, theory that Jung, Eliade, and Campbell are political reactionaries in and through the context of their academic endeavors. The dynamic focus of the theory is to be found in Ellwood's central contention that the "mythologists," perhaps unconsciously, utilized the object of their academic research and interpretation (premodern cultures and their mythic symbol systems) as an ideological foundation from which to draw negative contrasts, if not in fact initiate hostile critiques, of modernity. In his words: they "set the world of ancient myth over against the troubled world of the mid-twentieth century to critique its spiritual emptiness." The real strength of the theory, and the great merit of its proposal, is to be found in the degree to which Ellwood's theory is substantiated by documentation.

The seriousness of Ellwood's theory and the importance of the thinkers of its focus demand critical consideration by persons involved in a variety of disciplines. It has particular relevance to students of religion, psychology, and popular culture due to the enormous impact that Jung, Eliade, and Campbell have had on these respective fields. It has, perhaps, even more importance to students working in areas where these fields intersect and overlap. Finally, the theory may be of greatest importance to students working in either of two related areas of cultural inquiry: (1) that area of research and analysis that Paul Tillich termed "Theology of Culture," and (2) that far less stable and still ill-defined area of reflection and critique suggested by the term "post-modernism."

Although Ellwood's theory is of notable novelty and its substance presented with precision and clarity, the development of the theory may present two distinct though associated challenges. These challenges can be broadly classified under the headings of logical structure and methodology. While the stylistic design and rhetorical structure of the essay are effective, the theory might have been better supported by a more rigorously constructed logical framework. The paper is, after all, presenting an argument; and the strength of the theory rests in part on the warrants brought forward in the course of the argument that supports the theory. Warrants are not missing, there are reasons given for why these thinkers are political reactionaries. The warrants, however, are asked to do much indeed; they are called upon to support a theory that would substantially modify the interpretation of two seminal scholars and a great popularizer of religious inquiry. It may well be that the warrants are asked to do too much in the context of this introductory paper.

What seems to be missing from the argument is a significant quantity of examples from the extensive professional corpus of the three thinkers. Much of the evidence that is brought forward in support of the theory is biographical, anecdotal, and of a peripheral nature relative to the full breadth of their professional scholarly output. This is not to say that there are not examples from the original scholarly works (most notably in the case of Jung, and least notably in the case of Campbell), but such examples are often balanced by others (which Ellwood charitably offers) revealing contrasting or modified positions; and the examples from the original works are given equal standing with the biographical and anecdotal warrants.

In terms of the logic of the argument, the question raised here is: What counts as evidence? When entertaining a theory about a scholar's political position and its impact on his/her work, it could be argued that the range of evidence in support of the theory is best limited to the scholarly work itself. This issue is exemplified in the well-known (and still ongoing) debate about what might be called the Heidegger variation of the ad hominem fallacy. In short: Does it really matter what a scholar says or does outside the realm of her/his professional scholarly activity if that saying and doing does not obviously intrude on the scholarly activity itself?

The methodology of the paper may also present certain challenges; specifically in the different methodological approaches taken to each of the thinkers. The studies are really three different papers in themselves, each designed to offer support for the theory. In each case a different body of data is treated as primary; with Jung it is his original work and critical commentaries; with Eliade it is chiefly texts of a biographical character; and with Campbell the primary materials are critical texts and personal observations of persons who knew the man. As was the case with the question of logical warrants, the wide-ranging and diverse sources used might raise the methodological questions: What qualifies as the field of data for this inquiry, and how are we to read and interpret these different texts relative to the theory? Clearly the choice of data influences the process of evaluation and the conclusions that can be reached, and this is revealed in the manner in which the three thinkers are evaluated and judged.

The section on Jung is developed around an analysis of specific Jungian terms (collective unconsciousness, psychic epidemic, mana personality, individuation) and their relationship to both his encounter with alienated moderns and his own conservative political position. With its stronger reliance on primary texts (in which views contrasting with those that support the theory are cited), the Jung study appears the most balanced and least conclusive in its support of the theory. Jung's views on "minimal democracy" and his diagnosis of Germany's "epidemic insanity" appear to be fair enough reasons for him to critique modernity on the basis of individuality without necessarily revealing him to be a political reactionary.

The Eliade study, with its focus on biographical and subjective elements, reveals a politically ambiguous thinker who wrestled with competing ideologies and who, after 1945 (when he produced his mature and most widely read works), "no longer much committed himself publicly to any political or other myths." While the Eliade section may not weaken Ellwood's theory, and it does offer a critical mediation of some relatively recent data on Eliade's life, the precise relationship between the biographical elements and Eliade's scholarly work might be further developed for the sake of Ellwood's theory.

The Campbell study, which utilizes critical texts and personal observations, offers the best support for the theory and results in the most severe evaluation of the impact of reactionary political views on a "mythologist's" professional work. As Ellwood notes: "Joseph Campbell's thought can only be considered a collection of unassimilated fragments, many brilliant, some not thoroughly thought through, some frankly based on prejudices." It must be noted that Campbell's academic credentials and professional esteem are considerably less than those of the other two thinkers, and his greatest fame rests with his "media scholarship" – the popularly acclaimed PBS series *The Power of Myth*. In this regard the texts selected and analysis offered in the Campbell section seem the most appropriate from a methodological perspective.

The areas in which challenges are encountered reveal the novelty of Ellwood's theory and serve as invitations to both its further development as well as further inquiry into the work of Jung, Eliade, and Campbell. The theory and its development have something of a post-modern flavor, suggested perhaps in the citation of Lyotard's comments on "metanarratives," but more evidently revealed in the basic contours of the theory itself. The theory proper brings to mind some of the concerns that have been announced by Michel Foucault (see his *Power/Knowledge* and *What Is Enlightenment?*, for example). Here is a theory on which to base critical inquiries into the ideological motives of academic "mythologists" as well as other scholars engaged in research into and interpretation of the culturally volatile area of religion – whether archaic or contemporary.

That scholars may have hidden agendas (perhaps hidden even to themselves, as this paper suggests) and rightist (as Ellwood notes, or leftist as we must remember) sympathies cannot be ignored or trivialized. Scholars hold and exercise enormous power in the contemporary world by virtue of the political and social structures of this culture, and scholars of religion hold even greater power due to the culturally volatile character of their subject. To its merit, the post-modern school is concerned with the processes through which social power is gained and exercised, the (often hidden) agendas of those who hold power, and the diagnosis of the implications of such agendas. To its detriment, the post-modern school frequently is not properly theoretical, its claims and exercises more often merely disruptive and anarchic, and its tactics more often de-constructive (not of texts, but) of both academic and social stability. In this paper, Robert S. Ellwood has advanced a theory that seems at once genuinely post-modern, properly theoretical, and constructive in character. This is no easy task, but Ellwood reminds us that it is a necessary one for both the post-modern school and the greater academy in which it flourishes.

As the theory is further developed it may broaden out to include other sectors of academic research. It invites us to ask what are the motivating myths of historians, the nostalgic yearnings of sociologists, the primal tendencies of scriptural exegetes? It also asks us to review the type of logical support that such a theory might demand and the methodological structures that might guide inquiries based on such a theory. In this paper we have been told what to look for and why; we can now ask, how is it that we may properly see?

VIII.

A Theological Perspective on the Social Study of Religion in History

10

Historical Consciousness, Religion and the Social Order: Can We Make Normative Judgments?

Darrell J. Fasching[1]
University of South Florida, Tampa

Introduction

I am neither a historian nor a social scientist, and therefore I feel a little out of place giving a paper at a conference on "Religion and the Social Order: What Kinds of Lessons Does History Teach?" My own work is done at the intersection between theology and comparative religious ethics and is normative rather than empirical in nature. Still, my work is concerned with religion, history and society. Indeed, it could not be carried out in isolation from the work of historians and social scientists. My task, as I understand it, is to reflect on some of the normative lessons that the historical and social scientific study of religion teach. There are many perspectives from which to view this task. I shall confine myself to one which is both basic in the issue it raises and global in its impact, namely, ethical relativism and the profound impact that historical and social scientific studies of religion have had on our very ability to make normative judgments. *My thesis is simple – doing critical historical studies on religions and social orders demythologizes and deconstructs all our worldviews and seems to reduce us to a pervasive ethical relativism.* And yet I hope to make the case that the historical-critical study of

---

[1]This paper is based on material adapted from my most recent book, *The Ethical Challenge of Auschwitz and Hiroshima: Apocalypse or Utopia?* (Albany, 1993: SUNY Press).

religion and the social order, and socio-historical consciousness itself, have not so much destroyed our ability to make normative judgments as changed the grounds upon which we must make such judgments. Finally, I want to briefly suggest how this affects the ethics of doing history itself.

The Sea of Ethical Relativism – Our Present Dilemma

Our situation came home to me most vividly in 1982, my first year of teaching at the University of South Florida. There was one event in particular that stands out in my mind. In the first case, I was teaching a course on Judaism and Christianity after the Holocaust. One day, early in the course, I was explaining to the students how the Germans simply rounded up and gassed almost six million Jews and how we must never allow anything like that to ever happen again. In the middle of my lecture a student raised his hand and objected: "But Professor Fasching, maybe it was just the custom of Germans to kill Jews." I was dumbfounded. Had it really come to this? Had we educators, in an effort to promote "multiculturalism" – that is, to get our students to appreciate the diversity of social orders and historical traditions, left our students with the impression that *all* values are culturally relative? Is it true that if another culture chooses to round up and slaughter its own citizens, the best we can say is that, "I guess that must be their custom," and go on with our lives as if these "customs" do not concern us?

The study of the Holocaust has haunted my academic career as a teacher of comparative religious ethics because it presents us with a case study of a whole society losing its ethical bearings so that it was possible to make evil seem to be good and good, evil. After all, in Nazi Germany killing Jews and Gypsies was considered good and rescuing them was considered evil. To the degree that we get our ethical bearings only from the society around us, we remain as vulnerable as the citizens of Nazi Germany to such ethical distortions. We, too, can be led to commit atrocities and call it "good." I fear that our universities and professional schools, steeped in socio-historical consciousness, are forming persons without a sense of moral direction. We seem to live in a world without norms where all values are relative.

This situation which we find ourselves in was illuminated well in the very first paper of this conference by the rather grim picture painted for us by William Green. He characterized the situation of our academic world as one of living in an academic climate of multiculturalism accompanied by a "new ideology" (is this "post-modernism?") which sees all fields and methods as "confession driven." All pretense at objective neutral discourse is abandoned. He describes this new ideology as "conviction driven" and a form of "experiential foundationalism." Thus, he tells us that women, Afro-Americans, Jews and others, all claim to speak from their experience and that the "core experience" on which each builds their field is unassailable. Thus all fields are becoming like theology, conviction-driven disciplines. Now as a theologian, my reaction is – this may be good piety but it is bad theology and equally disastrous for any other field. It is intellectual and ethical suicide.

Robert Ellwood, in his paper delivered this morning, raised the same problem in another way. He examined the role of the mythologist as historian and "transcendent social critic" and asked whether such social critics could really differentiate the "sacred murder" practiced by the Aztecs from the "ordinary murder" committed by the Nazi Storm Troopers. Or to put it another way, can one live in a sacred world without ending up justifying "blood sacrifice" where the one who is to be sacrificed is all too readily identified by the division of the world into the sacred and the profane, those who are the same and those who are different? In my recent two-volume work on narrative ethics I have tried to address the questions raised by both my colleagues. Today I only have time to directly address the core question – Does historical consciousness disable our ability to make normative judgments?

Moreover, both Green and Ellwood are as troubled as I am about the teaching of religion, history and the social order. What are we to communicate to our students in the classroom? Are we to try to remain neutral as William Green suggests when he insists that we must not condemn the "otherness by exclusion" model in its supersessionist or other guises? Or are we to judge our scholar predecessors and find them wanting as Robert Ellwood suggests? Or to put it another way, in a "conviction-driven" academic world what possible purpose can the "intellectual rigor" that William Green called for at the end of his presentation serve? For in such a world how could one make normative judgments that would be of any use to our student befuddled by the murderous customs of the Nazis? In our situation, the retreat into methodological rigor simply becomes a way of dodging the issue.

Historical Consciousness, Ethical Relativism and the Death of God

Let me make my case more fully by shifting from a personal to a more socio-historical perspective. In 1965, a human being walked in space for the first time in history. On March eighteenth of that year, cosmonaut Alexei Leonov stepped into space for a ten-minute walk. He was followed in less than three months by the American astronaut, Edward White. Thanks to modern mass media we were able to see what was happening virtually as it happened. Thus on millions of TV sets around the world an image of virtually mythic proportions portrayed to us our contemporary situation. Cut loose from the earth's atmosphere, floating free at the end of a tether linking him to his space craft, the space walker symbolized the technological utopianism of an apocalyptic age. The decade of the sixties began on the brink of apocalyptic annihilation with the Cuban Missile Crisis and ended by putting a man on the moon. Thus despite an ominous beginning, the sixties ended in a utopian mood – seeing the astronaut as the symbol of our technological capacity to transcend all limits, creating and discovering new worlds without limit. Yet this symbol was not without ambiguity. Floating in space, without a clear sense of direction, the astronaut was also a reminder of the demonic normlessness of a technological civilization. This is the very normlessness predicted by Nietzsche's madman at the end of the nineteenth century.

Modern human beings, Nietzsche suggested, had committed a deed of world-historical import. And yet they remained ignorant of its reality because they had not yet experienced its earth-shaking consequences. As Nietzsche tells it, a madman enters the public square crying "I seek God, I seek God." Many who did not believe in God began to chide him – "Did he lose his way?", "Is he hiding?", "Has he gone on a voyage?" Then,

> the madman jumped into their midst and pierced them with his glances. 'Whither is God' he cried. 'I shall tell you. We have killed him – you and I. All of us are his murderers. But how have we done this? How were we able to drink up the sea? Who gave us the sponge to wipe away the entire horizon? What did we do when we unchained this earth from its sun? Whither is it moving now? Whither are we moving now? Away from all suns? Are we not plunging continually? Backward, sideward, forward, in all directions? Is there any up or down left? Are we not straying as through an infinite nothing? Do we not feel the breath of empty space? Has it not become colder? Is not night and more night coming on all the while? Must not lanterns be lit in the morning? Do we not hear anything yet of the noise of the gravediggers who are burying God? Do we not smell anything yet of God's decomposition? Gods, too, decompose. God is dead. God remains dead. And we have killed him. How shall we, the murderers of all murderers, comfort ourselves? What was holiest and most powerful of all that the world has yet owned has bled to death under our knives. Who will wipe this blood off us?
>
> What water is there for us to clean ourselves? What festivals of atonement, what sacred games shall we have to invent? Is not the greatness of this deed too great for us? Must not we ourselves become gods simply to seem worthy of it? There has never been a greater deed; and whoever will be born after us – for the sake of this deed he will be part of a higher history than all history hitherto.'
>
> Here the madman fell silent and looked again at his listeners; and they, too, were silent and stared at him in astonishment. At last he

threw his lantern on the ground, and it broke and went out. 'I come too early,' he said then; 'my time has not come yet. This tremendous event is still on its way, still wandering – it has not yet reached the ears of man. Lightning and thunder require time, the light of the stars requires time, deeds require time even after they are done, before they can be seen and heard. This deed is still more distant from them than the most distant stars – *and yet they have done it themselves.*'[2]

What is astonishing about the imagery of this passage, originally published in 1882, is how uncannily it corresponds to the image of our space walker in 1965. It is as if Nietzsche's prophecy of the deed which was yet light-years away from being acknowledged had now finally entered human consciousness. It is as if, in some uncanny way, Nietzsche had seen our astronaut floating in space and had grasped with utter lucidity the implication of that experience. It is as if he could foresee that the modern secular, scientific and technological civilization which was coming to birth in his time would lead inevitably to the death of God; that is, to a normless world "cut loose from its sun," cut loose from the bonds of gravity, adrift in deep space – floating and tumbling, without a sense of direction, suffering the consequences of the disappearance of the horizon as one breaks free of the earth.

Scarcely more than half a century after Nietzsche's madman had unleashed his prophecy the Nazis came along to embrace Nietzsche's vision of a normless *will to power*. Nietzsche had offered a vision of a new type of individual who would have to take charge of human history after the death of God – namely, the *Ubermensch* or self-transcending person. Such individuals would have the courage to "transvalue all values" and remake the world in their own image. Nietzsche, of course, had a somewhat aristocratic vision of these new individuals. But his vision was easily usurped by the Nazis who imagined themselves, the pure Aryan race, as the natural embodiment of this superior human being who would recreate the world through a *will to power*. The Nazi program of attempted genocide of the Jews is a logical outcome of this new normless situation expressed in Nietzsche's parable of "the Death of God." In a world where power is the final arbiter of values and *might makes right*, decide is inexorably followed by genocide.

In traditional or premodern societies religion played a central and public role in influencing the social order. What all traditional societies have in common is the belief that the order of society is part of a normative order of nature as structured by the sacred ancestors, gods or God. Since the order of society was considered part of the order of

---

[2]From *The Gay Science* by Friedrich Nietzsche in *The Portable Nietzsche* edited by Walter Kaufmann (New York, 1954 and 1968: Viking Press), pp. 95-96. *The Gay Science* was first published in 1882.

nature as divinely established, such societies were conservatively ordered. Society, like nature, was viewed as fixed and given and not an object to be manipulated and changed.

Our technological society differs fundamentally from all traditional societies. Neither astronomy nor chemistry nor even physics has produced the revolution in self-understanding in which we are caught up. The revolutionary sciences for a technological civilization are the human sciences – especially history, sociology, and anthropology. It was the new comparative socio-historical consciousness generated by the emergence of the social sciences in the nineteenth century which gave birth to a consciousness of society as a human product rather than an extension of nature. We now see society as an artificial social construct, shaped by human decisions, rather than as an extension of nature. The essence of technological civilization is not the transformation of nature, nor is it the proliferation of machines. It is, rather, the awareness of self and society as human constructs which can be shaped and changed.

The problem is that the very process by which human beings have come to think of society as capable of being shaped and changed is a secularizing or desacralizing process initiated by modern historical and social scientific criticism. The public order of traditional societies was stabilized by the firm belief that this order was part of a value-laden natural order determined by the gods and ancestors. Each society saw its social order through the lens of myth or sacred story, what Peter Berger calls a "sacred canopy," which made its social order appear to be a direct expression of the natural order. But with the emergence of critical socio-historical consciousness in the nineteenth century, the variety of cultures strung out through time and across cultural boundaries came to be compared. As a result the natural order of each society came to be seen as an artificial construct and all cultural values came to be thought of as relative. These values no longer appeared, as they had from within each society, as firmly fixed in a cosmic order. Now they appeared as subjective, culturally relative human options.

This is the point at which the fundamental crisis of modern society appears. Since human values in premodern societies were typically embedded in normative myths of natural order, their demythologization by critical socio-historical consciousness, which made it possible to think of changing society, at the same time undermined the very norms by which such decisions could be made. Precisely at that point at which human beings became conscious of their ability to shape and change society they lost access to the norms needed to make those decisions. It is this situation, which Nietzsche addresses with his parable of the *death of God*, which unchained the earth from its sun so that we now drift aimlessly in space without any sense of up or down. We have lost our sense of moral direction.

The world we have made for ourselves seems to be the embodiment of Babel – a confusing pluralism of voices and values. We live, it seems, in a sea of cultural and ethical relativism in which all ethical choice is reduced to arbitrary personal preference. With no rational way to adjudicate moral disputes such disagreements are reduced to ideological struggles based on the will to power. It is the tragic paradox of our time that the increase of our power over nature and society has been in inverse proportion to our capacity to discover a normative consensus by which to govern the exercise of this power.

The result is that we no longer believe that values are written into the cosmos. On the contrary, we now tend to think that values are a personal and a private matter and everyone should be free to choose their own morality so long as they do not impose it on others. However, to think of ethics and morality as private matters is a contradiction in terms, for ethics and morality are about our relations with other human beings and hence inherently public. To choose the values that will guide my actions in isolation from others is already to violate my relationship to those around me who will be affected by my actions. A private morality is inherently unethical. It violates the social nature of our existence. Ethical reflection by its very nature requires discussion, dialogue and negotiations with those others with whom I share existence. Hence ethics is always a public and social process – it can never be purely private and individual.

Therefore, we are faced now with what I believe to be the most serious and pressing challenge of our time: public dialogue and debate which will lead to the discovery and articulation of the philosophical and theological foundations of a normative social ethic whereby cultures themselves can be critiqued, and hence shaped and changed through those public policies and personal commitments which truly promote the human good.

Historical Consciousness and Human Dignity – Making Normative Judgments From an Ethic of Honor to an Ethic of Human Dignity

Despite this seemingly dismal characterization of our situation, the social and historical sciences have not left us without resources. While traditional paths to normative judgments grounded in the sacred order of the cosmos seem to be closed off, new paths have been opened up by critical socio-historical consciousness itself. As Peter Berger has argued, there is a fundamental difference in the ethical sensibilities of individuals in modern and premodern societies. "The [modern] age that saw the decline of honor also saw the rise of new moralities and of a new humanism, and most specifically of a historically unprecedented concern for the dignity and the rights of the individual."[3] The modern person, he argues, operates out of an ethic of dignity whereas the person from a premodern society is governed by a morality of honor. To fully understand the implications of, and reasons for, this shift we must understand the social and historical location of these contrasting value perspectives.

Honor and duty, says Berger, are concepts rooted in an understanding of self found in premodern hierarchical societies. These are precisely societies which understand both self and society as part of a sacred natural order. In such societies, the self is basically a clothed self. That is, the self is identified with or clothed in its social role which is given as its destiny at birth into a particular place in the hierarchical stratification of society. The sense of identity one has in such a society is basically collective. You would have the sense that your family and your clan reside within you, such that if you are insulted it is not just you but your whole family or clan who is insulted. Moreover, if you fail to live up to the obligations of your social status it is more than a personal failure. You bring dishonor on your whole family or clan. In both cases you may be expected to risk your life in order to reestablish this collective honor. An insult may require a duel or intertribal warfare. Individual failures entail a loss of face which may require reparations as drastic as suicide, as in the Japanese tradition of *hara kiri*.

It is very difficult for a modern person to understand this ethic because it is rooted in a sense of human identity totally at odds with the modern sensibility. Whereas the traditional self is from birth clothed in a culturally defined human nature (that is, a fixed set of social roles), the modern self takes off and puts on social roles or identities as if they were different suits of clothes. For the modern person, the self is never identified with its social role. The modern self is a naked self which identifies itself not with its roles but rather with its capacity to choose its roles. The modern self is an existential self, free to choose who to become through its choice of roles. Because the naked self does not identify with its social role, it does not experience insult as a threat to its honor any more than it experiences failure as a loss of face or identity.

In a premodern society there is a hierarchical ordering of human selves in status and value. The hierarchical order is a normative order, reflecting the sacred order of the cosmos. Thus one's place in society

---

[3]Peter Berger, "On the Obsolescence of the Concept of Honor," in *Revisions*, edited by Stanley Hauerwas and Alasdair Macintyre (Notre Dame, 1983: University of Notre Dame Press), p.173.

determines not only who you are but what your obligations or duties are toward your peers as well as those above and below you in the hierarchy. Such a hierarchy implies levels of humanity. The operative value governing human relationships is not equality but rather "to each his due." Those in higher positions having been given more humanity also have greater obligations of duty than those who are lower in the hierarchy, having less humanity. A very clear example of such society would be the classic Brahmanic caste system in India or the classical familial-hierarchical ordering of human relations in neo-Confucian societies. In both, one of the greatest sins is to violate the sacred cosmic order of nature by the mixing of castes or roles, ignoring the proper ritual obligations of caste or social position. It is a great sin because it violates the sacred order which makes life possible, introducing disharmony into the universe and causing the disintegration of the cosmos into chaos. In all such societies myth and ritual serve to legitimate the sacred order of society, reinforcing the obligation of everyone to perform his or her sacred duty.

By contrast, the naked self transcends it social roles. It is not that such a self is ever found without some social role or other but rather that the modern self views itself as prior to its roles which are understood as diverse opportunities for self expression. As a result all human selves are thought of as essentially equal, no matter what their social status since one's humanity resides not in a role but in an essential nakedness shared with all other selves. "Modern man [says Peter Berger] is Don Quixote on his deathbed, denuded of the multicolored banners that previously enveloped the self and revealed to be *nothing but a man*."[4] This is the essence of the modern understanding of human dignity which has replaced the notion of honor. "It is precisely this solitary self that modern consciousness has perceived as the bearer of human dignity and of inalienable human rights."[5] All selves have an equal human dignity and equal human rights because all selves are equally naked.

This understanding of self, while typical of modern society, says Berger, has its origins in such ancient precursors as the Hebrew Bible, Sophocles and Mencius. Its modern manifestations appear in the

> formulation of human rights, from the Preamble to the Declaration of Independence to the Declaration of Human Rights of the United Nations. These rights always pertain to the individual 'irrespective of race, color or creed' – or, indeed, of sex, age, physical condition or any conceivable social status. There is an implicit sociology and an implicit anthropology here. The implicit sociology views all biological and historical differentiations among men as either downright unreal or

---

[4]Berger, *Revisions*, p. 175.
[5]Berger, *Revisions*, p. 176.

essentially irrelevant. The implicit anthropology locates the real self over and beyond all these differentiations.[6]

The transition from an ethic of honor to an ethic of dignity, Berger suggests, can be viewed both positively and negatively. Conservatives view the decline of honor as a profound loss, while modernists see it as a "prelude to liberation." On the one hand, the naked self is in a situation of perpetual identity crisis, marked by excessive individualism and alienation from its social roles. On the other hand, this same deinstitutionalizing of the self makes possible "the specific modern discoveries of human dignity and human rights....The new recognition of individual responsibility for all actions, even those assigned to the individual with specific institutional roles, a recognition that attained the force of law at Nuremberg – all these and others, are moral achievements that would be unthinkable without the peculiar constellations of the modern world."[7]

Berger's distinction between honor and dignity as contrasting forms of ethical consciousness helps me make my case, namely, that while historical consciousness undermines one kind of normative thought – the ethics of honor – it facilitates an alternative basis for normative ethical judgments – human dignity and human rights. I would argue that religions in the past provided two different sources for ethical norms – sacred cosmic order on the one hand and experiences of radical transcendence on the other. While the experiences of sacred order give rise to an ethic of honor, those of radical transcendence elicit an ethic of dignity. Critical historical consciousness, I would argue, undermines the authority of the first but reinforces that of the second.

In most times and places throughout history religion and society were experienced as one, not two separate realities. Society was experienced as an extension of the sacred order of the cosmos normatively described in myth and ritual. However, at least twice in the history of religions experiences of radical transcendence forced a differentiation of religion from society resulting in the creation of holy communities. This seems to have happened in the sixth century B.C.E. both in India with the formation of Buddhist Sangha and in the Near East with the formation of Jewish synagogues most probably during the Babylonian exile. Our contemporary ethic of human dignity and human rights is both religious and secular, supported both by experiences of radical transcendence or holiness and by the emergence of socio-historical consciousness itself.

---

[6]Berger, *Revisions*, p. 176.
[7]Berger, *Revisions*, p. 180.

The origins of human dignity and human rights thought is controversial. I do not think it is either possible or desirable to trace a human rights ethic to a single source. Human rights emerge as a distinct theme of modern ethical consciousness as the result of the influences of a variety of sources both ancient and modern, both secular and religious. I would identify at least four such sources: (1) urbanization, (2) experiences of the holy, (3) socio-historical consciousness of the limits of all socialization and (4) the experiences of doubt and indignation and the questions they generate.

(1) Urbanization

Urbanization is a secularizing process which alienates the self from the sacred mythological order of nature, stripping the self of its collective identity and leaving it naked in its new urban world. Urbanization initiates an individuation of human identity by forcing people to deal with differences. While tribal societies were based on common myths and rituals and common work tasks, the city brought people together from different tribal backgrounds, with different myths and rituals, and at the same time created new complex levels of social stratification based on differences of occupation. Urban individuation breaks down the collective sense of identity that nurtures an ethic of honor and creates the burden of individual self-consciousness that is a precondition for an ethic of dignity. This process heightens the awareness of human individuality and the unique value of every individual. However, it also heightens the experience of alienation and meaninglessness as human beings are expelled from the womb of tribal myth and collective identity and, like Gilgamesh, must face the burden of personal mortality that accompanies individuated identity.

(2) Experiences of the Holy

In the ancient world, friendship between persons who were socially unequal was generally not possible, but it was viewed as a possibility within the holy communities of Buddhists and Jews, and later in Christianity, as is evidenced in their ethical traditions of hospitality to the stranger, the downcast and the outcast. I don't wish to exaggerate here, for clearly this possibility did not successfully bridge the gender gap, for instance. But the drive toward equality is inherent in the experience of radical transcendence or the holy, even when it is only partially or selectively realized. What these holy communities offered that was unavailable otherwise within a sacred society was the development of a language of inwardness to articulate an experience of the holy which breaks with the cosmological imagination – a language for exploring the openness of the naked self to the infinite. In the traditions of the holy communities the naked self created by urban secularization is not clothed in some new cosmological myth but rather discovers its emptiness. The consciousness of the equality of selves within holy communities is rooted in an awareness that all selves share a fundamental capacity for openness to the infinite. The self is understood not as created in the image of nature (with a natural caste or class identity) but in the image of the wholly other (for example, God or Nirvana), a transcendence which is unimaginable (that is, un-image-able) and hence can never be fully integrated into the cosmological/social order. The self, stripped of its natural identity, turns inward to discover that its nakedness is not the equivalent of an eternal self. There is no floor of Tao or Brahman beneath the self to legitimate sacred stories of hierarchical order, only an emptiness which is a radical openness to the infinite. All are equal by virtue of their empty or imageless condition. In this respect, the Buddhist speaks of the self as void or empty. Jews and Christians speak of the self as created in the image of a God who is without image.[8] It is no accident that such holy communities give birth to an ethic of hospitality that welcomes the stranger, the downcast and the outcast.

(3) Socio-historical Consciousness of the Limits of Socialization

Socio-historical consciousness generates an insight into human self-transcendence within a social order which, in some respects, parallels the religious insight into the emptiness and imagelessness of the self. That is, once modern socio-historical consciousness emerged with the appearance of the social sciences in the nineteenth century, the inalienable or transcendent quality of our humanity became visible not only to the religious eye but also to the secular eye. Once the distinction

---

[8]Eventually, Christians adapted this Jewish insight to the gentile world by using the Greek language of metaphysics to speak of being created in the image of a Trinitarian God. Like a Buddhist koan, the doctrine of the trinity defied the imagination, even as the doctrine of the incarnation affirmed that the human self, undistorted by sin, is a perfect image of the God who cannot be imaged. This insight, however, stood in tension with the hierarchical structure of Greek metaphysical thinking. To the degree that this way of thought influenced how Christians thought about God, Christianity drifted back into a cosmicization of the social order. This tension can be seen in the difference between Origen and Augustine's accounts of the trinity. Origen's account is ambiguous. One side of his thought suggests that since the son emanates from the father, the son is less than the father, and likewise the spirit is less than the son. Augustine, on the other hand, grasps that the trinity must not be thought of in terms of physical metaphors of "emanation" (for example, such as the sun's rays) but in spiritual terms, whose metaphors are the relations of mind to itself (for example, memory, intelligence and will). The result is that in the trinitarian God, all persons (divine and human) are equal. But even in Augustine this realization stands in tension with a hierarchical metaphysics of creation.

between the self and its social roles was made and the processes by which we become socialized could be studied, it became manifestly apparent that no culture or society has ever succeeded in totally socializing any self. There always remains some part of the self (the self as chooser of its roles) which escapes being encapsulated by society and reduced to its social roles. This is something every parent knows from practical experience – no child can ever be totally socialized. There is always some part of the child that remains holy (that is, "set apart"). Our legal tradition recognizes this under the rubric of the "right to privacy." It is the experience of self as holy or set apart which gives us an inalienable dignity (a dignity which cannot be usurped by the surrounding culture) and makes every human being a perpetual alien or stranger within its society and even to itself. And it is that experience of alienation which enables us to doubt, question and rebel.

(4) Doubt and Indignation

Doubt, socio-historical consciousness and emptiness/imagelessness belong to the same category of experiences – experiences of our radical openness to the infinite which create the gap between the self as self-transcending subject and self as cultural-institutional role. The abyss of the self, its emptiness, can never be filled or encapsulated by one's culture or society. Something of the self always escapes definition and encapsulation. The Upanishads ask, "How can the knower be known?," as a way of pointing out the impossibility of the reflecting self ever being so encapsulated even by its own reflection. The thinker always transcends that which is being thought about, especially when what is being thought is one's self. The mistake is to clothe the thinker in an eternal self. Augustine of Hippo came upon this same reflective paradox. Like the Buddha and other forest dwellers he turned inward, traveling through the "caverns" of memory of past life events (more than one life in the Buddha's case) and concluded upon exploring these caverns of his own inwardness that the mind is so vast it cannot contain itself and hence is un-image-able and radically open to the infinite as wholly other. Hence the mind discovers its own contingency, its own emptiness or openness to the infinite. In Augustine's case that lead him to the conclusion that God is not the mind but "the lord God of the mind" (*Confessions*, X, 25),[9] even as the Buddha came to insist that the experience of Nirvana is not an experience of an eternal self but radically

---

[9]*The Confessions of Augustine,* translated by Rex Warner (New York, 1963: New American Library, Mentor-Omega), p. 235.

other than all self– namely *anatta* (no-self).[10] In both cases the self is left swimming over the abyss of the infinite.

Doubt emerges out of the experienced gap between the self and its social world. Doubt is a secular experience of transcendence, whose religious correlate is the experience of the holy as the experience of emptiness or imagelessness. Doubt and emptiness give birth to the utopian rebel who calls the sacred order of society into question in order to bring about a new order of things, open to the infinite. At the reflective level, the experience of doubt gives birth to the philosopher even as the experience of imagelessness gives birth to the prophet and the experience of emptiness to the sage. And at the everyday level of common sense, doubt gives birth to the unreflective rebel, who, although he or she can't say why, feels the need to refuse the demand of the political, technological, economic or social order for total conformity. The rebel in the street is born in response to the violation of human dignity – out of indignation – as an intuitive visceral awareness of the silent yet commanding voice which witnesses to the irreducible dignity which all selves have in common.

The movement for human rights is rooted experientially in both the secular and the religious forms of the experience of the holy or dignity as irreducible experiences of openness to the infinite. Let me clarify this. I differentiate religious experience into the sacred on the one hand and the holy on the other. The sacred sacralizes the finite whereas the experience of the holy or wholly other desacralizes the finite in the name of the infinite. Drawing on the wisdom of Paul Tillich I would argue that while the sacred or "sacramental" identifies ultimate value with the finite, the holy calls into question this identification in the name of an openness to the infinite as experienced in either its prophetic, mystical or rational forms. The mystical experience criticizes the sacred in the name of the *radical otherness* of the holy which cannot be identified ontologically with any finite thing. The prophetic critique identifies the moral danger of elevating the finite to the status of the infinite for this is equivalent of identifying what "Is" with what "Ought" to be. Finally, secular rationality criticizes the demonic irrationality of every finite sacred order

---

[10]Insofar as Christianity and (to a lesser degree) Judaism allowed itself to be seduced by the Greek metaphysical tradition it of course tended to reduce "God" to an "Eternal Being" which denies the essential biblical experience of God as temporal-historical and without image. We find this tension in Augustine. The conflict between "Being" and the "Infinite" represents the fundamental conflict between the cosmological imagination and the experience of the holy. In Christianity, only with the Protestant Reformation did the holiness of God break free of the metaphysical imagination of being and then only partially and with ambivalence.

which seeks to limit what it means to be human to the parameters of that order and so forbids all doubt and questioning and demands uncritical, unthinking obedience.[11]

In this model, the secular and the holy are not alien to each other. On the contrary, they are dialectically united in their power to alienate the self from all sacred order in the name of a hidden transcendence we call human dignity. And the demand that the human dignity of all persons be respected and protected is in fact the basis for an ethic of secular holiness, an ethic which theists and a-theists (whether Buddhist or secular) ought to be able to construct cooperatively. For unlike the experience of the sacred which treats reason as the enemy of both religion and politics (demanding instead an unquestioning obedience), the experiences of the holy gives rise to critical reason, manifest through both the experience of doubt and the experience of emptiness. Secular holiness unites religion and reason in the common task of creating a public world ordered to the "unseen measure" of human dignity.

Human Dignity and the Emergence of Social Ethics

In the ancient world there really is no such thing as social ethics in the modern managerial sense of transforming the artificial social structures of society. Whether the world was viewed as defined by nature as one's unchangeable fate, or by sin, or as a world of samsara/illusion, etc. – it was viewed as a world which could not be significantly altered by human intentions. It is only when the peculiarly modern notion of society as artificial and managerial emerged in the nineteenth century that social ethics was born. The secularizing power of Greek rationalism converged with Jewish and Christian experiences of transcendence, and their accompanying myths of history, to finally secularize human existence and expose human beings to a newly invented critical social-scientific consciousness. This is the unique contribution of the West to the emergence of human rights. And this new socio-historical or technological-managerial consciousness radically alters the situation for all religious and philosophical traditions East or West, virtually forcing the anthropological traditions of both to develop a new dimension – social ethics as the ethics of human liberation.

Every ideology begins by defining the human in a sacral language of natural differences so as to separate the superior from the inferior, whether by race or sex or class, etc. Defining the human inevitably occurs only for the purpose of violating someone's dignity. But the human cannot be defined. To put it another way, the human can be

---

[11]Paul Tillich, in *The Future of Religion*, edited by Gerald C. Brauer (New York, 1966: Harper and Row), p. 89.

defined only by its undefinability. Our inalienable dignity resides in our undefinability. This means that the human self cannot be fully captured by the socio-cosmic or bureaucratic imagination and the social order it constructs. Consequently, the human self cannot be reduced to its social role in some sacred cosmic order.

The conjunction of experiences of the holy (emptiness or imagelessness) and modern socio-historical (or technological) consciousness with the experiences of doubt and indignation is hermeneutically and socio-politically explosive. It forces human communities to move from the conviction of *the dignity of the self* to an affirmation of *human rights* and finally to audacious acts of *human liberation*. For example, in the first century, Paul of Tarsus could say that *in Christ there is neither male nor female*. Nevertheless, Pauline communities, and Christians in general, continued to subordinate women to men in hierarchical social roles. Why? Because the order of society was seen as an unchangeable sacred order and therefore the statement of equality was taken as an eschatological statement of spiritual equality to be realized in the flesh only at the end of time. Or again, the peasants took Luther's preaching about the freedom and dignity of the Christian to heart and were inspired to revolt against oppression. But Luther, still sharing the conviction that society is part of a sacred cosmic order, explained to them that in this world everyone must know and keep to their place, only in the world to come will they be actually equal. But today, when a believing community reads Paul's or Luther's statements in the light of modern managerial consciousness, that is, with the socio-historical awareness that the social order is not sacred and unchangeable but secular and artificial, these members are suddenly confronted with a new level of moral obligation, the demand that society be transformed so as to allow for freedom and equality between the sexes and social classes here and now. The combination of consciousness of the holy and socio-historical (managerial) consciousness is at one and the same time both radically apocalyptic and utopian, for it leads to an ethic of human liberation which brings one's old world to an end in order to inaugurate a new creation.

The Historian as Storyteller and Ethicist

Like the bard of ancient times, the historian carries an awesome responsibility in telling the tale of times past. For the stories which are passed on shape the narrative imagination of a generation and with it its sense of future possibilities. We fail ethically in telling our stories of the past not only through what is said but also through what is left unsaid. Our stories violate human dignity not only by stereotyping the stranger but also by leaving the stranger out all together. The ethical test of a public narrative is how it treats the stranger. We are all prepared to acknowledge the dignity of those we perceive as being like ourselves. But unless the story we tell demands that we recognize the dignity of the stranger, it is simply an ideological expression of self-interest bent on protecting "our own." Ethno-centric (or gender-centric, or religio-centric) bias is the undoing of critical history. Critical historiography presupposes an ethic of hospitality to the stranger, a commitment to the dignity of the stranger. One must be prepared to enter into narrative traditions of the stranger and see the world through the eyes of the stranger.

As far back as we can see into the misty recesses of time and the human adventure, human beings have told stories; although, to be sure, the particular stories they tell are quite diverse. Human beings are not just storytellers, they are story dwellers. Stories are not something external to human identity, but the very substance of it. The choices we make, even the options we think we have, are governed by the kind of story we think we are in and the role we see ourselves playing in it. It is significant that prior to the modern period, all peoples everywhere conveyed their stories in song, drama and dance – that is, in mythic and ritual enactment. Their stories coursed through their veins and sinews and lived in their every gesture and movement. By dwelling in the story, by living *through* the narrative, one became human. To be human is to be like the gods or God or to do as the sacred ancestors did. That is why, in primal (oral) cultures the right way to do anything was the ritual way. For ritual is the archetypal repetition of those actions through which the right order of the world was created. It is significant that both the words *right* and *rite* are derived from the Sanscrit term ("*r'ta*") for sacred *cosmic order*. Morality in such a world takes the form of a cosmological ethic, in which *Is = Ought*. Ritual conforms human action to *the way things* are as established *in the beginning*.

"Modern" human beings, however, existing after the fall into socio-historical consciousness (especially since the nineteenth century), no longer understand themselves as living in a normative cosmos. They "know" that such cosmic stories are cultural fictions. Human beings are now historically self-conscious and "enlightened" creatures who can do without stories – or so the story goes. Such stories, it is thought, belong to the childhood and adolescence of the human race. Having reached the "enlightened" adulthood of the "modern" situation, contemporary individuals have put aside these childish stories. But as Stanley Hauerwas, the leading theological proponent of narrative ethics, has argued, the "modern person" is still living out a story, – one that is meant to put an end to all stories. The form of the story is modeled on the mystical vision of Joachim of Fiore, a monk of the late middle ages who imagined history as made up of three successive ages – that of the Father, the Son and the Spirit. In the apocalyptic last age of the Spirit, he suggested, the human race would reach a utopian maturity and institutions would no longer be needed (not even the church), as all would live in spontaneous harmony, guided inwardly by the Spirit. This narrative vision, in its later secularized forms, came to form the foundational myth of the Enlightenment and modernization. In its "modern" versions it drew on Lessing from the eighteenth century and Comte (the father of sociology) in the nineteenth century, to suggest a story of *the three ages of the human race* in which the *age of myth* (that is, story) is superseded by the *age of metaphysics* which is in turn superseded by our own *rational age of science*.[12]

The mythical stories which once shaped our sense of public order have now been replaced by scientific narratives, including the narratives of the socio-historical sciences. Where once our myths taught us that we lived in a sacred and normative order of nature, now our knowledge of history and the social order tell us that we have no direct and unmediated relation to nature. Instead all our relationships are mediated by language. Our world is an interpreted, socially constructed world. In this world the historian and social scientist have largely replaced the poet and the bard as the teller of tales of our origin and destiny – tales which construct for us a socio-linguistic world in which to dwell. And because historians cannot do history without telling stories they can never be "scientists" without also being "humanists." Critical history is the bridge between the social sciences and the humanities. Therefore, social historians have an awesome responsibility. Whether they like it or not, the stories they tell about the history of the human race have theological and ethical import. No matter how objective, secular and scientific they intend to be, their stories will inevitably reveal a religious imagination.

The fundamental ethical question to be addressed in the writing of history is whether the stories we tell will be governed by an imagination shaped by the sacred or by the holy. The sacral imagination forever seeks to define and confine our humanity to a given sacred order. The experience of the sacred is inherently dualistic. It divides the drama of human existence into a story of the children of light against the children of darkness. Whenever society and history are shaped by a sense of the sacred, the world becomes divided into the spheres of the sacred and the profane. A sacred society creates a sacred circle whose center is within itself and is defined by sameness. Thus all who are the same are sacred

---

[12]See Stanley Hauerwas, *Truthfulness and Tragedy* (Notre Dame, 1977: University of Notre Dame Press), p. 25ff.

and all who are different are profane. The stories of a sacred society and its historical traditions can be identified by their common characteristic – they have no place for the stranger.

A holy community, by contrast, is an alternate community (or sub-culture) whose values are shaped by stories of hospitality to the stranger. Hence the center of a holy community is not within itself but beyond its borders in the stranger. For the sanctified imagination, the stranger evokes the sense of the wholly (holy) other, the one whose ways are not our ways and whose thoughts are not our thoughts. The stranger, like the wholly other, remains undefinable and hence transcends one's sacred order. Thus in a holy community to welcome the stranger is to welcome God, or God's messiah or whatever symbolizes the transcendence of the holy as wholly other (for example, the Buddhist sense of Nirvana).

What separates the narratives of the holy from those governed by the sacral imagination is that unlike sacred stories, narratives shaped by the experience of the holy provide a place for the stranger who does not share one's story. In a sacred society those who do not share its stories are profane, less than human and beyond the circle of ethical obligation. Such a sacral worldview encourages the apocalyptic cleansing of sacred space to create "lebensraum" for those who are "truly human." In a holy community the recognition of the stranger as the bearer of the holy requires precisely the recognition of the humanity of the one who stands outside my story. Whenever historical narrative becomes ideological, demonstrating the superiority of one's own people (race, or gender, or religion, etc.) over the profane other, it betrays the presence of the sacral imagination. By contrast, whenever historical narrative calls into question such ideological interpretations in defense of the dignity of the stranger it reveals the power of the holy to shape the narrative imagination.

The sacral interpretation of history encourages the historian as storyteller to indulge in the ideological purification of history. The ideological historian tells a story of the past which is cleansed of everything profane (either by condemning or forgetting significant portions of that past) – even as the Nazis cleansed their history, including their Christianity, of everything Jewish. Critical history, at the same time both social-scientific and humanistic, by contrast, desacralizes such readings of history, recognizing the gender inclusive, multi-cultural and multi-religious history of every people. In so doing it expresses a narrative imagination shaped by the holy, namely one which makes a place for the stranger and welcomes the stranger into a common shared history.

Secular critical history is, I am arguing, deeply shaped by profound religious experiences. It is shaped by experiences of the holy as alienation from sacred history. To be alienated is as the Hebrew word for "holy" (*qadosh*) suggests, to be "separated" – separated or alienated from the sacred ideological order of history and society. The historian, both as a social scientist and as a humanities scholar, can only engage in serious scholarship through the experience of alienation – the experience of becoming a stranger to his or her own world so as to enter into the narrative world of the stranger, see the world (including his or her own) through the stranger's eyes, the stranger's stories and the stranger's traditions.

The academic study of religion is at the same time both a secular and a religious activity. And the historian of religions who seeks to understand the stranger and the stranger's narrative world is engaged in what I would call an ethic of secular holiness. The humanities embody two important characteristics of secular holiness – (1) openness to the infinite (wholly other) which gives rise to the audacity to question all things and (2) openness to strangers (holy others) from diverse times and places who have a story to tell. The humanities are "set apart" (that is, *qadosh* or holy) within the university as those disciplines and areas of study which seek to illuminate and protect the holy as disclosed in the unfathomability of human dignity. In so doing, the humanities go beyond analysis and description to engage in prescription – that is, to engage in ethics.

The humanities have a normative responsibility – a responsibility not only to sympathetically understand but also to critically evaluate and to be audacious in their defense of human dignity. The humanities ought to measure all worldviews by the measure of human dignity – the Socratic *unseen measure* of all things human. Our task is the Socratic one of the examined life which begins with a knowledge of ignorance, a knowledge which forces us to recognize that the human can never be fully fathomed or fully known – that we will always be, in some sense, strangers even to ourselves.

Through the humanities we attempt to distill from such human experiences in their moments of greatness the wisdom to live more humanly. Religious studies and socio-historical scholarship are themselves products of the alienation produced by a secular socio-historical consciousness which is itself the product of both urbanization and of the experiences of the holy. This modern secular consciousness alienates me sufficiently from my own tradition to be in a position to be both critical of my own and sympathetic to the traditions of others. To engage in religious studies, whether as historian or theologian, within the context of the humanities, requires that I desacralize all sacred traditions, beginning with my own, through a surrender to the critical questions of the scholar who seeks to understand. The purpose of these questions is not to profane these traditions but to secularize them. Secularizing the sacred narrative traditions of the stranger makes it possible for me to enter into these strange worlds, these other worlds, and see reality through the eyes of the stranger in order to come back with new insight into my own religion and culture.

As long as these traditions are considered sacred they can only be approached by their own initiates. But the wisdom to be learned from the religious experiences of human beings is too valuable to be held captive by the traditions in which they originate. To desacralize these narrative traditions, therefore, is not to desecrate them but to treat them as holy. A holy text is one that welcomes the stranger and the stranger's questions. A holy text and its meanings cannot be owned or possessed by any one person or community any more than the experience of the holy itself. Once they are desacralized the narrative worlds of the stranger become narrative worlds open to strangers – open to anyone who is human. Whenever historians as storytellers engage in such a reading of texts and traditions they are also engaged in the theological and ethical task of welcoming the stranger and affirming the human dignity of the stranger – even as they desacralize all historical ideologies that would justify the elimination of the stranger. In so doing, the historian contributes to the social transformation of our divisive and confrontational apocalyptic world into a more utopian world – a more hospitable world where each speaks his or her own language and yet each is understood by all (Acts 2:1-12).

Response to Darrell J. Fasching's "Historical Consciousness, Religion and the Social Order: Can We Make Normative Judgments?"

Siv Illman
Åbo Akademi

Professor Fasching's paper provides a beautiful entrance into the subject matter of accelerating pluralism, changing institutions and ways of life, and it casts light on the impact on the quality of life and on the quest of individual subjects for self-respect, solidarity and ultimate resort. Personally, I was much intrigued by the fact that a vision laid down in a paper beyond the horizon – or from my point of view in Finland, even *under* the horizon – that such an account has so much to say of common interest. The creative outlook as well as the attitude of openness to "the other" activate response.

My own field is theology and the psychology of religion. In passing I note that in Europe traditionally the study of the psychology of religion tends to be linked to theology and philosophy, whereas the link in America seems to be to general psychology and social studies. On the other hand, in America religious institutions from within their own work have expressed an interest in psychology, often with a background in depth psychology. For historical reasons religious life in the Nordic countries does not have the same features and dynamics as religious life in America. However, the interchange between theology and psychology is a fact. In general the two perspectives are seen to

257

constitute helpful correctives to each other, but it is felt that there is a fine balance to keep. Representatives for the church, for example, usually express the view that psychological points and methods can contribute to the understanding of the religious element, but that the institution should not end up buying its ideology from the outside at the risk of losing its own identity by a secularization from within.[1]

My comments address the paper indirectly by way of presenting some supplementary thoughts on the broad perspective envisioned. According to my interpretation, the paper discusses a basic need for human liberation, for balance and for life-supporting orientation. The outlook gives priority to aspects of human rights as well as to real differences between individual subjects and between cultural settings. The impression is that identity and well-being are constituted and maintained in the course of an ongoing, important interaction between intra-dynamic processes of an emotive type, and interpersonal and cultural processes with cognitive contents. Now, in the light of the broad theme of human rights I want to suggest some practical points bearing on the individual search for "self-culture" and for ways in which to invest in life together with other people. In a general way I base my reflections on my own study of religiosity in literary works, particularly on the interpretation of some novels where I could identify a similar formative process of interchange between "the single one" and the outside world, a process leading first to an inner change and, eventually, to a more resolved outlook on life.

Methods and definitions I use have to do with the aspect of research and the kind of material involved. I find creative literature very interesting. I consider it an ongoing discussion of reality. It constitutes a substance of its own and gives expression close to empirical life, as well. When fiction elaborates an existential thematic imminent in the text, the reading experience may function as a catalyst for new awareness. On the level of how symbols function, literature can offer material for the shaping of attitudes and decisions. Literature can increase insight, it can evoke impulses that link the individual subject to a collective area of thought and faith, or it might point out directions worth exploring. And, when traditional guidance falls short, literature, among other creative perspectives, can play an important role in providing formulation and in offering interpretation. Very often it is the literary work that articulates the questions of our own time, puts our doubts, our eagerness, into

---

[1]Interesting perspectives are offered by Scharfenberg, J. *Sigmund Freud und seine Religionskritik als Herausforderung für den Christlichen Glauben* (Göttingen, 1976). Owe Wikström, present professor for the psychology of religion in Uppsala, Sweden, has discussed the matter in many instances.

words. The artist, the writer who concentrates on the rules of art, also has the obligation to give personal realization to an inner vision. In this process a creative activity independent of prevailing or failing trends and ideologies is set forth, an activity which seems motivated by a challenging, basic drive to explore life conditions and to experiment with answers, statements and categories which formulate what is, ultimately, humane and rational. In literature, and in life, as well, we notice the human effort to come to grips with things, a search beyond the immediate pleasure and pain for something that is true and comprehensive, something that exists besides the individual, both before and after the self.

The fictive characters in the novels I refer to here typically went through intensive experiences in their struggle for solutions to live with. In addition to difficult life circumstances, these people were blocked from within by a Kafka-like inner isolation, and they seemed to need some sort of transitive assistance to help them reach a more gratifying modus vivendi. Their situation was marked by communication catastrophe. Their search for liberation and meaning had neither channels nor clear goals. They had nothing to really have faith in, but in the course of events an inner adjustment, a new sense of purpose, was activated and gradually established more firmly.

My interpretation leans on perspectives given by Martin Buber, among others. He argues that the field "between" people is important. What becomes clear, "real," between people who genuinely talk together functions as an existential encounter, and this, according to Buber, lays the foundation of the subject.[2] The encounter as such also works as a healing through meeting new aspects of reality. In the fictive description communication was created anew, or restored, and new ideas and engagements were integrated. This process made the individual whole from within and opened the person to the world. The change was initiated by friendly moves from the outside and was brought about in a dynamic dialogue with life events and in interaction with symbols and other persons. Basically, with these characters, it was a new perception of God that restored their sense of self and of being members of a living tradition, once again or for the first time. These characters had – as Emmanuel Lévinas puts it – been "directly exposed to being."[3] It was

---

[2]Buber, M. *Det mellanmäskliga* (Ludvika, 1990: Dualis), p 30. (Elemente des Zwischenmenschlichen 1953. In "Die Schriften über das dialogische Prinzip" (Heidelberg, 1954/1956: Verlag Lambert Schneider).
[3]Lévinas, E. *Tiden och den andre.* Översättning och inledning av Erik van der Heeg och Sven-Olov Wallenstein. Symposion. Stockholm/Stehag 1992, p. 55. (Le Temps et l'autre; Time and the Other, in Lévinas, E. The Lévinas Reader, ed. by Seán Hand (Oxford, UK; Cambridge, MA: Basil Blackwell).

impossible for them to flee, they had to be radical. From the novels you get the picture that man is more than just the sum of a genetical set and of a history in time and space, and that, usually, the question of meaning is added. The striving to realize what truly is the aim of one's own being, an aim that in some respects is shared by all beings, that is, perhaps, the humane about human beings. Self-consciousness, reflective thought and personal responsibility provide a person with *some* space to act, and the fact that ultimate questions are worked through most often helps pave the way for resolution.

From a practical, psychological perspective, questions are an integral part of life. The threats against life conditions and against the individual subject can be very severe. The symbols and rites of culture and religion give room for anxiety and pain involved in life experience. Symbols and rites can function as drain pipes for what is too much, and feelings and thoughts evoked by the encounter with symbols can activate, express and assist the working through of matters difficult to deal with in an ordinary day-to-day discourse. The symbols of religion, especially, give typified form to ultimate questions: they respond to emotional needs, treat cognitive aspects, mediate consciousness; they coordinate rationality with emotion and help include transcendence. A painful side of the breakdown of communication is illustrated by the symptoms in body and soul when a diffuse, long-lasting stress lacks symbolic articulation and confirming interpretation. These symptoms can, as a matter of fact, contain a healthy striving to "get better." But, their message needs to be heard. In a similar way the occupation, with human destructiveness, in many a literary work today, could be recognized as an effort to confront real problems, and, thus, be understood as a striving with a much wider scope and with constructive final aims. Analysis and interpretation of the human predicament to which literature and art give such vivid expression, suggest that considerate response from the outside world could help an individual subject into contact with an objective point of view, and that becoming in this sense related to a comprehensive structure of meaning gradually enables the isolated, alienated person to get hold of motivation and hope.

When I study religiosity I do not try to demonstrate religion, nor do I explain religion as a function of something else. The aim is to get a cohesive picture of the basic orientation identified in the text. The fundamental striving observed often takes the form of an urge to find formulation to ultimate questions and finds solutions somehow involving religious elements. Tentatively, therefore, the assumption is that the aspect of religion can contribute to a more comprehensive understanding. I assume that human beings, as well as religious phenomena, are so subtle that only theoretical approaches which integrate several perspectives and are tentative in character, are complex enough to match the expression of the text. Also, I do not range ideologies, but I want to know what they are about, if possible, because I believe that matter of substance and ways of presenting issues and relating to them influence each other – the principle being, as one might put it, the notion that "you don't fall in love with just anybody, there has to be *something* special about the person you feel attracted to, that makes a difference...." The research has to give room for the totality of "the other" and one should try to understand the striving from within. Theories and strategies do not always declare what their assumptions are and what kind of representations for the human being they operate with. Silent reasoning of this kind is a point of interest discussed by Maurice Friedman, for example, in his book *Dialogue and the Human Image*.[4]

With an inclusive starting point the concept of religion can be given a wide scope and openness to the most personal expressions, as well as to the ideological consciousness of the material. With further investigation more precise definitions become available. In order to describe psychological functions of the religiosity in the novels I have mentioned, I developed a theoretical construction which I call an "integrated object-relational" perspective. This approach draws upon role theory in Hjalmar Sundén's complex conception,[5] on views on the interplay between self-consciousness and culture, on theories dealing with the human need for meaningful answers to life questions, and on concepts of religiosity as a mature human engagement. Thus, an inclination from the psychoanalyst Melanie Klein, about a basic tendency for relating socially, was combined with the proposition of Donald Winnicott, also a psychoanalyst, that such a social tendency has to relate to factors in an

---

[4]*Dialogue and the Human Image*. Beyond Humanistic Psychology (Newbury Park, London, New Delhi, 1992: Sage Publications).
[5]D.M Wulff (in *Psychology of Religion*. Classic and contemporary views (New York, 1991: John Wiley and Sons, Inc.) gives an account of Sundén's theory that brings it close to a theory of social roles merely. It is in fact more complex. I have (in "Vere adest". The Theme of Presence in the Novels of Olov Hartman. An Interpretation of the Psychology of the Religion (Åbo, 1992: Åbo Akademi), dealt with the problem how to get more detailed theoretical description to the intrapsychic foundations of "social roles" in function. Nils G. Holm, present professor of Comparative Religion at the Åbo Akademi University, elaborates Sundén's role theory in two recent articles in two coming books on methodology: "Role Theory and Religious Experience" (in *Handbook of Religious Experience: Theory and Practice*. ed. by Ralph W. Hood, Jr. [Birmingham Alabama., in print 1994: Religious Education Press) and "An Integrated Role Theory for the Psychology of Religion: Concepts and Pespectives" (in *Theoretical Foundations for an Empirical Psychology of Religion* [Publisher at present not decided, in print 1994]; for more information write Professor N.G. Holm, Department of Comparative Religion, Åbo Akademi, Biskopsgatan 16, SF 20500 Åbo, Finland).

exterior world in order to make for separate being and actual contact with realities. This reasoning was linked to an interpretation of narcissism made by the British philosopher C. Fred Alford. It is argued that the Klein-inspired striving to relate has to surrender to socially shared reality and morally worthy causes in order to be in agreement with reality and with solidarity and self-respect. The concluding assumption is that the striving to relate in a creative way to life gets satisfactory orientation and goals through cultivation in the interaction with collective judgment on what, ultimately, is good and dignified. Alford, drawing on Melanie Klein, explicitly argues that mature humans "have an innate drive to make reparation. What is necessary is decent cultural values to channel this drive in morally praiseworthy directions."[6] Here concepts of religion suggesting positive functions to religious life were added, in order to bridge the understanding of the psychology of an equivalent need for reparation and recreation seen in the experiences of the novel characters.

The solution in the novels actually suggests that there is a place and a personal life for the individual in this world. The impression is conveyed that realities such as common sense, living tradition, the course of events, the behavior of fellow human beings, all give the individual pursuit impetus, cohesion and orientation. Slightly adjusting the words of a famous church father, Irenaeus, one could say: Culture does not destroy life, but perfects it. (*Gratia naturam non tollit, sed perficit.*) In Freud's well-known view of culture and morality, the demands of morality are seen to be external to man's nature, actually against man's innermost interests. Freud's view is deeply moral, though: man should choose to be rational and support morality, because it is better to learn to accept some discipline without giving up on who you are. Only, in Freud's outlook, culture, morality, religion, do not represent entities and functions which attribute "cultivation" a positive significance.

There are many ideologies underlying the various interpretations of a given life situation and of the human being, who as a self emerges like an ongoing narrative story himself. In light of the basic relational structure of the forms for the human pursuit, I would like to underscore the prospect of basic trust and of power-free communication as factors adding concreteness and attainability to the perspective of infinite openness and human rights. From a psychological point of view, trust, language and faith depend on the existence of a capacity in the

---

[6]Alford, C.F. *Melanie Klein and Critical Social Theory.* An Account of Politics, Art and Reason Based on Her Psychoanalytic Theory (New Haven and London, 1989), p 50. Alford on narcissism, in *Narcissism:* Socrates, the Frankfurt School, and Psychoanalytic Theory (New Haven and London, 1988).

individual to symbolize, and this capacity, theoretically, becomes useful to the extent to which a growing person has received attentive response. Therefore, the relevant ethic in the field of interaction – in the family, in the area of culture, tradition, history – in this "intermediary territory" where a person relates to his surroundings and takes in what will form self-conception and worldview – here the relevant ethic would be to respond both to one's own self and to "the other" person in such a way that human rights conditions are served and goodness is given form in reality. By responding morally, people subject their personal strivings to the cultivation of shared high norms, and by doing so, people benefit personally from a consolidation of life-enhancing values, as well.

Within his framework of thought Emmanuel Lévinas presents an "ethic of the face" in which it is argued that the face of "the other" addresses me with a challenge to reach out and take my responsibility "in the shaping of the other." Action for the other person's sake will also develop my own self, but I have to settle for a one-sided commitment: "reciprocity is the other person's business." I cannot decide over the other person – my business is to respond. In Lévinas's outlook I see a de-theologized account of the creation story, a secular perspective still holy by virtue of its catholicity. Here the face of "the other" gives the norm and a positive motivation for being there for the "other" is presented.[7]

The effort to include the transcendent and/or to preserve ultimate aspects of human dignity within life and discourse is differently argued in different contexts. In my opinion, the principle of the transcendent cannot be taken into a strictly scientific explanation.[8] The procedure does not feel right from the aspect of faith, either, if by the inclusion it is meant that transcendence is left entirely in human command. When the inclusion suggests openness to additional and new aspects of reality, openness to "the other" and to the unexpected event, thereby affirming a vision of the world as a place greater than human designation, a place to share, and one that might be God's world, too, then it is another matter.

---

[7]In addition to Lévinas there are theologians such as Knud E. Løgstrup, Jens Glebe-Møller, Henry Cöster, Tage Kurtén, among others, who deal with the understanding of the world today in relation to religion, theology and ethics. Løgstrup's phenomenological analysis, for example, stresses that human existence and "the universe" belong together; metaphysical thought is applied to everyday life in a way which brings the Judeo-Christian concept of creation into focus.

[8]Otherwise D.M. Wulff (in *Psychology of Religion*, 1991, p 639) who states: "Perhaps today we need a new principle, the PRINCIPLE OF THE INCLUSION OF THE TRANSCENDENT, to balance Flornoy's classic principle of exclusion.... Consistently applied throughout the literature, these principles might help to cast new light on a number of unsolved problems, perhaps giving the field a new coherence and a sense of direction."

Pluralism does not eliminate the need to see "the other," nor does it do away with the hope of "the single one" to be affirmed by others. Human rights are violated; they are both difficult to practice and hard to attain. Yet, they have not ceased being valid. There have to be norms for life. A basis for general agreement on what, in the end, is normative, can possibly be drawn from the conclusion that human conditions cannot be in just any fashion and still support life.

Normative Judgment and American Cultural Mythology: A Response to Darrell J. Fasching's "Historical Consciousness, Religion and the Social Order: Can We Make Normative Judgments?"

Darlene J. Corcoran
University of South Florida

Not only can we make normative judgments, we do make them. Thus, Darrell Fasching calls us to "public dialogue and debate," urging us to the consensus of a "normative social ethic" which will work transculturally to the good of humanity. His argument is sound, has great depth, and its logic is intricately woven. For this reason, I devote most of my response to the logic of the paper, before presenting my own commentary.

Dr. Fasching's argument that forming a normative social ethic "is the most pressing challenge of our time" rests on the presentation of two opposing facts. First, today's values have been reduced to personal and cultural relativism. Second, it is not possible for ethics to be subjective and private to the individual. His personal narrative, that of the student and the medical professional, together with his study of the Holocaust force him to ask whether today's morality is contingent upon one's culture and personal preference. He then correlates Nietzsche's parable of the madman with the act of putting a man on the moon. Although the man stepping onto the surface of the moon has become a symbol of the human capacity to transcend earthly bounds, it serves also as a reminder of the "demonic normlessness of technological civilization" which Nietzsche's madman predicted at the end of the nineteenth century, a civilization where God is dead and the world is without order. One must also note that the Holocaust, a great achievement of technologically advancing civilization, occurs between the two events. Thus, in Dr. Fasching's words, the Holocaust resulted from the "will to power...in a culture without counter-balancing norms to hold it in check." Furthermore, because culture is no longer understood as a result of natural order, but as human construct, values are no longer objective and universal; they have become subjective and particular to the individual. The problem is that ethics must always be determined publicly and socially because they involve relationships within a collective. Thus, the personal and cultural relativity of ethical judgment is in opposition to the very nature of the term.

Dr. Fasching explains that the reason for this dichotomy is the transition from one form of ethical consciousness to another. Prior to the emergence of social ethics in the nineteenth century, ethical consciousness manifested itself as a morality of honor in which the premodern self was identified with a collective which perceived itself as living within a "sacred natural order," which provided both a social role with a particular status and the obligation of each person to fulfill his or her sacred duty. This form legitimates the "sacred order of society" by reinforcing the status quo. Since the inception of social ethics, however, ethical consciousness has manifested itself in an ethic of dignity in which the self is identified instead with its capacity to choose roles. In contrast to the premodern self, the modern self is perceived as separate from and prior to its roles; human selves are thereby perceived as equal, giving rise to a social ethic of human dignity and human rights where each individual is responsible for her or his own actions. From this distinction, Dr. Fasching concludes that while the morality of honor results from experiences of the sacred order of society, the ethic of dignity results from experiences of "radical transcendence."

Tracing the emergence of human rights as a social ethic, he provides examples of "holy communities" which promote this experience of radical transcendence and an ethic of "welcoming the stranger." A distinction is drawn between the ethos of "sacred society" which affirms the social order with an ethic of unquestioning obedience, and that of the holy community which questions the status quo. From within holy community one can thus transcend social order to welcome the stranger through narrative which "provides a place for the stranger who does not share one's story."

In addition to this experience of the "holy" and the individuation resulting from urbanization, the alienation of the self from its social roles enables us to doubt, doubt being a secular experience of transcendence which demands that human dignity be the ground of an ethic of secular holiness. Through this experience of alienation, and the questioning resulting from doubt, critical reason arises. Dr. Fasching applies this process to those of us "engaged in Religious Studies and socio-historical scholarship" where sacred traditions and their myths are examined critically, thereby becoming desacralized and demythologized. This process provokes questions and doubt, yet initiates transcendence and experience of the holy. Experience of "the holy" encourages the revision of our perceptions of reality. Exclusive narrative, when reviewed and reinterpreted, becomes transformed into that which welcomes the stranger. He suggests that the historian can thus assist in social transformation and contribute to the improvement of the world by utilizing the same methodology.

This paper insists that, in order to allow room for the stranger, we must examine that which is often held most dear, the sacred narrative (whether "religious" or "secular"). In doing so, normative judgments are made only after transforming sacred narrative into holy narrative through critical examination, thereby allowing the stranger to enter the narrative with acceptance and affirmation. We who engage in religious studies scholarship experience the alienation resulting from close examination of our own traditions along with those of the "other." Ideally, this leads us to a summit of holy community from where we may engage in a discussion of social ethics grounded in respect for the dignity of humanity, and from where we may reach normative judgments rather than remaining in the valleys of social relativism which seem the sacred order of today.

As Fasching suggests, this does not only apply in the study of religion, but also in the writing of secular critical history. Taking seriously the request to use imagination in this response, I began to speculate, "What if...?" The "What if...?" I find most intriguing are the possibilities envisioned when one considers the demythologizing of American civil religion which is presently occurring through the desacralization of American narrative. The narratives of American mythology which include such figures as Christopher Columbus, George Washington, Abraham Lincoln, John Kennedy, and Martin Luther King, Jr. are challenged through the audacious questioning of that which has been in the past held sacred.

These heroes of yesterday, when closely scrutinized, are found to be individual human beings possessing the same imperfections shared by humanity as a whole. This means that "they" are on "our" level. "They" are no longer more adventurous, more ethical, more popular, more courageous, and more important than "we" are. This means that "they" and the mythologies associated with "them" are no longer held as sacred, on an elevated level of humanity or reality. *Anyone* can now become the next "hero" or "heroine." Thus, illusions become shattered and questions are raised; doubt follows, and transcendence becomes possible. American sacred narrative can then be recreated into holy narrative: honest, accessible, and welcoming to the masses of humanity who have arrived on its shores expecting this very thing. The American citizen, divorced from the sacrality of his or her cultural narrative and having experienced the transcendence of holy community, can begin to publicly engage in social ethics, pursuing the ideal of the preservation of human dignity. This can lead to the formation of normative judgment which provides for welcoming the stranger. This, in turn, could progress to an America which welcomes the stranger, providing acceptance and affirmation, rather than the America which now casts the foreigner off its shore, back into the sea.

Index

South Florida Studies in the History of Judaism

South Florida Academic Commentary Series

The Talmud of Babylonia, An Academic Commentary

243013	V, Yoma	Neusner
243014	XXXVI, Bavli Tractate Niddah	Neusner
243015	XX, Bavli Tractate Baba Qamma	Neusner
243016	XXXI, Bavli Tractate Bekhorot	Neusner
243017	XXX, Bavli Tractate Hullin	Neusner
243018	VII, Besah	Neusner
243019	X, Megillah	Neusner
243020	XXVIII, Zebahim	Neusner
243021	XXI, Bavli Tractate Baba Mesia	Neusner
243022	XXII, Bavli Tractate Baba Batra	Neusner
243023	XXIX, Bavli Tractate Menahot	Neusner

South Florida-Rochester-Saint Louis Studies on Religion and the Social Order

245001	Faith and Context, Volume 1	Ong
245002	Faith and Context, Volume 2	Ong
245003	Judaism and Civil Religion	Breslauer
245004	The Sociology of Andrew M. Greeley	Greeley
245005	Faith and Context, Volume 3	Ong
245006	The Christ of Michelangelo	Dixon
245007	From Hermeneutics to Ethical Consensus Among Cultures	Bori
245008	Mordecai Kaplan's Thought in a Postmodern Age	Breslauer
245009	No Longer Aliens, No Longer Strangers	Eckardt
245010	Between Tradition and Culture	Ellenson
245011	Religion and the Social Order	Neusner

South Florida International Studies in Formative Christianity and Judaism

| 242501 | The Earliest Christian Mission to 'All Nations' | La Grand |
| 242502 | Judaic Approaches to the Gospels | Chilton |